CEO OF INSANITY

THE RISE OF AN INTERNATIONAL PHENOMENON

DANIEL J. PRAZ

Hard Candy Publishing

CEO of Insanity
The Rise of an International Phenomenon
All Rights Reserved.
Copyright © 2019 Daniel J. Praz
v1.0

The opinions expressed in this manuscript are solely the opinions of the author and do not represent the opinions or thoughts of the publisher. The author has represented and warranted full ownership and/or legal right to publish all the materials in this book.

This book may not be reproduced, transmitted, or stored in whole or in part by any means, including graphic, electronic, or mechanical without the express written consent of the publisher except in the case of brief quotations embodied in critical articles and reviews.

Hard Candy Publishing

ISBN: 978-0-578-21601-0

Cover Photo © 2019 Chrissy Praz. All rights reserved - used with permission.

PRINTED IN THE UNITED STATES OF AMERICA

Table of Contents

Preface i
1. A Life of Learning 1
2. The "Great and Powerful" Silas Jones................................ 20
3. Calling All Loons 35
4. So Much for Hiring Family Friends................................... 49
5. More of the Madness 68
6. Power Struggles 89
7. Mutiny Conspiracy 107
8. All Things End.. 127
9. Let the Good Time Roll?... 142
10. The Competition Rises 164
11. Ending the Bad Run 182
12. International Salvation (or so it seemed)......................... 197
13. Shattering of a Dream 220
14. More of the Less 241
15. Take it to the Limit 259
16. You're Hired, You're Fired! 275
17. The Power-trippers 295
18. Cars and Gals 308
19. Crazy Clients 317
20. The Whacky World of Visitors... 335
Epilogue 349

Preface

The very first thing I need to tell you is that everything written here is true. I changed the names, locations and descriptions of characters to totally avoid anyone being able to be recognized. But there was no reason for me to have to embellish a single word of this true story because it was absurdity all on its own. No one could come up with such ridiculous and incredulous events.

Still, these are my recollections of the events. I recognize that others may have different memories of the events described in this book. I did not set out to hurt anyone in the telling of this story, but as a group, those involved are crucial to what transpired and there would be no story without including all.

When I set out to write of this epic journey, I had in mind just to tell what it took to launch an international franchise company. That would be Mr. Sandless, which offers wood floor refinishing without sanding, and turned into the largest refinisher in history. We were the first national refinishing company in the USA, bringing our service coast to coast, from Long Island to San Diego. We were the first national refinisher in Canada, going coast to coast in that country from Halifax to Vancouver Island.

In an industry dominated by sanding, Sandless refinishing truly was a revolutionary invention. In writing this story, I was trying to focus on the positives of what it took to take an amazing concept to a fully functional brand. What I found as the story unfolded before me, was that it was much harder than I ever dreamed it was. You see, when I was in the moment—in the heat of the battle so to speak—I was only concentrating on that moment and living through it. Now looking back, I am astounded of what occurred as well as how much I really endured.

When I first started this book, I began with the easy sections of the story which were employees, vehicles, and customers. But that didn't really work as a storyline. I stopped and went back from the beginning and told the story in sequence as it originally occurred.

All I really wanted to do was tell my story, which in and of itself is both horrific and amazing at the same time. What makes it so wild is a ten-year run of constant kicks in the groin by evil and horrible people that came at me steadily and relentlessly until I broke. Then it continued even after that. But more importantly, I continued after being broken, until I finally got through it all.

I read each chapter as I wrote it to both my staff and my kids. I would often look up to see their sad and depressed looks after hearing about terrible events in certain chapters. This reaction was not what I was telling the story for. I decided to include the funny stories with the bad ones so that you, the reader, don't get the steady dose of negativity that I received on this ten-year journey. The funny and crazy things were all happening to me at the same time throughout the journey.

To be quite honest, I felt as I wrote that the story would have a big ending. I swear I never really had an ending for this piece until I got to that end. I did not really know what that big ending would be until literally after I wrote it! It was right there all the time—right in front of my face—and I couldn't see it until after it was in print. As I re-read what I wrote the second time, I see that I believed this throughout the telling. Therefore, you will hear me prodding you on to wait until the end. I promise the payoff is worth the wait!

Make no mistake. This was a spiritual journey. I do not believe for one moment that any of this would be possible on its own. It is just too unreal to fathom. I hope this inspires you to take your own personal journey of growth and discovery—no matter how hard that journey may be or the years it takes you to complete it. Just imagine the story you will have to tell! Here is mine.

CHAPTER 1

A Life of Learning

YOU DON'T JUST wake up one day and find yourself as the CEO of an international company. Looking back, it is very easy to see now that each step I took in life brought me closer to this vision and company I created. Each adventure I explored added the pieces that I would need to be able to build and lead an international company, even though I had no idea of where my life was heading.

When I was a kid, I always hustled to make a buck, and when I say "a buck" I mean it! A dollar in the late sixties was a nice chunk of change. I started selling at the age of just seven. In the back of a comic book there was a company advertising that if you sold seeds for them (assorted seeds for flowers and vegetables) that you could earn money to get great prizes like fishing equipment. I was in!

I asked my Dad to help me fill out the information and before long, right around springtime, my seed kit arrived, and I began knocking door to door to sell my seeds. I did quite well with it, using my cuteness at the time as a sale's gimmick, and earned enough for a nice fishing pool, tackle and box. It was my first foray into selling, one of the most useful tools I have come to have in my personal arsenal.

I also played guitar and music became a part of my life at that time. A music store opened in the strip mall where my Dad worked, and on his lunch hour, he would go by and talk with the owner. My

CEO OF INSANITY

Dad always wanted to play guitar. So, he took me and my older brother down one night to take group lessons. I immediately excelled.

By fifteen, I was a professional musician and once people started to scream for me on stage, that is when I determined that this was what I wanted to do with my life. When I saw adults with their mouths open watching my hands as they went up and down that fret board, I knew I had a gift, and so I set my sights on becoming a "rock star". That was what consumed me for the next ten years. I know this could seem like the typical dream of a typical youth. But I really *could* play that instrument and my music is out there as a testament to this.

Often a starving artist, I had to take side jobs to sustain myself during those years. One of the situations I found myself in was a fire and safety company, where I learned to recharge fire extinguishers. It is also where I learned the finer art of selling I call "game on". The successful business was run by four Italian brothers who were often very loud and used boundless foul language.

These four brothers were all about "making money," even to the point of embellishing what they charged for their services. Their reasoning was that everyone one else did it, and that this was just their turn to get even.

"The butcher has his thumb on the scale," one of the loudest brothers announced to me. "The auto mechanic replaces a belt when there is nothing wrong with it! This is just our time to do the same!" They would perform tests on extinguishers that didn't need the tests, not test ones that needed to be tested, but then pass them without testing, and charged people for parts that were never replaced.

It was one day when this particular brother was screaming and cursing about a customer who ripped him off when the phone rang. He was yelling about everyone in the customer's family and that they could go "f themselves". His face was red and flushed and you could tell his blood pressure was high. But when he reached for the phone and answered it, everything changed in an instant.

"*Jonas Brothers, may I help you?*" he said as if he was never amped up in the first place. It was an instant change of demeanor, which later as I grew in sales skill; I came to call this "game on". No matter what mood you are in, or what is going on at that moment, that is not a customer on that line. No, that is money on that line! No matter how you feel on that day or at that very moment, when that phone rings, it is time to make money. That is a lesson I will never forget learning in that environment.

It was during this time that I learned to be much more outgoing. Up until that time, I was rather shy and reserved. This company set me up to learn sales from one of their seasoned guys, and while I could already sell at a high level, this was totally different. This guy was so outgoing and didn't seem to have a care in the world. I told myself that I wanted to be like that, and from there my salesmanship exploded. I grew to not fear anything.

This lack of fear led me to do some crazy things. It was during this time while working at this company where a certain type of fire extinguisher called a "soda-acid" was being outlawed. This thing when turned upside-down would mix water and baking soda with sulfuric acid to create pressure and squirt the water out of the hose and onto the fire. It worked great, but let's face it; it was easy to break into these things and get the acid. No wonder they were being outlawed!

Anyway, most of these types of extinguishers were solid brass and it just so happened that precious metals like brass were commanding significant money in the scrap field thanks to a super-high inflation rate during the Jimmy Carter presidency. Because of that, I went to the four brothers with what I thought was a great plan. We could offer to purchase the old extinguishers for a nominal fee and put that money toward the cost of the new extinguishers for the customer, then take the brass soda-acid types to the scrap yard and trade them in ourselves.

I was shocked to hear that the brothers thought my idea was "stupid" and back then, nobody called me stupid. I set out to show them just how wrong they were.

On the very next appointment I had where I was the lead salesman, the company I visited was replacing their entire soda-acid fire extinguisher line. I made up some nonsense about still needing the parts to the old soda-acids and inquired through the president of the company if we could purchase them for cash from him. He was very agreeable to the idea, basically getting cash for clearing them out of his warehouse. But I was floored to hear that he had one hundred and fifty of them!

I was led to the warehouse with the nephew of one of the brothers who was with me that day as my helper and co-worker. We discovered that nearly all one hundred and fifty extinguishers were solid brass. But it may as well have been a million for all it mattered. I had offered the president of the company three dollars each for the units, thinking there would only be a couple and that I could swing this myself. There was no way in the world I would be able to come up with four hundred and fifty dollars. Back then, that was more than I made in a month!

The only person I could think of who would have that kind of money was my helper's father who worked in a steel mill and made a great deal of money. He was a real nice guy who always liked me, so we drove to his house to see if he would loan me the money short term. His father knew I had some kind of scheme going on, but he said he trusted me and with that, pulled a wad of cash from his pocket and handed me enough to make the deal. I told him I would be back in just a matter of hours.

We rushed back to the company where I handed the money to the president, who slipped it into his trouser pocket, then to the warehouse where we filled the van up to take our bounty to the scrap yard. I had paid four hundred and fifty dollars for the one hundred and fifty fire extinguishers and got thirty dollars each for them as top of the line scrap brass. Four thousand, five hundred dollars for a couple hours work!

We drove back to my co-worker's father's house and I handed him six hundred dollars, then split the rest with the co-worker, because without his father's help, the deal would not have been possible. The four brothers already knew by the time I returned to the shop with the fire extinguisher order from the company. The scrap yard shorted me one hundred dollars and called, thinking I did the deal through the fire and safety company. Sure, the brothers were angry, but I told them it was their own faults. No one calls me stupid. The next day there was a company directive to offer three dollars for each soda acid exchanged. Wonder where they came up with that idea?

That's not the craziest thing I had ever done by a long shot. Fireworks were illegal in my home state of for years. Of course, everyone wanted fireworks that lived in the state especially around the fourth of July. I saw an ad in a music magazine that boasted they could ship to where I lived. I gave it a try, sending them a money order for about five cases of fireworks at the beginning of June, so that I could catch the biggest part of the July 4th season. They had a "buy one, get one free" deal, so I would be getting ten cases if it all worked out. Sure enough, I heard a knock at the door of my apartment one day and a delivery guy brought in ten cases. I sold out very quickly that year and made ten times return on my investment.

The following year I ordered ten cases and once again, the delivery guy brought me twenty cases of fireworks to sell. I used the money earned for a recording session at a high-end studio.

The year after that, going for the big brass ring, I lost my mind. The combination of the lure of so much money and my lack of fear had me order twenty-five cases, still with the buy-one, get-one deal going on. I would be getting fifty cases of fireworks! But this time I told the warehouse, located in a nearby state, to not ship them to me. Instead, I would drive across the state and pick them up myself.

The warehouse workers laughed and laughed when I pulled up to the dock in my Ford Maverick and a forklift dropped a skid of fifty cases of fireworks in front of me. I don't know how in the world I managed to do it, but I got them all in that car and made the eleven-hour ride back to the other side of my state. How in the world no one noticed the huge warnings labels on the boxes of fireworks that I was practically sitting on is beyond me. For the most part, I had boxes hanging out the windows of the car! I made a huge amount of money that year, but that was the last time I pulled this stunt. My music career started to produce income and so I didn't need to be as crazy anymore.

But as the story goes, I fell short of my goal of music stardom and as the music scene changed, I joined my now ex-wife in a home cleaning business she ran. My main focus became to simply make money. My ex and I worked hard enough at that to make it a reality. In a short period of time I went from being a starving musician, to being a successful business owner. From there, I moved to owning a janitorial company.

I told you that early in my childhood, I hustled to make money. I sold seeds door to door, Christmas cards door to door, newspaper subscriptions, worked as a dishwasher, and even sold vacuum cleaners. I cut my salesman teeth on these first offerings—I started to learn the art of selling.

Later, I worked at the fire and safety company where I had my first real dose of business. I learned to be outgoing. I learned that when the phone rings with a potential customer, it was "game on" and to be at my best always. My next foray came from the music world, where I learned two other important lessons. The first was how to sell myself. Everything in the music business is sales.

The second was how to manage people. It is amazingly difficult to get so many artistic type people to work as a cohesive group. When you have done that for ten years, you really have learned the art of management.

Then to the house cleaning company where I learned the next two important lessons. The first was how to run a successful business which I learned by reading every business book I could get my hands on. The outcome of that also taught me how to manage money, most especially cash flow, how to save and invest, and how to be successful.

Next was the janitorial company, where I started to show the signs that I was becoming a master of all these things. I used my salesmanship, my stage presence and my ability to sell myself to get great accounts. I used my knowledge of business to start to build wealth and success. And of course, I learned the next thing I would need—I taught myself to become a master of floor refinishing, because that was where the money was.

Then finally the culmination of all those things, I designed and launched Mr. Sandless. And there it is—it was the culmination of learning that led to me being the CEO of this incredible adventure!

I always felt it was an act of God that delivered Mr. Sandless to me. When I started working commercial janitorial jobs, one of my first accounts was a crazy doctor I wrote about in my cleaning book "True Dirt: Confessions of a Male Housecleaner" (Xlibris). He was obsessed with his floors, and he wanted them to shine no matter how I did it, no matter how many times I had to strip and recoat those floors. So, every Sunday for years—literally—I stripped this guy's floors and re-coated them. I tried everything I possibly could get my hands on, and basically, I became a master refinisher.

As I entered 1990, many potential customers were calling my janitorial company stating that the refinisher they used for their hard surface floor refinishing had "ruined" their floor. Back then, janitorial companies used aggressive and dangerous ammonia-based strippers to get the old product off the floor before they refinished it. While these products worked great, they worked a little *too* great, often stripping out the color from the floors they were used on. Most of these floors in my market were very old, some forty years old, some easily more than one hundred years old. It was nearly criminal to kill these floors and the owners and managers of these properties were not too happy. That's why they called my company.

I saw a huge need in this market to get away from the caustic strippers that were being used and come up with a better way to refinish this old, mostly asphalt tile floors to keep their color. That is when I developed the beginning stages of the Mr. Sandless system—a gentle way to refinish without stripping out the color of the floors.

Moving ahead nearly ten years later, this system I created already made me a success. Many churches and schools with old floors had become customers of my janitorial company. I had a regular rotation of clients that staff serviced as far as general cleaning, and I had staff and myself regularly refinishing floors on a contract basis. The profit was incredible, and I was making about three hundred and fifty thousand dollars a year with just a small staff, making a base salary of ninety thousand a year myself. I wasn't looking for anything else when fate dropped a new opportunity into my lap.

A church client called stating that they had a new rector coming in and wanted their parsonage cleaned. We set up the work and cleaned the entire home top to bottom. It was more than one hundred fifty years old, so it was a unique property. The church council asked if I could do something with the wood floors in the home. They had gotten a price to sand the floors at four dollars a square foot and they couldn't afford the ten thousand dollars it would cost due to the size of the home.

All my company's work to that point was tile. I had no experience at all with wood. On top of that, I couldn't believe the price they were quoted. I was making just thirty cents a square foot for my tile work!

I grabbed a janitorial book and read the recommended way to refinish wood. This would not be a true "sanding" but a screening of the floor and application of one coat of urethane which is sometimes referred to as a "light sanding" or "recoating". It seemed easy enough, so I told the council I would give it a shot. I grabbed a couple of my guys and headed over to the parsonage to try this process on one of the smaller bedrooms.

Immediately as I started to screen the floor I hated it! Imagine one hundred and fifty-year-old floors being ripped up by a floor machine with a dry screen on it. The sheer crap that was coming off this floor was shocking, especially that I knew that the old varnish or shellac that was on it was carcinogenic and toxic. The machine, my guys and I were covered in dust! But so was the room we so meticulously had just cleaned.

After cleaning all the mess up where we even had to vacuum the walls to get the dust off them, I applied the coat of urethane. It was thick and didn't want to move along the floor. It smelled of high heaven and was making me sick. It didn't self-level and I had to really work to get it to go on evenly. On top of all of that, it didn't even look good *and* it took us the entire day to do just one stinking room! I would be there for a month at that rate!

I went home that night and entered my garage which was my laboratory of sorts. I think I had more products that I had tried over the years on floors than the largest cleaning store in the world! I decided that I would give my wet floor system a try. Now I am not going to go into the details of how I came up with this, because it is part of the trade secrets of the company. But let me just state that I ran some simple tests that were eye-opening and led me to *know* that my wet system would in fact work.

The very next day we headed back to the parsonage. When I informed my guys that we would be trying my wet system on the wood floors, they were adamant that it would "f the floors up". I explained to them that I did tests to show that it would not ruin the floors and that there was no way in the world I was going to continue sanding. Since they believed I would ruin the floor, they opted not to help me.

"Fine, then just hand me the things I ask for and stay out of my way!" I barked at them. With that I began my wet process by applying a solution we used on tile floors that would allow for gentle refinishing. The absolute moment I started to apply it, I knew it was the wrong thing to use. I could tell by what it did to the floor that it was too harsh, and immediately I knew exactly what to use. That "light bulb" moment was the birth of the Mr. Sandless refinishing system.

I didn't have what I needed to use with me, so I decided to press on and see how this floor came out. I was finished in that room in under two hours, with nothing at all to clean up. I switched to a water-based urethane that was a much better product than the oil urethane I used the first time and this time I could use multiple coats.

I will never forget after I put the first coat on and stood outside the door of that room. The floor looked one hundred percent better than the first floor I did, with no clean up, with no odor, and saving six hours of labor. I pulled out this tiny calculator from my estimate book and began to visualize the amount of money I could make with a system like this. Repeatedly I typed in numbers because I couldn't believe what I was seeing. For a decade, I made my money earning only pennies for refinishing. There were some jobs back then that paid as low as just eleven cents a square foot! The only way I made any real money was sheer volume.

But with sanding at four dollars in my market, I could offer this system at half the cost and make two dollars a square foot. In just hours I would make more money than servicing a ten thousand square foot school. I projected out how much I could make in a year with the new system and then how much I could make in five years. It was literally millions of dollars! That kid who used to hustle just to make a buck had discovered a pot of gold.

The very next day I returned with a new concoction to try on the rest of the rooms, the one from the "light bulb" moment I had the day before. Once again, as soon as I laid this new mix on the floor, I *knew* I had the answer—the key to "Sandless refinishing" which I dubbed "grog". This product has nothing to do with wood or wood floors, and I called it grog to throw anyone trying to copy what I was doing in a different direction. They may think it is alcohol or some type of witch's brew! Anyway, we finished the entire home that day as my guys finally became believers and helped me. They kept saying that they couldn't believe it, but it was right there in front of their faces. The wet process worked on these floors like a charm.

Two days later when the oil urethane finally dried in the first room we did, I redid that room as well so that it would match the look of the other rooms. Then I called the church council to come over and see the work. Not only were they blown away by what I was able to do, council members started asking me to do *their* floors! I told them that the system was experimental but many of them insisted. I started booking their work and getting them on the schedule.

Let me tell you what I really had in mind with this system. Thinking about janitorial work where repeat customers were king;

what I envisioned to start was "carpet cleaning for wood floors". That is where yearly I could go back into the home and refinish them again for a low price, so that I had constant repeat business.

I also came up with my first slogan. It was "Fast Food for Floors!" The way I saw it at the time, we could be in and out in just hours, leave a remarkably better-looking floor and at a cost substantially less than sanding, hence the "fast food" idea.

That first year, through word of mouth only, I serviced ninety-five customers. One particular customer had a house that sat vacant because she couldn't sell it. It had been on the market for more than a year. We serviced the floors and a week later she called to thank me, saying that the house sold! I was also getting many people moving into a home that was new to them, so that they could get the floors refinished before they moved their furniture in. This would turn into my bread and butter customer in the near future.

Also, during that time, I developed the techniques to add to the system to make it even better—techniques that we still use today. Looking back, I was very fortunate to start this business in my market. Most of the floors are older and need more care, so much so that if I started this system in a newer market with more modern floors, I would not have any of the techniques I developed to handle the floors in my city. The market actually drove the development of the system.

It also seemed to be destiny that I'd be the one to discover this process. Not only was I constantly pushing the envelope to find new and better ways of doing refinishing, I had great knowledge of all the possible products in the marketplace for cleaning. That combination made it so without sounding too egotistical, I can't see anyone else coming up with the concept of Sandless wood floor refinishing. It is too "out of the box" from standard sanding for anyone in the industry to think of something like this—a wet process on wood—because everyone knows in the business that water is the enemy of wood. No one had the guts to try what I was doing successfully.

Within just a few months of doing the Sandless service, I considered how I would present it as far as growth was concerned. The main issue was, sure it was easy to me but that was because I was master floor refinisher. By that time, I had refinished literally miles of floors. I knew that I couldn't just give someone the system and that they would be any good at it. It was going to take a lot of teaching and support to get people to do this at a high level like I was able to do.

Given that, my first thought was expansion by the branch method. That would be where I would own all the locations, and one by one I would extend the reach of the brand. With that I looked at the difference between White Castle and McDonalds. White Castle was branch developed with four hundred locations at the time, McDonalds was franchise developed with over thirty-five *thousand* locations, even though White Castle was older! That ruled out doing this expansion by branch. I mean by that time, I was already forty! I didn't want to have to take that much time to build the brand.

I investigated licensing the system out to other janitorial companies which would have made me a fortune. But I met with one of my customers who licensed out their music system who told me they hated it because no one followed the system! Well that certainly wasn't going to work because you must follow the system in order to not ruin the customer's wood floor! I imagined all sorts of lawsuits if people didn't use the system correctly.

That left me with the feeling that the best expansion model would be franchising. Just as this was taking form in my head, I was servicing a client who had a strange home. It was basically three parts; a left side, a right side and a large center section. He had just installed brand new floors on the right side and he wanted something to be done with the old wood floors in the center section.

"Oh, that's a shame," I said to him when I arrived to service the center section. "What are you going to do when I make these old floors look like new and they look better than your new floors?" He seemed to think what I said was impossible, so we set out to work. After just the first coat he peeked at the floor, and he couldn't believe that what I said would happen really *did* happen. The old floors looked new and the new floors looked old!

A LIFE OF LEARNING

He began to explain to me that he was spiritually driven, and that God was telling him this was something he should get into. He asked if I was spiritual and I explained that I had a personal relationship with God. It was then he said that "this will make a great franchise!" While I already had come to this conclusion, I knew that God was moving in my life and confirming for me that franchising was the way to go, just not with this client. The brand and the concept were much too young to take anyone else on at that point and I told him that.

Of course, I knew nothing at all about franchising. Once again, I hit the books and to be honest, they were daunting, mostly written from legal perspectives by people who sounded as if they swallowed a legal thesaurus. I knew I would never get the "legal" end of franchising at the outset by myself and would need help in this area.

Meanwhile I started to develop the brand as a franchise with its look and feel. Many times I was servicing a customer, they would ask if it was indeed a franchise!

All during the first year, I wrote down notes on who my customers were, where they lived, what they drove, and their property value so that I could know the actual demographics of who our customers would be. After the first year, I went back and visited with all ninety-five that I had serviced except for the few who sold their home. After the first dozen visits, I knew the "carpet cleaning for floors" was out the door, as every home looked exactly like I just serviced it! It was going to last a heck of a lot longer than a year! For that matter, so was my new and still unused slogan because this service was way better than "fast food!"

It was right then that I decided I had to find a supply company to work with me on this adventure. I already knew it would be hard enough to run the franchise division, and that I knew I had neither the capital, space, knowledge, nor the desire to run the supply side. I would have to find a company to work with for the product supply as well as equipment and material supply.

I "went to the well" so to speak with this, looking at all the supply houses that I currently used for my janitorial company. I examined their size, strength, ability to grow and their product line as I only wanted to have one supplier "do it all" for the franchise system. There was one company that stood out among the rest, especially with customer service. They always answered the phone, took the orders and got everything out on time. I put in a call to Logan, the owner and president of the company.

This is probably the most incredible part of this beginning stage of Mr. Sandless. I explained to Logan what I was doing, what I envisioned for the company five years down the road, told him it would be a leap of faith for him to work with me, and that the risk of the product line at that point would have to be on him. The reward was going to come several more years down the road. Whether it was my passion that he read or that he was and still is a great business guy, or that he was just a trusting and sweetheart of a man, or all of the above, Logan agreed to be the supplier for my new brand. Without him, his partner and his team, there would be no way for Mr. Sandless to have grown as quickly as it did, and I will never forget that. This also once again shows that this was destiny. This partnership between my new concept and this supply company was about the only ray of sunshine to come along in the early stages of Mr. Sandless. Everything else was such a battle.

Once I determined that the system produced floors that were going to last years, everything changed! During that year and since it was experimental, I charged only forty-nine dollars per room for the service! As I started the second year, I began to test market the system using my janitorial company rather than the brand name I had come up with. I will explain the brand name in another section of this book, but for now I was running this Sandless refinishing business as an offshoot of my Major Cleaning Company. I raised the price in these advertisements to one hundred forty-nine dollars per room and by the end of that first year; I was up to one hundred ninety-nine dollars per room. Believe me, no one balked at the price!

The goal of the marketing tests was to determine the best way for a new franchisee to advertise to get their business going. I tested every single form of marketing out there with just samples going to small areas I knew were hot for the service, so that I could track the return on my advertising dollars spent.

One such mailer brought a call from a woman with a living room, hall and stairs she wanted refinished. After I explained the service, she didn't seem to really understand, and so she asked if I could speak to her husband that evening about it, because "he will understand this more than I do". I agreed to call and speak with her husband that evening.

When I called the husband that night and once again explained the service, he didn't seem like he was listening to me. I asked him what he was thinking about.

"F**k my floors," he replied. I didn't know how to respond to that except to let him continue. "This would be *great* for us at work!"

"Where do you work?" I asked.

"I head up the Apartments for the University" he replied.

"How many units do you have down there?" I asked.

"Two thousand," he said. I about fell over.

Up until that point, I had not even considered the commercial applications for the system! It was already crazy enough with the residential customers and I certainly was not looking to expand to commercial work when I hadn't even officially launched the brand yet. Still, I would have had to be insane to turn away from such an opportunity. I made an appointment to meet with the head of the property maintenance for the company, a very nice guy with an interesting name to boot: Tim Floor.

Tim showed me two units that needed floor refinishing. They would normally refinish the floors after someone moved out. I told him I would service one at no charge and that he could sand the other, and then compare the two. I said that if he wasn't happy with my service that my finish would sand off as well, and he could sand the unit I was doing. He agreed to my terms.

Honestly these apartments were perfect for the Sandless refinishing process. All they had been doing is screening and coating and my service as I proved with that very first job was way better than screening. On top of that, we completed the entire apartment in less than four hours. I could do several of these units in a single day.

I wanted to apply four coats to make sure the floor really popped when Tim came to inspect it. As I was just about to put the fourth coat on, a realtor stuck her head in the doorway of the unit.

"Oh, I forgot you were doing the floor today," she said to me. "I have a couple that wanted to look at the unit".

"That's okay, they can come in and see it," I replied. The realtor looked a bit shocked because you can't walk on the floors the sanding company was doing for at least two days!

"This is a different kind of service. I promise you can walk on it!" With that the couple came in to examine the apartment. It wasn't much of anything to be honest. There was a small kitchen, a main great room, a small hall and a closet. Still there were some interesting features as the place was built before electricity. I jumped right in to show the couple all the interesting historic items in the apartment. Right after I finished, they turned to the realtor and said, "We'll take it!" The realtor gave me the thumbs up sign, and I finished the final coat.

Like a shark seeing blood in the water, I was pumped up about this account! I mean I nailed it with the unit being completed in just four hours and the place rented. Two days after the job was finished I had still not heard back from Tim and I couldn't take it any longer. I called him to check on the results.

"Tim, this is Dan from Major Cleaning," I said. "What do you think?"

"I don't know yet," he replied. I almost couldn't believe what I was hearing. My apartment unit floor came out looking brand new and I had before and after pictures to prove it. *How could he not know?* My heart sank as I immediately thought that I was being presumptuous and that the account was not going to be that easy to land.

"What do you mean you don't know?" I asked.

"The sanding company isn't finished their unit yet," Tim answered.

Okay, well now that was a different story! A huge smile broke across my face. In fact, I am sure that Tim could "hear" the smile when I spoke again.

"Do you know mine rented already?" I said confidently.

"Yeah, I know," Tim said, seemingly smiling as well.

"Are you going to call me?" I inquired.

"Yeah I will call you." he returned.

Two days later Tim did call.

"Come on down again. I have three units for you to do and I will pay you this time for them," he said. Seven hours later, all three units were completed. All three looked great. As we were finishing up the final unit, Tim stuck his head in the door, looked at the floor and announced "Okay I fired the sanding company. The account is yours!"

We serviced one hundred and fifty units for them this second year I was doing the Sandless service and nearly three hundred the third year. Between working the other clients I had in Major Cleaning and this account, plus still testing residential work, I was working eighteen hours a day. There were times where I laid in the halls of an apartment building, put a "wet floor" sign over my head, and slept right in the hallway!

Logan and his team did an excellent job configuring their product line to my system including keeping the product line "green". I would give them feedback on each and every product they sent and then they would tweak it to what I was seeing. The end results were amazing—great, affordable products that were perfect for a franchise system that were completely kid and pet safe. I always used safe products in my company. To me, it would have been really stupid if I invented this ultra-cool system for refinishing without sanding, and it ended up killing me! Green and safe products was the only way to go; for my safety, for my staff and for my customers.

We set up a "franchise kit" of all the equipment and materials a beginning owner would need and as we entered our fourth year of prototype testing, the time was just about right to launch the brand.

By then, my Sandless refinishing was dwarfing my contract

cleaning income with thirty thousand-dollar a month the norm. Once I amped up the advertising, the price was raised to two hundred ninety-nine dollars per room and customers handed the money over without blinking an eye. While I was still about half the way to the two dollars a square foot mark, which I knew I could get, I figured I would take hold of the market first, and then slowly raise the prices. After all, there were one hundred seventy-nine other wood floor refinishing companies in the region—one *hell* of a lot of competition.

I set up the corporation to run the first and original Mr. Sandless. The goal was to show the viability of the actual model and to use that to propel franchise sales. It was June 4, 2004 when Mr. Sandless, Inc. was created, nearly five years after I discovered Sandless refinishing. There is really a very simple explanation of why I waited so long to launch the brand. To be dead honest, I was waiting for the "shoe to drop" so to speak.

Every single customer we serviced was thrilled! We had five years of perfect client satisfaction. That was nearly unheard of and so I assumed that something would happen to burst the bubble of my excitement for this system. But it never came. I count myself as honorable and there would be no way in the world I would offer this service as a franchise to anyone else unless I was absolutely sure it would be viable to them as well.

The next two-year period could be described with one word: madness. It was sheer, utter madness. Nothing in my life to this point had ever come easy to me. Life was always a constant struggle. But this time it was not "life" that was the struggle. It was the people I encountered on the way who brought grief, pain, misery and yes, through it all, success for the brand.

There are two things that I have to say about myself to "toot my own horn". The first is that there was probably no one else in the world with my uncanny common sense, who due to choosing a music career over college, who then was forced into cleaning and refinishing to make a living, who could have come up with Sandless refinishing. I was just the right person, in the right place, at the right time.

The second is, due to my life struggles to that point, there arguably was no one better suited to lead the insanity of this company to success than me. Again, right place, right time, right person. I can now introduce a key player in the launch of Mr. Sandless, who was tied to me through the initial stages of the company in the most bizarre way and how I came to name the brand through my work with this enigma of a man.

CHAPTER 2

The "Great and Powerful" Silas Jones

FLASH BACK TO 1997; two years before I came up with Sandless refinishing. One morning I was reading the local newspaper, and in the entertainment section was an article about a local musician doing a gimmicky tour to promote his brand of music. His name was Silas Jones; at least that is the name he went by for his music. He had a long last name: "Montefusco", so I assume he changed it for the very reasons I changed my last name in music.

I don't know what it was, but I was compelled to reach out to him. What do I mean by "compelled?" It is this strong feeling that I "need" to do this—that something will come out of it that is meant to fulfill my own or someone else's spiritual growth. I had been compelled before to do certain things and found the events to always be extraordinary. While this story is not about my personal relationship with God and I will save that for a different book, this topic does come up as a theme for where I will eventually go with this journey. I set out to tell "the truth" about my adventure here, and so I need to say that I recognized that God wanted me to reach out to this guy Silas.

I "get it" if you don't believe in God, or if you do, that you do not believe that He reaches out to people still even this day, or that maybe you even think I am in fact crazy. I have asked people who have told me in the past that they were "God fearing" individuals, to tell me a time when God moved in their lives. They respond with a blank look on their face. And this is from someone who believes they have a personal relationship with God. If you don't believe, believe passively, or are a staunch believer but still can't see God compelling anyone to do anything, I get it. All I ask is that you keep an open mind and that by the end of this book, you can make a better decision if what I am saying is true, or if I am indeed out of my mind, or maybe even a combination of the two.

Because of this compulsion, I actually took the newspaper up to my home office and left it there so that to remind myself to contact this guy. He lived a few towns away from me, so he was relatively close by. But for whatever reason, I got distracted and never got back to it, probably because that was the year my son was born, and he didn't sleep more than an hour per night!

Two years later, 1999, once again I read about Jones in the same paper, doing the same stupid tour to once again try to spark his music career. Once again and much more powerfully, I felt compelled to reach out to him and this time I followed through. Now this was after I had discovered Sandless refinishing. I had no time, no need, and no desire to get involved in this man's career. But I contacted him anyway—it was something I felt I *had* to do.

I found his music website and wrote him a lengthy email, to tell him what I thought he was doing wrong. Perhaps not the best introduction, but after all, I just called his tour "stupid" and I felt I should tell him why I didn't see this working for him. I mean let's face it, if it did work, it would have worked the first time! Here it was two years later, and he was doing the same gimmick again. Besides I had just had my book "Making It: Fifty Secrets of Successful Musicians (Xlibris) published and I did know a thing or two about the music industry. I didn't fail in it because of lack of talent. I just could never find a great singer to write for.

As expected, he responded that he didn't believe a single thing I said, but he agreed to meet with me to discuss things. I expected this reaction because I wanted to lay it out there to get his attention. I also knew that he didn't know what I knew about the music industry, otherwise, he would be taking a different path in his attempt to be discovered and to be a star. So, the idea of "making it" since my book was just published and was fresh in my mind. I knew completely that what he was doing was never going to work.

Silas was nothing much to look at; short, round and balding. He wasn't going to have any sex appeal that is often required in music. I listened to the album that Silas was trying to promote and thought it was very good. The one main issue about it was; it was not the genre that I was used to. I played in the rock field and all my top connections (and I had some *great* ones!) were in rock. This was a totally new genre for me. While many of the ideas I had would be perfect for him, I couldn't be sure that they would work with this type of music.

Silas worked a very good job at a huge company in another town a bit further away. Apparently, he had always put his music first, even before his family, as he had quit even better jobs in the past to promote his music, only to fail and have to return to work for someone else. He dreamed of the day he would be his own boss and be successful on his own without working for someone else, and he believed and hoped that would be through his music.

Next, I went out to see him perform live, still being compelled to "help" this guy for some strange reason. To once again explain what this is like, it is like a "weight" or "pressure" on me. I wake up to the weight, I have the weight on me all day long, and I go to sleep with the weight the last thing in my mind. It is the kind of thing where you *must* do something about it because you can't keep holding the weight—you very much want the weight gone! So, I am not going to tell you this is a pleasant thing. It is almost like to make certain you don't miss that which you are supposed to do. I was most certain there was something I was supposed to do with him or for him, and something that was important.

Silas was quite good live and played to an upper end "coffee house" type audience in an establishment that housed very big names. The place was packed for him and he ate it up. But I recognized this would never be enough. One guy on stage playing a guitar and singing to a recorded track just wasn't big box office entertainment. I pretty much had the plan outlined for how to give this guy a shot at stardom—thinking this was the reason I was being pushed to get involved with him.

But once again my biggest concern was the genre. Someone once said that this type of music was like "performing in one's own living room". Not a big money venture for sure and it was going to take some serious coin to make this work.

For the next two months, the compulsion to help Jones was very powerful. I knew, absolutely *knew* that God wanted me to help this guy, but you know something? I said "no" and that I didn't want to do it. First, I didn't know the genre. Second, I would have to become his "manager" so to speak. Third, he had no money, so I would have to "invest" in him as well and it was going to be substantial. Fourth, I was already swamped in my own life. There was no sound reason why I should do it and if anything, there was plenty to say that I should just walk away. I didn't just want to walk away, I wanted to run!

Yet the weight on me continued until I couldn't take it any longer. As I saw not a single redeeming reason to focus on to do this, I prayed to God and asked for a "deal". As I wrote earlier, I understand you may think I am insane for such a belief in God or if you do believe in God, you may laugh thinking He doesn't make deals. Again, this part is for another book. Nonetheless, I asked for the deal.

I asked that if I did this, since I had no real concrete reason to do it, that God reveal to me before I die, why I did it. I mean Silas did not appear to me at all to be spiritual and God-fearing. So why would God want this to happen for him? What was the purpose of helping this guy pursue his music career? It just didn't make any sense to me at all. As I prayed this, the weight lifted off me for a moment and I knew that meant the deal was struck. Great, now I had to work with this guy to make him a success and with my own money. Some deal!

I outlined the plan of attack for Silas and as I grew to realize, he disagreed with everything! *Now* I understood that this was the reason he didn't believe a single thing I wrote in that original email. He was just such a contrary person. He spoke the word "no" more than any human being I have ever encountered in my life, so much so, that he would repeat it multiple times. "No, no, no, no," was his most quoted line.

Anyway, the plan was to get Jones a live band to perform with him, to have his album "mastered" by a professional sound engineer, to get copies of the new mastered version of the album, to pick a single to be distributed, and to promote the album on the radio, which is the real way to breakout. I personally knew some of the top radio promoters in the country.

Jones didn't argue that much with the band because he understood he needed to make money playing live, and people don't pay for shows with a guy and a tape recorder. But he totally disagreed with the mastering of his album. What mastering does is prepare the album for the big leagues. It compresses it for radio play, so that it stacks up with all the other top artists, as well as to balance the equalization to make it a more pleasant and dynamic listening experience. An un-mastered recording sounds *dreadful* on the radio. I know this for a fact. I released two such recordings that when I heard them on the radio, they sounded weak and pathetic compared to other artists with mastered works. This would also mean that his other copies would then be junk—if the mastering came out as well as I told him it would.

But I convinced him to at least give it a shot because after all, *I was paying for everything*! What in the world he had to be contrary about when I was paying was beyond me. I had a connection in the city of the top master engineer in the region and booked the session for Silas. Jones brought his original tape and the engineer got to work. The result was startling and was so much more powerful than what Silas had been promoting. It was a game changer!

Silas reluctantly agreed it was a lot better. I ordered a thousand copies of the new mastered album and five hundred singles of the title track which was the one I had decided to promote, thinking it was the best "breakout song" on the album. We pulled together a bunch of musicians that we knew to form a decent band for him, and I hired a promoter who worked in his genre to promote the new single on the radio. One of the musicians was a friend of Silas by the name of J.R. which wasn't really his name but some sort of nickname. J.R. would eventually come to work for me, but that story will be coming up a bit later. J.R. didn't have a drop of common sense and this led to many funny stories about his time in my company. Meanwhile, the stage was set for Silas.

I couldn't possibly have done any more for this guy. The promoter did a good job getting airplay and the first Silas single made it to #2 on the small charts, #26 on the mid-level charts, but did not break out to the top. I hired a producer and we cut a thirty second commercial for the album which I then had played on a music television station which was a very popular music cable channel at the time. Due to his popularity, I pulled some strings and got Silas on the cover of the mid-level charts magazine, which was a big deal. Only twelve artists per year got the cover. Everything seemed to be coming together.

I hired a great photographer I knew from my music days to take a picture of Silas to use for the cover shot. Of course, as usual, Silas was negative about a new picture and wanted to use some old photo he had been promoting for years that screamed "I am a dork!" I wanted something much more edgy that would catch people's attention because for heaven sakes, it was the cover of a very prestigious music magazine, read by the entire industry. And here he wanted to go with a picture that looked like something you get when you buy a picture frame!

I booked a room at a local bed and breakfast in a country county that had an antique decorated room with a four-post bed. I hired a smoking hot model/singer who was also trying to promote herself to be the love interest for Silas in the shot which tied into his first single. There we are in this gorgeous appointed room, Silas sitting on the edge of the four-post bed, with my model brushing her hair at the vanity directly behind him. It was the perfect shot...except for Silas, who looked like he was about to have a vasectomy!

After a couple of shots were taken, the photographer looked at me and shook his head. I shook my head in return and I knew it was up to me to do something to make this shot come to life.

"For heaven sakes Silas," I announced. "You look like a freaking two by four! You are a radio charting artist, in this gorgeous room, with this gorgeous woman and you look like you are about to have a root canal! I mean the woman you wrote the song about; pretend this is her. This is it! This is your chance! What emotion do you want her to see out of you? I know it isn't *death*, so could we please get a little more excited?"

The best word I could use to describe Silas Jones was "stiff". He *was* a freaking stiff! His music was great, his performing was great, but his personality was the equivalent of a dried sun flower seed! Somehow, he loosened up enough for the photographer to get the shot that ended up as the cover of the magazine.

Along with all of this, I set up a huge show for him to play on Valentine's Day promoted by a local radio station that had his single on rotation. We sent out posters and promotional material for the station to promote the event, the band practiced hard and was ready for the entire two-hour show, and I provided all the sound and light systems which I would run myself to make sure Silas and company looked and sounded great. I had hoped that this would launch a potential tour for Silas, so he could start earning money as I was bleeding to death on this project to that point!

As the radio DJ took the stand, she announced the beginning of the show that night.

"Ladies and gentlemen, WWHY is proud to present, local recording artist Silas Jones!"

With that, Silas started the show to an audience that consisted of... no one! Not a single person came out to see him despite all that radio play and announcements. It was what I was told it was; like playing in your own living room, literally! I could see that performing was never going to work in this genre.

Within six months, everything came to a head with this effort. I booked a massively great gig for Silas and the band. There would be a day-long event with thirty some bands performing in front of *twelve* record labels. These labels were not looking for "rock bands" but for unique niche bands that was exactly what Silas had to offer. I was very fortunate to be able to get him on the bill.

But it was way more than this. Despite everything I did to promote this guy, the weight was still on me. I failed to complete whatever task it was that I needed to complete! I dreaded the thoughts of continuing to funnel money into this project when I knew it was already dead in the water, but by that time, I was already in too deep. I had no choice but to continue.

After thinking hard on the matter, I realized where I had gone terribly wrong. I had made one major mistake in this entire effort and if I hadn't made this mistake, I would have already completed what I needed to do and could have ended my investment. I *totally* misread the assignment. I wasn't supposed to make Silas Jones a star. In fact, this wasn't about Jones at all! I was supposed to get one of his songs out there—*that* was the real goal. When it came time to pick the single to be released, it was a tossup between the title track, which had the best breakout capabilities, or another song on the album which I considered the best "radio" song on his album. I went with the title track and that is where I knew I made a mistake. Had I realized that Silas was not the main focus, I would have gone with the radio track and my work would have been completed.

By that point of time, I believed I had the mission completely figured out. I believed that somewhere "out there" there was someone who was down and out, who was at the end of what they could carry, that they were broken, maybe even suicidal, who needed to hear that particular Silas song to pull them out of the funk they were in. I believed that this person would go on to do something great, and that God wanted them to continue to push on. That upbeat Silas tune was what was going to do this for this person, in the most bizarre path imaginable with me pulling all the strings.

Silas Jones would have never been able to do this without me, this mystery person would never hear this song without me, and God wouldn't be able to move in their life without me. Why that song, why that time and who that person is has not been revealed to me and to this day and at that point, I was still waiting for my "deal" to be fulfilled. At that time, I honestly expected that in some time in my life I would hear this person explain that when they were down they heard this one song that pulled them out of that funk and then I will know.

I paid for the copies of the second single and received the contract to promote it on the radio. I will never forget the day I signed it because the entire world seemed to open up that very moment. I signed the form to promote the second single and faxed it to the promoter, then headed up to a church I had to service that afternoon for my janitorial company. The very moment I faxed the form, the weight lifted off me! I was free of the task I was supposed to do and now could move on from the Silas Jones project after it cost me more than fifty thousand dollars!

The moment I opened the door to the church, the name of my brand popped into my head. I would call the service "Mr. Sandless". The name was perfect! I am a big believer in not making potential customers "guess" what your company does. The name should say it all. Also, since our customer demographics were 70% female, I wanted to pick a title that would give some authority. Mr. Sandless was perfect! I felt this was a gift from God for what I had so reluctantly done. I probably should have never fought it to start with because I know the outcome to these things are normally incredible. I felt like whoever I was supposed to save through a Silas Jones song, that person was saved. I know it sounds insane. I guess if you're in my shoes you would understand and believe it as I do. But remember this moment, as it is the most important to my story which will come full circle by the end as God fulfills the deal and reveals to me know why I was to do this good deed to start with.

I immediately filed for trademark protection for my new name and purchased the URL to use. It was unfortunate that I didn't have a good lawyer back then, as the trademark office would only grant me using the term "Sandless" with the "Mr" and not alone. The reason they say was because there were "sandless water fountains". This I was to learn later was sheer nonsense. I invented Sandless refinishing and both the service and the word did not exist prior to me coining that term and creating that service. Even to this very day, Sandless comes up as "miss-spelled" in all writing programs! Not getting this trademark protection would open the door for knock-off companies using my term for their businesses in the future. More on that coming up.

But there was even more to come! The lukewarm believer Silas received a gift as thanks from God as well. It was not going to be the kind of gift that Silas would want or as I learned, even accept. But none the less it was a blessing for his song. Once again, I was compelled but it was to tell Silas the message I had for him from God and I called him that night, extremely excited for him in what I now believed.

"Silas God has a message for you," I started. "Something huge is going to happen to you at the record company showcase that I got you in. God wants me to tell you that He is going to reveal something to you in such a fashion that you will see His hand moving and you will have the answer to your life's question. This gig, it will be revealed to you if you are going to be a star or not! I am absolutely positive something is going to happen there to give you an answer to this question!"

Now telling this to someone who may or may not even believe in God, I already knew the reaction was going to be passive at best. But I was convinced that God would move that day to show Silas something. Because of this, I worked the band like dogs to make sure the music was perfect, the vocals were perfect, and the timing was perfect. I wanted no excuses if this didn't work out and by making sure there were no loose ends, if in the end things failed, it would not be from lack of trying. But the only thing was; I couldn't be there for that show! I had to attend my in-laws fiftieth wedding anniversary party that day, and so Silas and the band would be doing the show without me.

Now if at this point you believe I am way over the top when it comes to God and this kind of thing, this is your chance to see if that theory is true or false and maybe even set the stage for the rest of this book. To make a pronouncement like I did to Silas about this particular show would prove what I am saying about "God moving" in someone's life or it would not. It will prove that maybe I am not at all crazy. Let's face it. If *nothing* at all happened at that show after I made such a strong statement, after I received such a strong message, then even I would think I was insane. Here is the chance for you to decide for yourself. Just know that this is not coincidence! It is *impossible* for me to have pulled this out of thin air and everything I write here is the absolute truth.

The Sunday after his event and the anniversary party I attended, I called Silas in the afternoon to find out how the gig went. To be dead honest, I was really excited, again because I *knew* that something was going to happen, and I believed and hoped it was going to be a positive thing. Silas recounted the day like he was telling me a trip he made to the grocery store; like it was nothing extraordinary.

Apparently, despite my warnings to "get there early," Silas and the band were late getting to the city where the event was being held. From there they had trouble locating the sign-up booth. There were nine venues on the ticket for that day, all within walking distance, so that the record company executives could walk between venues and the times were set up for each band to play at precise times so that they wouldn't be missed. Being late was not a great idea!

When they found the venue they were to perform at, they had to hustle to get their equipment in and set up because they were soon to be on. As they were removing the equipment from their vehicles, a thunderstorm blew in, which was extremely rare in this part of the country in February—the dead of winter. It was already cold and damp out, but now it was a torrential downpour. It rained just long enough that not only were they all soaked, but it strangely stopped the moment they got the last piece of equipment in the place. Then they had to carry the equipment up three flights of stairs because there was no elevator in the old building.

I sat there listening and thinking to myself, "Why in the world is Silas so calm retelling this story, for this is no trip to the grocery store!" Anyway, since the rain stopped, the record labels made it to the venue as Silas Jones and the boys started the first song. Three lines out of his mouth later, Silas totally lost his voice! Between the rain, the cold and damp, and then climbing the stairs, not only couldn't he sing, he couldn't even get a word out! It was like his voice was completely taken from him! J.R. had to take over the vocals and that was the end of that.

There is so much to say here at this point, but first things first. If you don't see this as a "movement" I don't know what else to tell you. While all of us hope that when God does move in our lives it is a positive outcome I can see that initially this could be read as a negative. But it really isn't at all. This was in fact a gift from God to Silas. Imagine if you spent years and years of your life chasing a "dream", and if you didn't know better, you kept on chasing that dream for years after it, putting everything second to this dream, wouldn't it be better to know that it wasn't ever going to pan out? If someone came along and proved to you it wasn't going to work out, as heartbreaking as that may be, wouldn't that be better than continue to sacrifice your life, your energy, and your family for this dream that was never to be?

I knew at that moment that Silas Jones would never be the star he hoped to be and even more so, that he would never have the success in music he so desperately craved. It's a funny thing but I was faced with a similar situation many years before this. I prayed and asked God how I could walk away from music knowing I was so damn talented on the guitar and writing music and singing. The answer I received then was for me to give it my best shot, and that once I did that and didn't "make it" that I could then walk away and never look back. I gave it my best shot. I got close but didn't break through and I walked away, never to look back again.

When I explained all these things to Silas, he said he totally disagreed! He said that he took this as a sign that his road was going to be a tough one, but that he needed to continue. There is going to be much more on Silas coming up, so I am going to save the punch line to this one until a bit later. Remember that I owe you this one!

Now through this entire period two things occurred. The first was that I continued to test and refine the Mr. Sandless brand as I described in the first chapter, along with running my janitorial company, along with doing all this Silas Jones nonsense. As I said, this time period was sheer madness overall in my life. The second thing was that Silas's family and my family grew close. Silas to me was like an abused dog that I took in, and I grew to love him. I considered him my best friend at the time. His wife and mine at the time grew very close. We went out to dinners together, had each other's families over our houses, and did barbeques and parties. We grew to be like "family" to one another.

This all occurred over the three-year period I was testing Mr. Sandless as a prototype offshoot of my janitorial company and takes us up to the time when I was preparing the brand for the official launch. I had known Silas for nearly four years to that point. When I told him the name of the brand would be "Mr. Sandless," he *hated* it! While some of this was just part of who Silas was, it was more than that. I actually believed *he* wanted to name the brand as he emailed me several names in an effort to try and get me to change my mind. But that name to me was my reward for what I accomplished in my "deal" and I knew it was the right one.

It was more than this for Silas. He thought I was playing off a moniker that he used for his music style: "Mr. Silhouette". Many times he played out, he would be introduced as "Here he is, Mr. Silhouette, Silas Jones." Even in the commercial I had produced for him, the announcer said, "Mr. Silhouette, Silas Jones new album." Who knows, maybe that is why it was in my head, but does it really matter when I knew the name was going to work? Well it didn't.

As I moved forward with the business and brand, Silas Jones

would not be the force of positive reinforcement and support, but the voice of negativity and challenge, which I learned to use as a positive. Since he disagreed with absolutely every step I took, I got to be able to have a more balanced look at everything I did because I only looked at things in a positive light. Now I can't tell you a single time ever that Jones was correct. He *never* was, and I was always on point. This was just my way of turning his massive negativity into a positive.

I did everything right at that time. Since I had a full demographic breakout of our "average customer" I hired a logo company to design the Mr. Sandless logo. They did an excellent job and sent me thirty to choose from. I picked out ten that I thought had the best potential including my favorite; a huge arm holding a lightning bolt, crashing it down on a floor with sparks flying out the sides!

There was a mall marketing company that for very little money would test the logo. I bought two hundred movie tickets as giveaways to use. The marketing company would walk the mall, find someone that fit into our demographics, have them pick the logo they liked the best, and then that person would receive two movie tickets.

When I got the results, I scratched my head in disbelief. How many people in our demographic group picked my logo? Zero! It was unanimous the choice that was made, this swoosh over a shell looking thing with a strange font. Unanimous! While I knew that the choice was perfectly clear, I had no idea what the heck the logo even was. To be honest, I think our demo picked it because the "M" in the Mr. Sandless looked like a woman's ass!

Next it was back to the mall marketing company to take my new logo and put it on six of the most popular vehicle colors so that I could get the demographic tests to pick the best color for our vehicles. Unlike the logo, I had no real preference for the color of the vehicles except to be sure that our potential customers would like the logo and color combinations. The end result was that 90% picked the color silver and with that I had our logo and vehicle color.

Next was the website development. Not only did I give the development company our demographic details, I actually hired a company that fit the demographics for the site. The result was an absolutely wonderful site with warm, earthy tones and a warm, comfortable feel so that our potential customers would want to stay on it. I wrote all the text for the site, using all my sales and marketing skills. I also came up with several slogans, including a combination of words so that people knew what they were getting with Mr. Sandless. Remember this, as this slogan would eventually lead me to trouble with another company.

Silas for his part as my friend disagreed with the logo, disagreed with the vehicle color, disagreed with the website, hated the slogan, and more. But when I asked him for what he would do, it didn't line up with anything that I believed. He never had any better ideas besides his desperate attempts to insert himself into my new company.

Now that the logo, color and website were completed, I started looking for a unique vehicle to launch the system with. I wanted something modern and progressive, economic and eye catching and settled on a new brand called "Scion" made by Toyota. They had a version called the "XB" that was a very small boxy looking vehicle that came in silver. The sides were plain, straight and like a billboard, perfect for what I was looking for.

I contracted a company to create our vehicle decal based upon the logo that was chosen. Again, to keep it progressive and innovative, I wanted the vehicle to really stand out. I had them create a pin stripe from the logo which grew larger toward the back of the vehicle until it was a flame, as if the vehicle was a rocket ship taking off! It was extreme as much as it was extremely eye-catching. I measured the back of those Scions a dozen times to be sure I could lower the back seats and fit all the equipment. Once I was convinced, I purchased three of them to launch my Mr. Sandless, and ordered three full franchise kits from Logan's company to fill them with supplies.

The brand was about to be launched! Little did I know what was to follow. Now that I have set up the rollercoaster, hold onto your hats as the coaster is about to leave the loading dock!

CHAPTER **3**

Calling All Loons

THIS NEXT APPLICANT into the foray of Mr. Sandless was a friend of my family for years. This family friend Henry heard about my new venture and offered up to me a friend of his by the name of Caden. I knew Caden since he was younger as he always hung around this family friend. He was rather tall and very thin with a full head of long blond hair. As he grew older, Caden was troubled to say the least, with drug use and heavy drinking that he participated in along with Henry. Henry told me that Caden cleaned up his act and would be a good "lead tech" or manager for me at Mr. Sandless, and he urged me to meet up with him.

Long prior to this, I ran into Caden in a bar years earlier. He told me he was down on his luck so to speak and as it just so happened, my janitorial company was exploding at the seams. I asked him if he would like to come to work for me and told him the kind of money he could make with this type of work, which was way more substantial than anything else he was going to find. He readily agreed, and I gave him my contact number and told him to show up Monday morning. He never did and blew me completely off. I certainly wasn't too thrilled at the prospect of hiring Caden for my next adventure after that experience.

But as luck or providence would have it, I had a large Sandless job in a converted mansion for a Sunday which was the only day the business that used it was going to be closed. None of my other guys from my janitorial company would be available that day. I called Henry and Caden to come out, work with me that day, that I would pay both, and then they could see the system for themselves.

During the job, I told Caden straight up that I wasn't too thrilled that I offered him a great opportunity before and that he blew me off. He explained to me that he was really "messed up" back then, that he was now "clean and sober" and hadn't had any drugs or alcohol in several years. On top of that, he was diagnosed with some other malady and was on medication for that. From what I could see from working with him that day, he was like a manic Chihuahua with OCD! But it seemed like he would be a good worker to add to the system, someone I could have as my "right hand man" despite other obvious flaws.

The moment we finished the job, Caden yelled "I'm in!" By that time, I had a darn good system worked out and the results were startling. I could tell Henry seemed a bit put off that he was not being included in this new venture; so, let's talk about Henry for a little bit here.

Henry was a short and stocky ginger with terrible skin, blisteringly orange hair, and married to a very wealthy woman. She was wealthy in the most bizarre way imaginable. While it seemed as if their family was already "blue blood" and came from old money, as well as the father and patriarch of the family being a well-known doctor, I am talking about wealth *way* beyond that. Henry's wife Drusilla, an enormous woman with black hair and a butt so big I often wondered how she fit into any chair, stepped into wealth without doing a damn thing to earn it. She earned it just by existing—simply by being in the right place at the right time! When the family was young, they lived next door to an older couple who had no children. These older people became like family to Drusilla's family, even going so far as to call them "Grandma and Grandpa".

Grandpa started work in 1938 for a new delivery company. Instead of taking pay, he took shares in the company, which grew to be the largest of its kind in the world. In fact, it grew to become a sixty *billion* dollar a year business! Basically, by that time, Grandpa owned this company and on top of that, it was privately held. There would come a day when it would move to become publicly held and the shares would increase to ridiculous proportions.

Over the years, Grandpa gave shares of his company as gifts to his adopted family. For Christmas for example, each family member got ten thousand dollars' worth of shares. As the company kept growing, the shares kept increasing in value. Drusilla, who was the youngest child in the family was worth over seven million dollars by the time she was to marry Henry, an amazing amount of money for someone in their mid-twenties. And this is before the company went public! Heaven knows what she was worth after that split!

I saw Henry right before his wedding to Drusilla. There didn't seem like there was any passion or love of any kind shared between them. In fact, Drusilla despised most if not all of Henry's friends, so much so that when he handed in his list of friends to be invited to the wedding, she nixed several of them without telling him! He found out when he bumped into them and they expressed anger for not being invited to attend.

It seemed clear to me that Drusilla would be wearing the pants in that family and that Henry was willing to go along with this thanks to Drusilla being worth so much money. Of course, Henry also told me that "they", being "the family", made him sign a prenuptial agreement—in case he was a gold digger. I knew he wasn't that. He was just a spineless individual who believed he would have a life of luxury through his wife.

I attended the wedding; you know one of those "affairs" at a super-posh country club with ten groomsmen and ten bridesmaids, ice sculptures, a thirty-piece band, flaming baked Alaska and probably exceeding a couple hundred thousand dollars in cost. The only remarkable thing at the event that I can recall is that they didn't even look like they were in love!

Well as it turned out, the life of Reilly was not what Henry was going to live. After his wife pulled some political strings, he got a job with a township where he would head their maintenance department. This was a political job placement where apparently the family had connections as well as wealth.

Henry told me while working with him that day that Drusilla "made" him take that job. He said he hated it, hated the smell of the trucks every day and the diesel fuel odor that came into his office. This couple had more than enough money so that they would never need to worry about it again. But Drusilla wanted Henry out of the house and out of her hair and again, she wore the pants in that household. I grew to learn that Drusilla was very "tight" when it came to money and she didn't want to spend a dime of "her" funds. She actually expected to live on Henry's income!

Right around this time, I listed my janitorial company for sale. There would be no way I could keep both companies running as the janitorial company took up way too much of my time. Besides that, I absolutely hated a great deal of my customers. We could do thirty location's floor refinishing in one night, and they would call to bitch about being five minutes late to one of the stores. Five freaking minutes! I started to joke back then that I would take a candy bar for the company. If you want to see what I mean, read my book "True Dirt: Confessions of a Male Housecleaner (Xlibris 2004).

I hired a guy to replace the work I did in Major Cleaning. His name was Jack and he was a real nice guy, a bit older than me, very tall with broad shoulders and a boatload of experience in the maintenance field. It only took me a week or so to get him train and he totally replaced me in my own company so that I could launch Mr. Sandless. But it wasn't long before I realized that Jack and I had a strange connection.

He came to me a couple of weeks later and said he was home with his wife and kids, and that when he told them who he was working for, the kids said, "We know that guy!" These two kids were Jack's step sons. Jack was married to their mother. As it turns out, Jack was married to a woman from Italy, Missy, the ex-wife of none other than

Silas Montefusco. How about that for strange coincidences? Not only that, I heard the real story of what happened between Silas and Missy. Missy told me that Silas cheated on her with his current wife and after he left Missy and her two kids he married his mistress! Now how about that news? Silas of course never said a word of this to me.

Since we had that huge account with servicing the university apartments, I made sure to switch over my contact and billing information from Major Cleaning to Mr. Sandless so that I could retain this account even when my janitorial company was sold. While the new owner would get my tile refinishing system, they would not be getting anything to do with wood refinishing and would even be banned from servicing wood. The brokers I hired said it would take at least six to nine months to sell the janitorial company, so during that time I had to deal with managing both the new entity as well as my old.

I started Mr. Sandless just as I felt a new franchisee would so that I could see how it would go. How could I tell someone else how to do this if I didn't experience it for myself? I started from my home office and figured I would grow it slow and steady from there. I would release all my other employees to the new owner of the janitorial company accept two that I would keep for my new venture.

The first of those was another close family friend by the name of Matt who was short with an average build and completely bald. He showed up on the doorstep of my house years earlier when he was just sixteen. His parents were divorced, and he lived with his mother. I suppose this was why he was so wild as he loved to drink and party. I gave him a job in my janitorial company and he worked well through his high school years. But once he was in college he really turned wild, and the drinking and drugs got way out of hand.

Over the years he worked for me, I fired him at least a dozen times! But I always took him back. To be dead honest, I grew to love the kid like he was my own son. I tried my best to be a father and mentor to him, but he was already damaged goods before he even came into my life. And so, my efforts really didn't mean much and all I did was basically become an enabler for him.

CEO OF INSANITY

Luke was a friend of Matt's who I also hired. As far as workers go, he was beyond exceptional! He was a stocky kid with a big back and arms and could really hustle on the job. While I took Matt with me from the cleaning company because of my feelings for him, I took Luke because he was such a great worker. This would be the team I would build Mr. Sandless on to start.

Matt and Luke were so good on floors that none of us needed to talk about the job as we worked. We would talk football, or politics or music or whatever, and each of us knew exactly what job we needed to do, in what order we needed to do it, and how to not get in each other's ways. We were the perfect team and proved this by doing three full house refinishing's in just one day! I would never find a better team than this.

The first month of the new Mr. Sandless, I had no jobs at all. It was like I said; I followed the guide in the handbook I was writing so that a new franchisee would know exactly what to expect. That month I was meeting with advertising vendors to start the marketing plan I came up with to begin to grow the business.

The second month my new Mr. Sandless had no jobs. The third month, I started to get customer calls, but a strange thing happened right away. Potential customers said that they had never heard of me before and asked if I had any references. Despite all the planning and all the perfectly laid out things like logos, trucks, supplies and equipment, it never dawned on me that I would now be having credibility issues. There were many people back then who told me their husbands said that Mr. Sandless was an "internet scam"! Great—just what I needed.

While I totally wanted to separate Mr. Sandless from my other company, Major Cleaning, I couldn't do it until Mr. Sandless could stand on its own two feet. For the first six months or so, I had to explain to people that the system was five years old, that we serviced more than a thousand customers with 100% customer satisfaction, and that I ran it as a prototype offshoot of the main company, Major Cleaning, which had a stellar reputation. If that didn't seem to work, I would drop the "university" name. While servicing all those apartments for the university, we also got to service many of the professor's homes. That became my battle cry; that if we were good enough for the university, we would be good enough for them. Thankfully it seemed to work!

Matt, Luke and I serviced eleven jobs that third month and in the fourth month, we serviced eighteen. I had to develop another trick to get the women calling me to book. I called it the "husband challenge".

"My husband said this is *impossible*," said a woman I was trying to book. "He says it is just an internet scam!"

"I have a deal for your husband; a challenge if you will," I replied. "You book me to do the service. When I come out, I will hand you a one-hundred-dollar bill. Your husband needs to leave one hundred dollars as well. I will service your floors. If they do not come out to your liking, you can keep my hundred, you owe me nothing, and you can put my money toward the price to sand your floors. My finish will sand right off just like urethane. If, however, the floors come out to your liking, you must pay me, and I get your husband's one hundred dollars as well. Ask him if we have a deal". After using this gimmick six times and winning the extra hundred six times, when I made this offer to women who called, I would tell them I am "six for six" and then they would book without taking the bait!

It was so maddening listening to people tell me they thought it was a scam and that it is impossible to be refinishing wood without sanding it. For heaven sakes, I had been doing it for five years by then, more than a thousand times and it worked every time. It just got so old to hear! I had this one guy waiting for me at a job who announced he was a carpenter.

"You are going to f*** my floors up!" he said confidently to me. I offered the one-hundred-dollar challenge, but he said he would just be hanging around so that when I ruined the floors he could tell me he "warned me" that I would ruin them. When he came up from the basement after they were finished, he had the most dumbfounded look on his face I have ever seen anyone have.

"It's *impossible*!" he muttered repeatedly. "It *just can't be*!"

"It *is*, and if you could get my check now, I can be on my way," I said to the rocket scientist carpenter. This happened so many times. I would have people yell at me from their vehicles as I drove by them saying it was impossible to refinish without sanding!

I stopped at an estimate I needed to do at an historic building that was being rehabbed. I was just getting through with a presentation and I was in a suit and tie. The floors were old maple but covered with construction debris. As I spoke to the foreman explaining the service, the "boss" showed up and spoke to me like I was a piece of trash.

"Throw this charlatan out of here!" he barked to the foreman. "This is absolute *bullshit* that you can refinish without sanding." I told the guy I wasn't too happy that he was calling me names without knowing anything about me, and he was so bent out of shape that he got into my face as if he was going to kick my ass! He was a big SOB too!

I challenged him that I would do a three by three-foot section of the floor right there and then to prove it works. With that, he grabbed a bunch of junk that was on the floor and slammed it against the wall to clear and space for me and barked "Here!" for the spot I was to do. I took my coat and tie off and headed to my Scion, which I was thankful I was driving with all the materials. In about an hour, I had a single coat of finish on the floor and it looked amazing. When he saw it, his entire demeanor changed.

"Get a price from him for doing the entire property," he whispered to his foreman. I sent them a bid for $10,000. I wasn't about to work for this total jerk! But this was the kind of thing I had to put up with back then.

When things heated up more, I called Caden and told him I would most likely be able to start him in four weeks. That was at the end of the fourth month. One day later, I told him to start in a week. One more day, I told him to start that next Monday! I booked thirty thousand dollars in business in just two days, booking out the fifth month completely.

When Caden showed that Monday, I handed him a handbook to follow for the service and sent Matt with him, while I would take Luke with me on another job.

"What, no training?" Caden asked in a panic. Who could blame him? He had only done that one job with me to that point and I wasn't even training him at that time.

"No time to train Caden. Matt knows what to do. Follow the handbook, call me for tech support and you will get through it," I replied. From that point it got even more maddening. I put an advertisement in the paper for more help, and immediately began a search for a small office to get out of my home. With Matt, Luke, and Caden all driving to my house plus the work vehicles, it was getting way untenable. I had to get this business out of my house!

The problem was, at that time the economy was still expanding and hot. There were very few offices available anywhere in the region. I found one in my town that was six hundred square feet that had just become available. I gave the first month rent and deposit and signed a ridiculous lengthy lease from the landlord who lived in the complex he rented—not the best scenario but I really didn't have a choice. I got some desks, a phone system, alarm system, fire system and passed the stupid borough inspection, then moved in all the supplies and equipment, and moved the three trucks into the lot. I could not believe how fast the business was growing!

It was at that time that I got a call from Henry who asked to work for me. He had heard from his friend Caden how much we were growing and that we were looking for immediate help. I told him straight out that I didn't think it was a good idea. I did *not* want to get involved in his marital issues with Drusilla who pulled a lot of political strings to get him that cushy job with the township. He whined and cried to me on the phone about the fumes in the garage and the smell of the trucks and that he felt this was beneath him. I told him I would have to think about it.

To reset the stage at this point, my new business Mr. Sandless was exploding, my old business was busy as hell, I had two young children at home to spend time with, an office to manage that I couldn't even be in, tons of calls to make, supplies to order, workers to hire, people to train and on top of that, people started calling in to purchase a franchise to become a Mr. Sandless dealer! To get everything done I had to get done, I worked on four hours sleep each night for that first year and a half! Now you understand why I was telling people I would take a candy bar for my janitorial company instead of the six figures it was listed at! I was literally losing my mind.

At the six-month point, the brokers found a family that wanted to buy my janitorial company. I was elated! In between all the other madness, I took these people around to all my vast accounts and showed them the business, explained how they could work it, and how they could continue to grow it. They said they would pay me cash for it.

But before I could celebrate, the business brokers called me in for a meeting. They asked if I just wanted to get out, or if I wanted the business to continue after me. When I asked why they wanted to know that, they told me that in their opinion, that this family would run the business into the ground and that they believed they didn't know anything about business!

It didn't take me much thought. I had a great staff and I loved my workers. All the gals who worked for me did a fantastic job, never complained, and always showed up for work even if they were not feeling well. I could never do that to them, so I told the brokers to tell the family I wouldn't be selling to them. This bodes very well for their honesty and trustworthiness because these brokers would not get their commission until the sale. But for me, this was like putting a hundred-pound sack on my back again. The burden of doing the juggling things would continue.

Now, on top of all this other madness, I had Henry calling me again to come to work for me. It was then I received a call from none other than Drusilla who proceeded to bitch me out for ever considering hiring her husband! She told me that she pulled a lot of strings to get him that "great job" and that how dare I interfere in their lives. I could barely get a word in edgewise, but I was able to say that *I* was not the one asking Henry to work for me; that it was the other way around. With the ever-so-un-scary threat of "I warn you" she hung up on me.

The very next call I received was from my mother, God rest her soul. Okay I must explain my mother for a moment here. Mom had a "pecking order" in our household. My father, God rest his soul, was *not* number one. That position fell to the oldest son. Then my dad was number two, and the chain continues downward until it hits me being in the dead last position. For whatever it was, I was always "the black sheep" of the family to my mother. She had absolutely no respect for me and I never really was able to figure out why.

She did however have massive respect for Drusilla and her family. That was the family my mother had always dreamed of belonging to, with Drusilla being "the doctor's daughter" and their maids and wealth, my mom ate that right up and did everything she could do to weasel her way into their lives. She just simply loved the idea of being "rich" like Drusilla's family was, and she was more than willing to take crumbs from them just to feel that way.

Now I will just relay one story of my mother, so that you see what I am talking about when I say she had no respect for me. Even though I am telling one story like this, I have many that I could share. But this isn't some type of psychiatric confession, so I will keep it to just one. I have long ago forgiven my mother of all offenses against me.

It was around the time of Henry and Drusilla's wedding. My mother needed to get a dress for the event as did my now ex-wife. I agreed to take both dress shopping, which I would have rather simply jumped off a tall bridge. After picking my mother up some forty minutes away, we visited the first dress shop. My ex-wife was able to get a very nice dress right away there. But not my mother; oh no. Everything she tried on, no matter how great she looked in it, it was "junk" so that we had to move on to another store. And then another, and another until we were miles away at our eighth store and there was nothing whatsoever to show for it.

That was when my mother told me that she really had her heart set on this dress in a little shop five freaking minutes from her house! Here we were heading to our ninth store, now more than an hour from her home and she finally decides to share this information with me. It wasn't like I had anything else going on in my life at the time, so I turned around and headed to the tiny dress shop.

Mom came out of the dressing room with "her" dress and looked like a million dollars. That is exactly what she wanted to look like to "represent" to Drusilla's family. I told her that she may as well get the matching shoes and matching earrings as well, and I paid the bill in full, two thousand seven hundred fifty dollars. She didn't even thank me when I dropped her off.

Okay this is not the story yet. We all went to the foo-foo, fa-fa wedding, mom looked great and the baked Alaska was over-cooked. This wedding cost me a small fortune, for my tux, my ex-wife's dress, my mother's dress, earrings and shoes, and for a room I had to get for two nights just to be able to attend as well as a "big" cash gift because mommy dearest told me I had to "represent" our family with pride and dignity.

Now here is the deal. My mom did *not* want me to buy her that dress and the other items. What I heard through the family was that she wanted *Henry* and *Drusilla* to buy her the dress. My mother had such disrespect for me that she *never* wanted to accept something like that from me. Now, I had already heard just how cheap the multi-millionaire Drusilla was as well as I already heard that she *refused* to take my mother dress shopping. Where it stood at that moment was with my mother telling Drusilla and Henry how much I spent on her, with Mom hoping that these two would "reimburse me" for the cost. Then mom could be proud again, knowing that she wasn't wearing something paid for by the black sheep.

Think I am kidding? I'm not. After Drusilla told my mother she was not giving me a penny toward the dress, my mother called my now ex-wife to her home.

When my ex got there, my mother threw her the dress.

"Take this thing, I don't want it!" she said angrily. "I never looked good in that thing anyway, so you take it." You see, in my mother's head was this notion that by giving me back the dress I paid for, her and the black sheep were now "even", though it was worthless as my wife and my mother were not the same size.

Now back to the phone call that day. The "wrapped around Drusilla's little finger" mother of mine, was told by Drusilla to talk some sense into me and get me to leave her husband Henry alone. Remember, none of this was my idea! Henry is the one who approached me, not the other way around.

Immediately as I answered my mother's call that day she lit into me. How dare I involve myself into rich Drusilla's poor pathetic life and that I needed to leave poor, poor distraught Henry alone because I was causing a problem for him. Not only that, my dear loving mother told me straight out that my business was a joke.

"That business is going to fail!" she announced all-knowingly to me. "Nobody is going to want to get their floors done during the summer because they go on vacations. You are a fool giving up your cleaning business." She had no idea that I had tested this for years at that point. She had no idea that the new business was already exploding and that I couldn't even keep up with it. I don't even think my mother knew that my IQ was ranked in the top 1% of the world and honestly, she wouldn't have cared anyway. But that is what you get when someone has no respect for you.

"Thank you for your vote of confidence, mom," I deadpanned. Then I explained *again*, that *Henry* was the one who started this, not me and that I didn't offer him a job, nor did I give him a job. The moment I hung up, I dialed Henry.

"Thanks to your wife and my mother, there is no way in hell I am hiring you Henry!" I exclaimed. I was so pissed off.

"It's too late!" Henry returned. "I already quit. I will see you on Monday." With that, he hung up on me.

So my new business Mr. Sandless was exploding, my old business was busy as hell, I had two young children to spend time with, an office to manage that I couldn't even be in, tons of calls to make, supplies to order, workers to hire, people to train and on top of that, people were calling in to purchase a franchise to become a Mr. Sandless dealer and now I had to deal with Drusilla and my freaking mother! Simply unreal. Little did I know that the stage was set for a series of nightmares a horror writer couldn't image! If you think this is bad, we haven't even started.

CHAPTER **4**

So Much for Hiring Family Friends

EIGHT MONTHS INTO launching Mr. Sandless we were at five trucks! I had to get two more vehicles—silver vans this time—hire several new workers and order more equipment and supplies. By that time the business was earning sixty thousand a month and I still couldn't keep up with the volume.

When Henry showed up, I threw him a handbook and sent him out with Luke to do his first job. I know and understand that you may feel that instead of taking Henry on, that I should have given him a good swift boot to the rear. I hope this shows through; that I am a good man. There are plenty of people who would have simply not hired Henry and told him to go away, so I get that. If things weren't already crazy enough, I had to take both Caden and Henry's calls during the day so that I could give them tech support on the jobs they were on, while I tried to train three other guys on the job I was on while I tried to get that job done. It was all so maddening!

To keep the peace, I made Henry "acting vice-president" of the company, so that it would at least appear to Drusilla and my mother that he made a unilateral move—you know—as if working on trucks all day was equal to being vice-president of this new revolutionary brand. But that did in fact keep them off my back, because Henry told both his wife and my mother how busy we were and that we had people lining up to take franchises.

It was already into 2005 and I needed to get out of the truck and start to focus on franchising. I had already proven that the business model was very powerful and was ready to be franchised. I had ten guys who were all somewhat trained, and finally came the day when I would be able to stay back in the office and start to get organized. All those months before this point I was running the business from my cell phone. Back then the cell phones were like blocks of wood. I had a plug-in earpiece, so I could keep the thing in my pocket and work on a floor while I still did business! On one job, the thing shorted out and nearly electrocuted me as it singed my ear. Blue tooth wasn't invented yet in case you are wondering. I used to tell people that I was applying finish on a floor while I talked to them and that was the truth!

I will never forget the day that I reach the end of what I could take to that point. I was doing an entire home in a town a few miles from our offices. The floors were really in bad shape that day. I had the office calls forward to my cell, and the phone just kept ringing and ringing non-stop. I was frantic writing down names, addresses, phone numbers, the scope of their job, the price I gave them and the date I put them on for service. Thirty-six calls in a row! On that thirty-sixth call, I felt so bad for the woman on the phone.

Allow me to explain. The name "Mr. Sandless" was an absolute winner. Rarely did anyone who saw our ads, website or vehicle ask *what* we did. But they always, *always* asked *how* we did it. I had to give the elevator pitch countless times and to this day it drives me crazy. There I was on this terrible job that day, thirty-six calls in a row, mounds of disorganized papers with names and other information, and this woman asked the million-dollar question "So *how* do you do it?"

Almost to the point of a nervous breakdown, I said this.

"I'm sorry, I can't tell you."

"What do you mean?" she inquired.

"Listen I have given that answer so many times today that my head is spinning, and I can't say it another time!" I said as I feigned crying. She laughed, and I continued. "Let's just pretend that I told you, then you can tell me about your job, I will get you a price and get you on the schedule, then I will call you in a week or so and tell you how we do it. Is that okay?"

She agreed, and I booked thirty-six out of thirty-six, then shut my phone off as I couldn't take another call. We were booked out a full month and that was with five trucks. When I finished up the job for that day and was returning to the office, I turned my phone back on and took a call from the university apartments giving me five units that had to be serviced. And we were already booked solid. What a freaking nightmare. Friends were saying to me, "*Hey* be happy this is great that you are so busy." Oh yeah right. Just try juggling all that I was.

When I got back and opened the door to the office, I couldn't believe my eyes. There sitting in the manager's seat was Silas "Jones" Montefusco.

"*What* in the *world* are you doing here?" I asked him.

"I quit my job to come help you out!" He replied gleefully, as if I would be happy with this bit of news. "I knew you were really swamped, so I figured you could use the help to get organized." I was so exhausted and worn out, that I couldn't fight him.

I need to take a moment and explain to you the psyche of both Henry and Silas as they both have the same "M.O.". I never had a hard time reading through people and so at least I knew where I stood, even if these two never said a word. Why did Henry, with a wife who was worth millions, want so badly to quit his cushy job and join Mr. Sandless? It is simple. He saw the growth potential and knew it would grow to international stature. By getting in at the ground floor, he had a chance to make his own way, so that he would have his own wealth and not be just another subject in Drusilla's castle.

As for Silas, it was nearly identical. This was his opportunity to get in on the ground floor of a great opportunity and to make money for his music career. He was all set to cash in his friendship with me for his own good. While I recognized this, I couldn't just tell him to get out. He was my best friend at the time and he had young kids and a wife to take care of. On top of all that, I *was* inundated and kind of welcomed the help.

But now for the real kicker to this part of the story. I started paying Silas $70K a year, Henry $50K a year, and Caden $40K a year, but did not take a salary at that time for myself. Since I still had my income from my janitorial business, I did not need any money for myself from Mr. Sandless. I reinvested the rest of the profits to go toward the cost of setting up the franchise system. The only problem with having Silas was he was going to be doing the job that *I* had set out for myself—managing *my* Mr. Sandless! I would be relegated to going back out on a truck! On top of that, I hired Silas's friend J.R. to be a field tech because Silas said he needed work and another guy Willy who had a lot of sanding experience. These two will get their own stories a little bit later.

I taught Silas the phone script and the schedule and made him the manager of my business. Again, so that you don't beat me up here, if I wasn't so piled-on and exhausted, I wouldn't have taken him on. But it was a bit of a relief to have educated help because Silas was the only one in the company to have a college education. Because of that, he quickly got the hang of things and the office ran better than ever. That freed up my time to not take any more calls during the day, do just a job per day with a helper and concentrate on franchise development.

It was at this time that the name "Timmy" became part of the Mr. Sandless lexicon. During the summer months, my former company serviced many school floors, normally one school per day to fit them all in. On occasion, we would run into a school that had just been used. They were supposed to be clean and ready for us to just service the floors. When they were used, we would have to clean before we serviced the floors, which would really be a downer for my staff.

For several years to cheer up my refinishing staff when we found a

SO MUCH FOR HIRING FAMILY FRIENDS

school had been used, I would go on a tirade about "Billy and Susie", two evil kids who trashed the place on purpose. My rants were so funny that my staff completely forgot about the misery of cleaning the school before we serviced the floors.

One day, a school we were doing was trashed beyond reason. It looked deliberate. I went on a tirade saying that this was not the work of "Billy and Susie" but a much eviler child. "This is the work of *Timmy*!" I yelled.

Later that day as we pulled out a shelf, a name tag fell to the floor. Low and behold the tag boasted the name of "Timmy". "I *knew* it!" I yelled. "It *is* the work of evil Timmy!" That tag has been in my office for the past 18 years on top of the cartoon character "Timmy Turner".

Only a couple of days later at another school, I was directing one of my guys to go and get the machine from the van; but was stumbling for the word "machine". Instead, I said "Just go and get the damn Timmy!" Well the worker instantly knew was I was talking about and suddenly the floor machine became "Timmy" and it stuck.

A few months later, I was yelling at one of the guys to get the Timmy and stumbled for the word "van". I said, "Get the Timmy out of the Timmy." Suddenly "Timmy" was now the name for both the machine and the van! This went on for years, with my crews calling just about everything Timmy.

As I was launching Mr. Sandless, we had a fleet of silver Scions. The problem was; they all looked the same, so no one knew which Scion they were taking out for the day. I directed Silas to go out and purchase some kind of decal so that we could put a sticker on the bumper to know which Scion was which.

When I returned to the office, Silas had the decals already on the vehicles. He labeled them as "Truck 1", "Truck 2" etc. However, he only used a "T" for each: "T1" "T2" "T3" "T4" and "T5". When I saw all the Scions lined up with that "T" I immediately exclaimed, "OMG, they are Timmys!" Hence the Timmy moved from my other company to Mr. Sandless. So, if you see a reference when I say something that is "Timmy" it is just homage to that wicked kid from my old company!

Since I needed help in the franchise department, my brokers introduced me to their franchise owner who built his company up to some two hundred locations. This was the kind of guy I needed to help me get the franchising going. I contacted Damon and we met to talk about how he could assist me.

He promised me he knew what he was doing and as proof, offered up his two-hundred-unit brokerage franchise system as his one and only reference. He said that writing up a UFOC, which is the disclosure document needed to be able to franchise, would be easy for him and once I had that, I would be able to franchise. Damon asked for fifteen thousand dollars to do the work and I wrote him a check. I mean my brokers already vouched for him and were happy franchisees of his system, and the guy did have a successful and large broker business. I figured he could whip this out in a month. Then all I needed to do was start a new entity for the franchise division, fund it and get an audited financial statement and I would be able to start offering franchises.

It was right around this time that two guys from the mid-west visited with us, Colton and his business partner Xander, to consider coming on board with Mr. Sandless. I made our shoebox of an office look as brisk as it could get. I filled up all the back shelves with things like water and snacks for the guys, to try and show we had money to burn, and filled as much product in as would fit. I completed a presentation for offering franchises and was immediately upfront with them that since I did not have a UFOC, I could not offer them anything at that time. I told them that the information I gave them was just that and not an offering of any kind.

I thought the meeting went well. Caden was in there with me so that I could "pretend" that he was a lead tech and that I was the "boss". Little did they know that the very day before I was out doing an entire home including full furniture moving, yet another job I will never forget. I had a guy call me on my cell begging for us to refinish his home floors before he moved in that day. I called all our other crews, but everyone was busy with a full house on their own. There was no way I could do it because I was stuck with this skinny kid who could barely lift anything. For the first time ever, I had to turn down work. There was just no way I could get to this guy.

Anyway, the job was memorable for two reasons. First this woman client had a hole in one floor board in her family room about the size of a dime. She told me that would need a board replacement, but I told her I would hide it in the floor. She was adamant that she would see it. I bet her one hundred dollars, that if she saw the hole when I was done, that I would take off the money from her bill, and if she didn't she owed me an extra hundred. She agreed.

Second, in that same room was a piano. One of the wheels was missing on the leg on the right-hand side, and so to move it and refinish behind it, we would have to lift it. El Skinny that I had with me that day could not lift his side of the piano. I had to lift one side and move it, then go to the other side and move that and keep doing this until I moved the piano out myself.

Now when returning to inspect that room, the woman first looked for the hole. She looked and looked and couldn't see it, said "Damn it" and put a hundred-dollar bill in my hand. As I was moving back the piano by myself again, she said that she had the wheel for the leg and that it was her chance to get it back on. As I lifted that side, she got on the floor between my legs to insert the wheel. She was literally between my legs and her head was up in my crotch so that my "balls" literally rested on her head. It was the most awkward thing in the world! All I kept saying was *"Hurry up!"*

Back to my meeting, I thought it went as well as it could go. Caden took me aside and gave me "his" dissertation on how he thought it went. He said I didn't make enough eye contact with them. Now to be honest here, Caden on an intellectual scale with me would put him completely on the opposite side of the spectrum. Not only that, he knew nothing about selling. My presentation was loaded with subtle overtures to let these two know exactly how successful my Mr. Sandless was. But that all went over Caden's head.

What I believe Caden "felt" was my uncomfort of trying to sell a franchise to these guys in a shoebox office. The kind of business I wanted to present would have been from an opulent office, with a receptionist and an actual meeting room. Instead, we were crowded in this tiny ten by ten shoe box pretending it was a meeting room and these two prospects were greeted by Silas, which was more like Igor letting you in than receptionist. Not many people that I know could talk a "big game" under these conditions and not what I had envisioned for my first franchise meeting for sure.

There will be more on Colton and Xander coming up. But the next meeting a couple days after that was with Doobie, a Canadian who wanted to take a franchise with us. Unfortunately, I could not make that meeting and had to leave it to Silas and Caden to manage. That morning of the meeting, I had a kidney stone and had to go to the hospital. It was a massive thing that really tore me up. The night before, I let my daughter paint my toe nails pink. Laying in the hospital bed that day, I thought I had to explain this to the male nurse attending to me, who got his training in the army.

"Sir your private life is none of my business," he said in military voice, with a smile on his face.

Once I got back in action was when things even got crazier. Matt was arrested for a DUI for the second time in less than a year. Now this was a serious problem because I needed him to drive one of the company trucks, plus he was the most seasoned guy I had on the team for doing the service. Apparently, the first time he was arrested, he was at a party and got drunk, then instead of going home, he went to a beer distributor to try and get more to drink and that was when he was caught. He retained a lawyer to represent him, got a year probation, but got to keep his driver's license.

This second time he came out of a bar drunk and supposedly was just sitting in his car when he was approached by the police and was arrested, saying he was never actually driving. He retained the lawyer again to fight the charges.

Meanwhile, Henry showed up at work announcing in front of the entire staff that he was up all night doing cocaine! Caden was freaking out because of his "clean and sober" attitude now, he had zero tolerance for anyone drinking or doing drugs and yelled to me to do something about this. I went out on the job with Henry and a helper that day. Henry was worthless and slept in the truck the entire time while I did the job. On the way back to the office, I made it perfectly clear that he needed to clean up his act.

When I talk about drinking and drug use in a nonchalant way, please understand. I grew up in a southern suburb of the city, blue collar all the way, and basically both my parents and the entire neighborhood consisted of the "working poor". Drinking was far and wide, and drug use was as well. Then from there, I moved to the music industry where drinking and drugs were the norm. When I encountered this in business, it was not only no big deal, it was almost expected. It wasn't like I was working with college educated people with degrees. I will explain more about drug use in the chapter about employees.

Anyway, the next day, all the other employees came in early to talk to me about Luke. Now Luke was an exceptional worker for years for me. What in the world could be so wrong here? The other guys told me they believed Luke was "cracking up" and that he told them all that he was just diagnosed as being "bi-polar". They were all afraid to work with him and so I told them I would speak with him. Apparently from what I read, it typically strikes someone in their mid-twenties; Luke's age.

I pulled him aside before he went into the field that day and asked if he was okay. He seemed a bit agitated, but otherwise he seemed fine and said it was no big deal. I told him to try and stay calm on the jobs and just concentrate on the work. He agreed.

Just as I got him out, the landlord burst into the office to announce that he couldn't take us anymore. There were too many cars coming and going in the lot and he said the other tenants were complaining of a lack of parking spots. To pacify him, I agreed to keep all the trucks in the back lot and to have my staff put their cars back there when they came to work. I mean no wonder. I had ten workers, plus Silas, plus my car, plus visitor's vehicles. We *did* in fact take over the parking lot. While I didn't blame the guy, I certainly didn't need any more to worry about!

If this wasn't enough, Matt started to act very strangely. I had played professional music for more than a decade and have seen all kinds of drug use. There was no doubt in my mind that he was doing drugs, however, I had never seen anything like this before. I knew it was something I have never encountered. I told him to meet me over at my house after work, so I could talk to him in private and find out why he was acting so strange.

To recap, Mr. Sandless continued to explode, I still had to run my janitorial company, I had two young children to spend time with and believe me I was a hands-on dad, an office that I was barely in, my sleep down to just three hours a night, Silas doing my job, people wanting to purchase a franchise, not hearing a peep out of Damon, a wife who didn't give me a lick of support during this time and who ignored our marriage, Matt with his drinking and drug problems, Henry with his drug problems, Luke with his mental issues, the landlord bitching about our parking lot takeover, and there I was like Atlas holding all this on my shoulders. I unfortunately learned that things can always get worse.

I met with Matt on a Friday afternoon at my home and told him I knew he was doing drugs and asked him if it was heroin. He didn't say it wasn't and wouldn't look me in the eye when talking to me. If anything, he was evasive. I tried to father and mentor him and told him how much he meant to me, but it seemed to fall on deaf ears.

The next Monday, Matt was a no-show for work. I called his cell phone and had to leave a message. The next morning, Luke came storming into the office screaming about the job he was on so that the veins in his neck were popping out. I tried my best to calm him down and told him to come back that day to speak with me, so I could see if I could get him some help. He was scheduled to go out with J.R. that day on a job. He grabbed his clip board with his assignment and him and J.R. left.

The next thing I knew, I heard screeching of tires and the roar of

SO MUCH FOR HIRING FAMILY FRIENDS

a car engine in the parking lot. As I exited the office, I was horrified to see Luke doing donuts in the parking lot with J.R. in the passenger seat of the Scion next to him. Luke's eyes were bugging out of his head as he went around and around. I yelled for him to knock it off and a second later, he exited the parking lot without stopping and without looking, driving up the wrong side of the highway! It was a miracle that no one got killed, as that was a very busy road.

I immediately dialed him on his cell phone and left a message for him to return to the office. He ignored my demand. When he returned later in the day, he was shocked to find that I was furious. He cried when I told him he needed to get help and that he was fired until he did. I told him he could come back once a doctor said he was sound enough to work, but that I could not allow him to put his life and the lives of his co-workers at risk. That was the last I heard from Luke ever again.

A day after that I received a call from a member of my family, which was a very rare thing. This family member was very close to my mother who had indoctrinated him against me, so he too had zero respect for me. Once he had me on the phone, he told me to hold and then he patched in Matt. Then he said to Matt "Tell him".

Matt proceeded to tell me that he had lost his driving license due to the DUIs. He had been driving the company vehicle for six months without a license. He also completely lied to me about his situation. It seems that night at the bar he wasn't in his car. He was involved in a fight outside the bar and that was when he was arrested—trying to flee the scene. Not only that, he was hauled before a judge and was belligerent and unapologetic. The judge was going to throw him in jail for nine months, but Matt's lawyer, who was friends with the judge, got him a deal to serve time for nine months each weekend. He would have to report to prison every Friday right after work and be let out late Sunday evening so that he could come to work on Monday.

It was a beautiful weekend that just passed, and Matt decided that his ass didn't need to be in jail. He skipped out and went to the beach instead. Monday morning, a warrant was issued for his arrest. I was dumbfounded with what I was hearing. This was all news to me. Matt had totally kept all these events hidden from me with deception the likes I had never seen before.

I heard that Matt's father took him to prison to turn himself in. Since he violated the terms of his release agreement, he would have to serve nine months in jail. It was at that time that his father saw "track marks" on his arm and questioned Matt about heroin use. My suspicions about him were confirmed. Just like that, I lost two of my best workers and the only two guys who really knew the Sandless system.

I went back into the field again to train new guys to replace Matt and Luke. The next month was just a blur of floor refinishing and all the rest of the madness. Henry seemed like he was continuing to slip further into drug use and I tried my best to get him to straighten out. I told him that he could start going to the gym with me and getting himself healthy. Being a spineless individual, he would always agree with me, but nothing ever changed. Henry blew in whatever the direction the wind went.

The next month I was back in the office. I had not heard anything from Damon and so I repeatedly call him and left message after message asking where the first draft of my UFOC (Uniform Franchise Offering Circular) disclosure was. He finally sent me an email with a couple of lines that basically said he didn't owe me anything! I couldn't even grasp what he was trying to say, so I wrote back to him that it was imperative that I speak to him. He agreed to take my call the next morning.

That day I had to do a huge job in Wilmington Delaware. We were short-handed, so J.R. said he had a friend who just got laid off who could help. I told him to get him in as well and I would go on the job too. That morning I got to the job early and sat outside to call Damon. It was one of the most frustrating calls I had ever made. This guy turned into being a total prick. Whether this joker was messed up on drugs or just a freaking loon, he told me he did not work on a single thing, was not going to work on a single thing for me and would never give me my money back! Can you imagine the nerve? I would have to sue the SOB to force him to return my money. He was nothing more than a total thief.

The job that day was huge. It was to move all the furniture, rip up all the carpets, install quarter round, and return the furniture throughout the entire home. The furniture was all antique and there were some great pieces. The woman who owned the home had a total crush on me. The entire day I kept her occupied so that my guys could get the work done. I only had the opportunity to work on one room with them, and the guys were all making fun of me because the woman was all over me.

The new kid that J.R. brought in was an exceptional worker and a real hustler. He reminded me a lot of Luke and the way he worked. I took the team out for lunch that day and I asked this guy if he would like to come to work with me full time. He agreed.

"The only thing is, you have to have a clean driving record so that I can put you on my insurance," I told him. "Do you have a clean driving license?"

"Absolutely!" he stated. I told him I would run his license when I got back to the office and if it was good, he was hired. We always did this for all new employees. The way I see it, if they have a clean driving record, chances are they have a clean criminal record as well. I ran the guy's license and it came up with two warrants for his immediate arrest! Seems he stabbed somebody and that he had been ducking the law for some time. Simply unreal.

In life, especially when things look bad, it is for reason and purpose that you can't see yet. This was one of those times. Ironically Drusilla sent in to the office with Henry a magazine that devoted an issue to franchising. There was an ad for a law firm that specialized in franchising and had in their advertisement that they could get a new franchise a UFOC. I immediately called them from a job I was doing with Henry that day. The last person on earth that I thought would ever help me was Drusilla. Maybe this was a reward for making her husband V.P.

I spoke with the head of the law firm, a pistol of an attorney, and explained to him my plight with Damon, and that I had people who wanted to franchise and had no UFOC to show them. He assured me that this is what they do, and I set up a meeting with his team to get this franchise thing rolling. You have to love lawyers. No, actually you don't. They wanted fifty thousand dollars to get me a UFOC and I had no choice but to pay. They also charged me another ten thousand to get a full release from Damon who they were afraid would try to come after me in the future when the franchise system was larger. They got him to sign the release or they threatened to sue him for the money he stole from me. Thankfully he signed. Years later, Damon sent me an invitation to join his business network. Can you imagine the balls on this guy? I sent a scathing reply and called him a thief in response. But you will see a recurring theme here. There are countless times people I discarded would somehow come back into my life!

At the end of that summer of 2005, I finally sold my janitorial business. It was a mother and son team who took it and I felt confident they would continue with the growth of the business. I liked the spunk of this kid a lot. In another time, I would have offered him a job with Mr. Sandless, but that would have defeated the purpose I needed him for at the time. This kid took my business national and five years later he sold it. He called me to thank me for the opportunity and said he made out very well with it. He then launched a construction company and became a customer for Mr. Sandless. It is strange to have a business out there that I created from scratch!

Jack wanted desperately to come with me and not remain with my janitorial company. But by that time, it was too late. There was a clause in the agreement that I couldn't hire any of my old employees for a period of six-months. I told him he would have to wait the six-month period and then I could get him into Mr. Sandless.

He would stop by my office weekly to let me know how things were going and the moment he was at the six-month period, he gave his notice and I hired him. We have been friends ever since and he has traveled around the world with me doing the great Mr. Sandless service.

As we were moving into October of 2005 I received another rare call, this time from my dear mother. What I was about to be told would be the very last communication I would have with her for the rest of her life. Since it is now many years later, I have the full story, but back then I just assumed these things by the evidence. Now I know that what I thought was indeed true.

Matt, who was hooked on heroin, was having a rough time of being in prison that first month. He was desperate to try and get out somehow so that he could get high. No one was visiting him in prison from his family and so he reached out to my mother. She went to visit him, and he told her this wild made-up story that Mr. Sandless was a front for drugs, specifically cocaine, and that I was a "drug kingpin". He asked my mother to go and talk to the warden so that he would give me up in exchange for a reduced sentence, so he could get out!

This guy, who I loved for a dozen years turned into a Judas and wickedly stabbed me in the back like no one had ever done before to me. As my mother filled me in on her "discovery" I left the office to walk out in the parking lot to cool down, otherwise I knew the conversation was going to turn bad. The worst part of this story was my mother, *my* mother, believed every single word Matt told her! She told me she "*knew*" Mr. Sandless was a front and that there was no way it could be a legitimate business. She told me I should be ashamed of myself for getting Matt hooked on cocaine, even though he was hooked on heroin and was in jail for DUIs, not coke. And of course, she said she was disgusted by me for being a drug kingpin. I've been called a lot of things in life, but drug kingpin was a new one I never thought I would hear.

I told her that I had ten guys out in the field that very day refinishing floors. I told her to go to whoever she wanted with that ridiculous story and they can come and watch us refinish floors. Then I said if that was how she truly felt about me, then we were done.

"You are not my mother," I said to her that day. "You know what *my* mother would do after hearing that? My mother would have stood up and slapped Matt's face and told him that he is in jail because of his own actions, and to say how dare you blame your mess on my son! That is what *my* mother would do!" That was the last time I ever spoke to her.

We used to have a running joke when I worked with my guys in my janitorial company. I was telling them several of my antidotal stories involving my mother one day while we were on a large job working. I said that my mother had such disrespect for me, that she would believe I would be capable of murder. My guys were going to put this to the test. They were going to call her and say that they suspected I had killed their manager because I was having a problem with him and then suddenly he disappeared, never to be seen or heard from again. Of course, my manager was right there when we came up with this.

"Go ahead and call her!" I said confidently. "I will tell you right now what she will say. She will say, "I *knew* he was a murderer!" She will eat it right up!" *Now* you understand the relationship I had with my mother. How in the world could she take the word of a two-time DUI earning, jail hopping, drug-shooting felon over her own son who was and had been an outstanding businessman? *What kind of mother would do that?*

The next two months were a blur of business and just trying to keep everything moving forward. The new lawyers were working on the first draft of the UFOC, and I set up a new corporation to be the franchise entity. We were already past our first-year mark and heading to the end of 2005. The business income was astounding with $660,000 in revenue for 2005! Believe me I needed every penny of it. The more I made, the more it seemed I needed. Everyone had their hand out!

To reward everyone for a job well done that year, I booked a club to have a massive Christmas party for all the staff and their families. I also had large bonuses to give to everyone, a three-hour open bar and tons of food. Silas and his wife and children attended, as did

SO MUCH FOR HIRING FAMILY FRIENDS

Caden and his live-in girlfriend and kids. We were about halfway through the event when Drusilla and Henry stopped by for a "guest star" appearance. Right away I could tell something was out of sorts. It seemed that Drusilla and Henry were not getting along.

The next day I heard what had happened. It seemed that Drusilla suspected Henry of using coke. She went through the house looking for evidence. She found that he had cocaine hidden in nearly every single room of the house. She found a ton of CD plastic covers with coke on them along with straws and razor blades. It was then that Henry admitted to her that he was a coke addict; a six hundred dollar a week coke habit!

I didn't know what to expect that Monday, so I got in early, so I could talk to him. I will never forget it. He pulled his car right up to the front door of the office and got out, but wouldn't come in. I went out to talk to him. He took the office keys out as well as the truck key he had and threw them to me and said he was "out".

"*That's it?*" I asked. "Just like that you are quitting after all the crap I took in getting you in here?"

"That's it," he muttered as he got back in his car and drove off. I stood there for a moment shaking my head in disbelief. He lasted just six months and didn't bring a single thing to the table of Mr. Sandless. Unfortunately, this is not the end of this story. Two days later I heard that Henry *confirmed* what Matt said, that Mr. Sandless *was* a front for coke, that I got *Henry* hooked on it as well as Matt, and that I was indeed a drug kingpin just as Matt and my own mother believed! Because of the total BS get out of jail free stunt by Matt, I lost my own mother and now Henry and all of Drusilla's perfect wealthy family who all thought I was a total piece of crap. And I didn't even do anything!!

Shortly after that, I was working on an apartment in the city for a huge management company. These guys were real sharks as far as customers would be concerned. But if I could win them over with this one job, I could gain serious apartment work in the city. Of course, the unit they gave to "test" me on was a disaster. It was half painted.

Normally old floors are painted when they are totally shot. I just knew that what was under the paint wasn't worth saving. I had my newest worker with me, Hunter, who I will tell you more about coming up as well. We killed ourselves for five straight brutal hours only to decide we had to color the floor to hide all the damage in it. The coloring system I had back then was brand new, experimental, and fairly terrible looking. It would take several more years before we eventually had the colors we still use today. So, the floor did not come out nearly as great as I wanted it to.

On top of that, it was excruciatingly hot in the place with no air circulation, and the rug in the hallway was infested with fleas, so I had bites up and down my legs. Nothing like being tortured while you work!

Six hours into this madness, the family member who forced Matt to tell me the truth called me. He called only to tell me that he was done with me, that he knew that I not only was a drug kingpin but that I was a massive user as well. He "knew" all these things even though he hadn't seen me in several years. To be honest, I didn't have it in me to fight or argue with him. I told him that I didn't understand how I got anyone hooked on drugs. I asked if they told him that I held them down and blow the coke up their noses, because that is the only way I could be responsible. I said he could believe whatever he wanted to and with the end of that call, that would be the last time I ever spoke to that guy. The body count for this one huge lie was really adding up. But you know what? None of these people really cared about me anyway, so it wasn't like I was losing anyone of substance. None of them brought anything to the table of my life.

A week later, I came to the office on a Saturday to clean up all the trucks. The landlord literally had all my things out in the parking lot: the desks, phones, computers, machines, table, and all the supplies. And the locks were changed as well. I had only been there eight months! I ran and got a newspaper to look for another office that very day. I couldn't believe that this total jerk of a landlord didn't give me a stinking bit of notice!

It was a miracle that I found something. I called an ad that said they had retail space and I drove to the next town over from me to look at it and meet the guy renting the place. The moment he turned the key I said, "I'll take it!"

"It's just a shell!" he said back.

"My guys are all carpenters. We can build out what we need. I'm desperate as my computer and desks are sitting up in a parking lot! I can give you a check for the deposit and first month rent right now, and then we can sign the lease on Monday. He agreed, and I went back to pull all my things into the new office and lay it on the concrete floors. There were no walls, no phone lines, no computer lines, no floors, nothing!

That Monday I worked as fast as I could to get up and running. I rented both the upstairs for the franchise division and the downstairs for my Mr. Sandless. I quickly had phone lines and a phone system installed and got new numbers to use. I had to change all my advertising to the new number and turn off my old ones. The numbers would forward to my new lines for the next six months, so I was okay there.

Next, I had an alarm system installed in both places, and kept my best carpenters back from doing floors so that they could fix out the office for use. They built walls, created offices, installed carpet and flooring and before a month was out, we had our new office. This would be the year we were about to begin franchising and an entire new set of problem arose that I did not expect. While I was still way overburdened, I was amazed by my own drive and fortitude in carrying all I did to propel the business forward, always looking to the next day and never looking back to what was behind me.

CHAPTER 5

More of the Madness

AS I PRETTY much knew, the choice for the Scions, the logo and color schemes on the vehicles were all a flat-out winner, so much so that I let many of my guys drive the company vehicles home so that I could build the brand faster in the region. The more people who saw our vehicles on the road, the busier they thought we were, and this would help me start to dominate the market for refinishing.

I can't tell you how many episodes I had driving one of these vehicles. One such time, I was going forty-five miles an hour down a four-lane road, when a Mercedes got in front of me, slammed on his brakes and forced me off the road! I jumped out of the car and was furious and the owner of the Mercedes knew I was pissed.

"No, *no*!" he shouted to me, believing I was going to kick his butt. "It's just that I was going to sand and I don't want to go through all that, so I had to stop you to get a business card!" I handed him one, still not believing that he just ran me off the road for a business card!

Another time, Caden was driving me down to our franchise attorney in the city, when a crazy woman pulled up alongside of us flashing her lights and honking her horn. I lowered my passenger side window to see what she wanted.

"I don't have a pen!" She yelled across to me. "I need a card from you, so I can call you!" I reached for one of our sales cards and hung out the window a bit so that I could hand it to her, while we were going fifty-five down the freaking highway.

"Don't hit me or my car!" I yelled to her. She pulled a bit closer and was able to get the card out of my hand. "Thank you!" she yelled back as she pulled away. I was just thankful she didn't smash into us.

Another time I ran up to the fast food place to grab lunch for a bunch of us. As I was at the window and started to take the food into my vehicle, the car behind me started honking their horn and flashing their lights. I motioned to let him know I still had more food coming, but the honking and lights continued.

"Dude, *I'm still getting my food*!" I yelled back.

"No, I just don't want you to pull away without giving me a card!" he yelled back.

There was another time that Caden was pulled over by a police officer who said he just wanted a card. One of my other guys reported this happened to them as well. If these things weren't bad enough, constantly when someone saw me in those vehicles, they would ask the "how do you do it" question. It seemed I couldn't go anywhere without being interrogated!

One guy saw me and told me he was a local firefighter and asked if I could come look at his floors. I agreed and drove to his house, following him. When I entered the home, I saw the floors were ruined. Someone had tried to sand them and didn't know what they were doing. They sanded them down to the nub and now the floors looked like an ocean of dump marks and unevenness. They were ruined.

"Wow, who did this to your floors?" I asked him.

"You are talking to him!" he replied.

"What made you think you could properly sand your floor?" I asked.

"Well, they rented me the sander at the big box store," he returned.

"They would rent you a bazooka too! Does that mean you would go and fight in Iraq?" I replied jokingly.

There came a time when I said I would never drive a company vehicle ever again. After countless times of people interrupting my routine while driving these things, I reached my limit. It was very early in the morning and I was headed to the new office. I stopped at a gas station to fill up. Immediately the guy next to me looked like he was going to start up a conversation.

"*Don't do it man,*" I said to him. "I haven't had my coffee yet."

"*No*, I just want to know how you do it," he replied.

"Just call the office and they can explain it to you," I answered.

"I just pulled the carpets up in two rooms and need to know what this service would cost me, as well as to find out how you do it," he again stated. I had no choice but to respond. That was the last time I drove one of my own vehicles!

The "over the top" vehicle design was not always a big hit with the owners coming on board. Mainly it was the flame part of the decal that they didn't like. Initially four out of ten owners would ask me to have it removed from the vehicle decal package. After I explained of the many times we got jobs from our vehicles, I asked them to just try it and see for themselves.

Always they would call to tell me how many times they were stopped for business cards! In fact, some of them even got card holders to put on the outside of the vehicle so that people could just help themselves!

As the franchising was starting to heat up, I went and leased an expensive vehicle and got one that was as ostentatious as possible. The offices we now occupied were not very "corporate" so to speak. To give the appearance that I was doing exceedingly well, I figured a flashy personal vehicle would certainly help. As usual, this sales trick worked as it seemed every visitor we had for franchising remarked about my vehicle.

By the beginning of 2006, we were finally able to franchise. I signed up for advertising with just one online portal—Entrepreneur.com—for the franchisee leads we would get. The upstairs office where the franchise division would be housed was fixed out and ready for occupancy, even though I was paying rent for it for months by then. The plan was to continue with the "appearance" of success by having

Silas become Vice-President, and Caden as "franchise trainer and support" with me being the President of the company. This should at least give us the appearance of a corporate entity.

I needed to replace all three of us from my Mr. Sandless, so I appointed Hunter, a guy I hired as the new lead technician and I hired a new manager to run the show there by the name of Cora. Over the next year, I came to call her "Crazy Cora" because she always seemed to look for trouble more than peace. Then I added an assistant manager by the name of Katherine, who pronounced her name "Kathereen." I set the franchise fee at what I thought was reasonable at twenty-five thousand dollars. But there were no takers; even the ones who visited with us already wouldn't buy at that price.

I lowered it to twenty thousand, then fifteen thousand, then to just ten thousand and still no takers! We were six months into the year and I couldn't sell a single franchise! The goal was simple: get a few up and running and making the kind of money my location was making, then the rest would be history. I fully expected to be able to raise the price to fifty thousand or even more once I had a few under my belt. But no takers. It seemed there was a lot of "fear" with no one else being a franchisee. No one wanted to be the first! I had no choice but to lower the franchise fee to just five thousand dollars. At that point, I thought I may have to simply *give* away the first couple to make something happen! I was running a company for six months that was making no money! I don't know how in the world I was able to do this with no investors or loans and thankfully my own Mr. Sandless was so successful that I was able to keep everything going through the profit earned there.

The five-thousand-dollar mark seemed to be the winning combination to jump start the franchising of the brand. In six months, we brought in twelve sales in various markets, who I affectionately dubbed "the dirty dozen". We had Doobie from Canada who took a franchise in the Canadian metro suburb. Doobie was much like Henry and moved whichever way the wind blew in business. The next was Colton and Xander who took a large franchise for most of a single smaller state. I will tell you more about both sets of these guys later. There was a guy Noah who took a mountain region and two women; Clara and Elizabeth, who were in a relationship took a site down south.

I personally trained all the people who took a franchise to be sure we had the best possible start of the franchise system. Clara and Elizabeth seemed very much in love and at times were affectionate with one another during the training. That was interesting to say the least, but they were both very likeable.

One job we did for their training stands out as one of my worst. We were servicing an upstairs hallway, small set of stairs, and a large living room/dining room combination. The crazy thing about this job was not the floor but the client. The client was a guy maybe forty years old, who as soon as we got there offered us all a drink from his bottle of vodka. He was loud and obnoxious to the women, going so far as to be sexual with his comments to them. I had to tell him to back off. Then he retreated to the basement where he "huffed" glue until he passed out!

Meanwhile, in a room upstairs was his dementia-crazed mother, who every time there was a sound, would scream out from behind a bedroom door that she was going to come out and kill us! I don't know how it is possible to be quiet when refinishing a floor, so it was maddening to put up with this woman screaming bloody murder every five minutes.

Thankfully we got through the job and it came out very well. The guy, who by that time could barely stand, asked me if I would take a check. I told him no; that I would only accept cash for a payment. I didn't trust this loon as far as I could throw him! So, he got in his car and went to the bank to get the cash, even though he was totally plastered on vodka and glue. I kicked myself for letting him go, because I thought he could kill someone, but the SOB made it back with the money. With that we ran out of there as fast as we could.

The next owner to come on board was Leo, who took large metro where he lived. Leo was a perfect example of how the brand developed on its own. He lived locally and was retiring from the work he had done there for twenty years, to move to another state. He wanted to get the maximum amount of money he could get by selling his house. He did all the needed repairs and upkeep, then he contracted with my Mr. Sandless to do the floors.

It was a Friday when my guys showed up for the service. Leo called his realtor and told him to list the home that very day, stating that all the work was done except for the floors, which would soon be completed. The realtor told him it was a soft market and to not expect a bid for at least two months; noting that Leo was asking for top dollar for the home.

That weekend a bidding war ensued on the home. Five people wanted to buy it and Leo ended up selling the place for five thousand dollars more than he was asking. The reason? Everyone said the floors were drop dead gorgeous. Based on this knowledge, Leo took a Mr. Sandless for the town he was moving to. But this is not the end of the story.

I allowed our owners to work outside of their owned territories, knowing this would help build the brand. Not only that, as the franchisor, I directed the online advertising for these initial owners. I had huge areas turned on so that something like this would happen. It was a brilliant strategy if I say so myself. My owners got plenty of work and created new owners for me at the same exact time!

Many, if not all service franchises make their owners work in their owned territory, and for my reasons above, I thought that was a mistake. Who wouldn't want happy clients, happy franchise owners and new owners as well? Anyway because of this, Leo went down to another city that was not his territory to service a floor for a truck driver, who then loved it so much, he took a Mr. Sandless franchise for there. He was not one of our original dirty dozen owners, but just an example of how I grew the brand—through our great work and through allowing owners to work outside their owned territory. And of course, the advertising which I directed.

The next to come into the system in 2006 was a firefighter from

Canada by the name of Nathan. He came down to visit with me to see the service prior to coming on board. That day I did the franchise presentation with him but got a call from Cora saying that there was trouble on a job site. Apparently, she had to send four helper type workers to an entire home job and since none were lead technicians, the job was chaos. I asked Nathan if he would like to go with me to that job and he agreed.

When we got there, the guys on the job, led by the totally incompetent J.R. were running around like a pack of blind mice. I straightened them out by giving them clear instruction of how to manage the job, then told Nathan that there would be no way in the world they would get the job done that day without my help. I asked if he would like to help me do the stairs and large living room even though both of us were not dressed for floor work. Nathan rolled up his sleeves and I showed him how to work the stairs with me. Once they were completed, we started working the living room. While kneeling next to him, I spoke softly so that the home owner wouldn't hear me.

"This is what we call polishing a turd!" I said. The floors of this home were one hundred fifty-year-old plank pine. What they used to do back in that day was to cut the pine trees down on the property and mill the boards right then and there for the floors. They were random width plank pine, just a real basic floor and not particularly a fantastic wood by any stretch.

"But wait until you see the color of this floor pop when we are done," I told Nathan. "These floors are going to look *amazing*, even as bad as they are right now!" As I said this, the owner walked in to inquire how the job was going.

"You have the "A team" on the job now!" I announced to him. He shook his head as if he knew he was in good hands, and then made a pronouncement.

"Nothing like polishing a turd, is there?" he asked. I looked over at Nathan and we both laughed out loud. I had just whispered this to him two minutes earlier!

"You are not going to believe this floor when we are done with it!" I told him. I had done many of these plank pine floors and they all came out great with the Mr. Sandless system. The wet process just makes the colors pop! When Nathan saw that floor finished, he was in!

The next franchise sale was with John and Jay, two friends who took an entire metro region in my state. John would stay behind and not train as he was going to manage their office, while Jay and his friend came out to train. I have several favorite John and Jay stories, but a few stand out. First was their training. By that point, I had trained several dozen people in the system without a problem. These guys were just very difficult, so much so that they actually were *arguing* with me like they knew more about the system than I did! They were arguing with me!

By Thursday of that training, they still didn't grasp the system basics, which was a first for me. We were doing a kitchen floor for a woman in a small town. This floor was about a hundred twenty-five years old and boy did it have a history. Where the refrigerator was, there was a deep black square outline where an old ice box used to sit. The ice would melt, and the water ran right into the floor, causing all the boards around the ice box to turn black.

There was a basement door that someone years ago had varnished. You could see where originally, they had the door wide open to varnish that side, because I could clearly see the outline of the can and the splatters there against the wall. Then they closed the door and moved the can of varnish so that it left another ring on the floor closer to the closed door. The floor was raw wood and that varnish was really on there!

If all of that wasn't bad enough, there was a ten foot by one-foot section of linoleum crossing the middle of the floor. It was actually very old linoleum, with *second* section of linoleum over that. This would have to be removed and was the first order of business for the day. We would have to use some very heavy stripper I had in the system at the time to work this stuff off the floor and since the rest of the floor was raw, we had to move fast. We couldn't let the stripper sit on any part of the bare floor or it could damage it.

Jay and his friend did not know the meaning of the word "fast". I clearly explained to them that we could not let the stripper sit too long on the floor. But it didn't matter as they moved as if they were sitting out on a veranda, sipping iced tea, and waiting for a harness race to begin!

While this was going on, the woman of the house was driving me crazy. Every five minutes she would pop her head into the kitchen doorway and ask me if I saw something or other on the floor; every five minutes like clockwork. The first time she did it, she asked about the black boxy stain under the refrigerator. I explained to her that it would not come out, explained it came from the ice box from years ago, and explained that it went all the way through the boards.

The next time it was the linoleum. The next time the varnish. The next time a bit of paint by the stove. The next time the wear area by the back door. The next time the grease spill next to the stove. The next time a black mark by the doorway. She would ask "If I saw" these things. Of *course*, I did! That was what I was there to do!

The best thing about this floor was it was heart pine. That is the center of the pine tree, where the wood is the hardest. It has the best-looking grain of pine and the best color and is my absolute favorite floor. I knew that I could make this floor look like a million dollars. But between this woman and Jay and his friend, I grew so tired of being distracted. The next time she popped her head around, I yelled at her.

"*Honey?*" I asked very loudly. "Do you want me to make this floor look great?" With that she nodded. "Then you have to leave me alone!" I told her. "You are *driving me crazy!*" She finally stopped her nonsense. After I got the linoleum off the floor, the rest was fairly cut and dry. After the first coat was on, I went to have lunch in the truck by myself and Jay and his friend stayed to have lunch with the client. By that time, I couldn't stand all three of them.

When we got back to coating, they told me she didn't believe what I said about the black box in the floor. She literally crawled under the house with a flashlight to look at that section from underneath.

"He is *very* mean," she told them. "But he does know what he is talking about. I can see the black stain under the floor just like he said."

When we were finished, the floor was magnificent and went from looking one hundred twenty-five years old to brand new. The customer signed off and paid. The very next day she called the office to complain…about *me*! She told Katherine that I was mean, that I yelled at those "poor dear men like dogs," and that I treated her like she was my "girlfriend." I guess that is because I called her "honey". Believe me, when I said that, I *did* mean it in a derogatory fashion. But I only say something like that when I am pissed off! I've also been known to call someone "hon", "sweetie", and "chief" as well. Anyway, I was standing there when the call came in and Katherine put her on hold to tell me.

"Ask her how the floor came out," I told her. Katherine asked, and the woman said the floor was fantastic, then she put the customer on hold again.

"Tell her to go f herself!" I said. With that she told the client she would report to the boss her complaint.

"Consider it reported!" I responded.

Later after being launched, John and Jay told me they wanted to do a commercial on cable television. During my proto-type tests, I had proven that cable television ads were ineffective, and I reminded both that if this worked, we would have it in their marketing plan in the handbook. It wasn't there for good reason—it didn't produce work.

When they sent me the draft ad, I asked them if they were doing this for vanity reasons, and they responded that they were. I already had a very good ad that could be run, but they wanted their "own" commercial. That was why I thought it was for vanity, you know; that they just wanted to get their faces on television. I said that was fine and for them to "not spend a lot of money on this".

But the ad they sent me was horrific. First the announcer had a lisp and was saying the brand name incorrectly. Imagine if you will, "Mr. Sand*less*". Next, they used all low definition pictures. I knew on my high definition television that this ad would look tremendously foul! Then at the end of the ad, was their entire company standing by their vehicles. If they were all in uniforms and lined up, this may have worked. But it looked more like a line up at a police station or a gang of thugs on a street corner.

I got them to make all the changes and approved the ad for use. About eight months later, John called me to ask what else I recommended they do for marketing (even though we gave all owners a full step by step marketing plan) because "we spent thirty thousand dollars on this ad and it didn't work!" This is unfortunately franchising! You give them a marketing plan that is proven to work, and they don't use it. You give them an ad that is proven to work, and they don't use it but make their own. You tell them not to spend a lot of money on it and they do. Welcome to franchising, a strange Twilight Zone episodic place where getting owners to follow the system is like herding gerbils.

Now back to the dirty dozen list, there was a friend of Caden's brother who worked in the automobile industry who wanted a change. He came in and took a franchise where he lived. He was so happy the first year that we put him in a print ad in Entrepreneur magazine to advertise for more owners. Next was an ex-stockbroker who took a small franchise in a large metro suburb, a woman who took the same type and in the same state, a guy who took one down south and a guy who took his hometown in the mid-west.

It was right after this that I realized this was not going to follow the growth that I had predicted. Let me see if I can explain. Long before I started to franchise, I created a "bell curve" graphic to determine what an "average" franchise location would make. On the right side of the curve, I put what the original model was averaging: $50,000 per month. The service was in high demand, it practically sold itself, and the logos, vehicles and website all worked perfectly as did our script, database and marketing plan. What could go wrong?

To be almost ridiculously fair, I had *zero* on the left side of the bell curve. I figured that there would be some dud owners for sure, maybe even five percent who didn't make a lot of money with their Mr. Sandless. By putting zero in as the low factor, I *had* to be covered so to speak. That meant the average owner should easily make $25,000 per month, or $300,000 per year. Certainly, owners in large metros would most likely make well over this and closer to the original, while all the rest of the smaller markets would make less. But all should average out to that $25,000 per month number.

With this in mind, it was easy to see when the company would become a dominate player in the industry. When we reached just one hundred owners, the gross company income would exceed thirty million dollars. There would be plenty of money to advertise nationally for new owners as well as for customers for our current owners. There would be nothing stopping us from a total sell out of all markets in a ten-year timeframe.

In anticipation of this, I began to further market the system. I set up a YouTube channel and started to record videos to put online to promote the brand. This gave us a huge footprint in the industry because no one ever did anything like this with a wood floor refinishing brand before! On top of that and as I said earlier, I ran the online ads myself for the owners, turning on large areas to not only give them the most leads, but to also attract new owners into the system from open areas that were close to our owners. Both by-products of my advertising worked perfectly, with fifty new owners coming in within just two years of Mr. Sandless franchising, ranking us as the third fastest growing franchise system in the USA!

Unfortunately, it became quite clear that after six months of operations, these initial franchise locations were not going to do *anywhere* near the bell curse average I had predicted! I have never encountered a time in my life where mathematics failed so miserably! That first year, the best posted month reached by only one owner was a horrible $13,000, with the average being *under* $4,000 per month! It just didn't stand to reason. If they do the same service, follow the same marketing, use the same sales script, and use the same pricing, then how can earnings, in markets far superior to mine, *not* make more money than the original? How *was that possible*?

While my location did close to $700,000 in 2007, no other location was even close. The average location per month of 2007 came in at just $13,000. Thirty owners that year did only $3.2 million in sales, when the original Mr. Sandless did $700K! That meant the average owner did only $106K in business for the *entire year*. My original Mr. Sandless earned nearly seven times that amount!

By the second year of franchising, I determined that market had nothing whatsoever to do with a franchise location's success. The success of the business was primarily all about the owner. What I determined is that what we gave them was a race car. We had race car drivers, we had owners who drove the race car like a family sedan, owners who pushed the car, and still others who parked it in the garage. This made no sense to me why someone would go through all the trouble and expense to open a business and then to do nothing with it, but we had owners just like this.

But it was even more than that. They did *everything* wrong! They would answer their business phone with "hello." They would not only *not* follow the script, they would bastardize it to make it sound horrible. They made up things to say out of the clear blue sky! And I am not talking just one or two owners. *Most* of them simply made things up!

They wouldn't practice the sales script. Their phone messages were not on script and sounded like they were serial killers! They wouldn't ask for the sale, wouldn't use the company provided database system, and wouldn't follow up. In other words, other than the floor system, they did *everything* one could possibly do wrong! I believe that they all focused way too much on the work doing the floors, then the work of actually running their businesses. When you are doing the work, you were working "in" the business. When you are working your business, you are working "on" the business, not in it. That is the ticket to success and that is exactly what the model called for. But since they didn't follow what the model called for, what difference did it make?

It also seemed quite clear that only two out of every ten owners seemed to be the race car driver. The clear majority were anything but, holding true to the 80-20 rule where twenty percent do, and eighty percent don't. Believe me, I tried to get the eighty percent to run their business correctly. Every so often one would and that made it worth it, but the majority went right back to doing it their way—the wrong way. One owner for example just needed to follow the script instead of the madness he was telling customers. He made the change, and for the next two months, doubled his income to that $25,000 mark. Then he slipped back down to $13,000 the third month. I listened to one of his calls and he was right back to his old nonsense. Even money and success didn't work as a motivator to these guys.

This unfortunate discovery led to a huge change to the system. Up to that moment, I vetted every single person who wanted a franchise. If I got the slightest inclination that they were trouble, I would turn them down. For example, I caught one guy lying to me. I immediately told him I would not give him a franchise.

But with this new understanding and underperformance of the franchise system, I changed to say that if someone had a pulse and a check, we would give them a franchise! I figured if the quality model did not work, then I may as well go with a quantity model. I raised the price after our first year to ten thousand dollars and half way through 2007 I move up to fifteen thousand, where the fee would remain for years to come. I tried so hard to work with owners that were doing poorly, but to be honest, most of them just didn't seem to care. In fact, I believed I cared more than they did!

Take the guy from the mid-west. He had a region where he could service all the best parts of the biggest city in his state. He averaged around three thousand dollars a month. His absolute best month was a paltry six thousand dollars. What was his problem? He sounded like Eeyore the donkey from Winnie the Pooh, but a seriously depressed

Eeyore! I got him on the phone and explained to him that sales were emotion based and that if he couldn't do a better job on the phone, to find someone who could. He was fine doing the floors, but on the phone, he was a disaster. Did he make the change? *Of course not!* Why someone in business wouldn't want success was beyond my ability to understand.

Another owner had the same exact problem. He and his girlfriend showed up in my office to ask me why I thought they were not selling enough, after all, they were getting plenty of calls for work.

"Did you ever hear yourself on the phone?" I asked him. He replied that he didn't. I played him one of his calls. Not only did he answer the phone "hello," not only didn't he follow the script, he sounded like he was selling a casket rather than wood floor refinishing. I told him to put his wife on the phone instead of himself. Did he? Of course not! Franchising is like trying to herd gerbils.

Around this time, Silas and Caden settled into their jobs at corporate. Silas handled the paperwork, map creation, website posts and changes, and as much as he could get his hands on because he was turning into a real control freak. I could sense that he was getting *way* too carried always with "locking things up" so I had my eyes wide open to prepare for trouble.

Caden who was excellent at the service by that point took over for me with training so that I could continue the growth of the franchise system. We were growing at a great pace, even if the new owners were underperforming, and in 2007 we held our first annual convention in St. Petersburg Florida where all thirty owners attended. I paid for Silas and Caden to both attend including all their family members and treated them to a day at Busch Gardens Tampa as well as multiple dinners.

The best part of Mr. Sandless was running one. I loved selling the service, talking to clients and having them call me to tell me how great the experience was. I loved being challenged like when we did a one-hundred-year-old floor for the university where they had a section of flooring that popped out of the floor. We were to put new boards in there and we promised them they wouldn't notice. They said they doubted it, but when they returned at the end of the day, they could not see the patch. They couldn't believe it! I stuffed the old boards into my bag and later made a floor model so that I could show people what our products looked like on antique wood. The patina of that old wood was amazing.

But like I said, running the franchise division and ignoring my own Mr. Sandless was not much fun at all and just like I said, like herding gerbils. Still in 2007, I was very happy with the progress I was making and thought things could only continue to grow, getting over that bad start with Henry, Matt and Luke. I had peace from the time after Henry departed until the middle of 2007. But peace in this venture was not meant to be; certainly, not meant to be lasting.

As we were approaching the summer of 2007, I set up an enormous open house to entertain for the day some thirty people who were interested in joining Mr. Sandless! It was exhilarating being able to coordinate that many people to visit on a Saturday to see if this was the right business opportunity for them. Along with that, I had the "group" factor on my side for sales. People are way more apt to move to purchase when they see this kind of pull and excitement. By that time, I had a killer franchise presentation, and now that we had actual owners making money, it would be easier than ever to get more people in.

That morning, Caden and Silas got everyone situated in our conference room while I reviewed my notes prior to starting the presentation. As I exited my office, ready to walk down the hall to introduce myself and start, Silas stopped me.

"I have some problems with the way you do the franchise presentation," he said to me that morning.

"What?" I replied as if the words were punched out of my diaphragm.

"Yeah, I have a list of three things you say that I don't like during the presentation," he continued.

"Are you f'ing kidding me Silas? I am going in there right now to start! What is *wrong* with you?" I could not believe that with thirty potential sales on the line, that this guy was going to try and take me off my game right before I was to start! It was unimaginable!

Luckily, I was able to put his nonsense out of my mind quickly and went on to have a great presentation. One couple wanted to speak to me alone and I took them into my office and closed the door. They told me they felt compelled to do this—to join Mr. Sandless. I told them of my belief about God, that I felt this was a gift from God, and that I too have been compelled in the past to do things—some that I didn't even want to do. Then explained that once I did them, it was always great. With that, they took a franchise.

There was another guy by the name of Johnny who was interested. He was a major in the army and now retired but found retired life to be boring. And so, he was considering coming on board with us just for something to do. For several weeks after the open house, Johnny called me to talk about the business. He really didn't need to work, but he couldn't shake the feeling that he needed to come on board, that he was being compelled to join the team. I told him my experience and once again, he signed on.

Right after this, for some totally unknown reason and certainly without even asking me, Silas hired his son to work for my Mr. Sandless. This was strange for many reasons. First, Silas himself was swamped and if anyone could use the help, it would be him. His son would have made a good assistant for him. Second, I did all the hiring for my Mr. Sandless. Silas was never involved in the least other than to insert himself into my business originally. Third, we didn't need the help in the capacity that Silas hired him under, which would be for sales. This kid grew to be an extraordinary man, but at that time, he was very shy and very quiet. He was not at all a salesperson type.

If all of that wasn't bad enough, *Silas* decided what to pay his son...with my money! Can you image the nerve? To say the least, I was not thrilled at all. I mean again, there wasn't a problem with the kid and it wasn't his fault, but I couldn't believe Silas did this without even asking me.

My biggest concern was I didn't want to lose business in my Mr. Sandless by putting a twenty-year-old on the phones with no experience at all in sales and I confronted Silas with this.

"Listen Silas, he's a nice kid and all but he has no sales experience. Wouldn't he be better off working up here with you to get a feel for the business before we put him on the phone?" I asked.

"That's why I want him to do it. This is what he needs to break out of his shyness and be more outgoing," Silas answered.

"This isn't a social club Silas and it's not a school!" I replied. "We are not here to shape personalities, but to make money and succeed in this business." With that, I agreed to try the kid out on a very short leash basis. If he was going to cost me money, then I would put my foot down and maybe even up Silas's ass.

After just one week, Cora came to me and said that Silas's son was not only not working out, she was fielding complaints about him from potential customers. They were saying that "the kid doesn't know anything about the business" which was exactly what I was worried about. I went to Silas to inform him that I couldn't let this continue, but again, to show the kind of man I was and still am, I did not fire the kid.

"Silas, you are the one who needs help," I told him. "Let's get your son up here, get him a computer and you give him all the little stuff that he can do so it clears your plate and frees up your time. He isn't any good on sales, but he is highly educated, and he can pick up this stuff very easily. That frees you up to do more of the high-end things you need to do. Have him up here tomorrow and we can get started training him. I will even spend time with him to show him what he needs to learn."

It doesn't get any fairer than that. I figured to give Silas the night to speak to his son about the change.

But the next day when I came to the office, I was shocked to see his son still downstairs and on the phones. I threw a look to Cora who rolled her shoulders as if she didn't know what he was doing there, because I told her I made the change.

"What's going on?" I asked him. "Didn't your dad talk to you last night?"

"He said that I was staying down here no matter what anyone said," the kid told me. This is what I call the "jackpot" pull. It is where someone pushes all my buttons in the proper manner and pulls the final lever to have me go totally off. I immediately fired his son but told him it was not his fault but his father's fault. I told him I wanted him to come upstairs and work with us, to help take the burden off his father and that I was even going to spend time with him to teach him the business. Then I told him that for his father not to make this offer to him and demand he stay where he put him was totally unacceptable.

When Silas came in, *he* was the angry one but by that time, I was on ten and I ripped into him. I told him that the offer I made to him for his son was more than fair, especially that he hired the kid without even asking me—that he paid the kid without even asking me! I told him that the kid was fired and would not return and then I did something I had never had to do at any point in my life; not in the decade of running and managing my band, and not in the eighteen years I managed my janitorial business. I had to say that I was not only the boss, that I owned the business from top to bottom, lock stock and barrel because it certainly seemed to me that Silas had forgotten that.

Caden too was giving me problems. Some people are born to lead and some people; the power goes right to their head. Being in the third position of the company, Caden took it upon himself to denigrate the other workers. We had booked a huge job which could lead to a lot of work with a national clothing store chain. I instructed Caden to go to the job and "manage" it so that it was completed before they were to open the very next morning. Somehow this made the job go bad. I received calls from Bob and then Max, two of the guys I trained for my Mr. Sandless, saying that Caden was being a "tyrant" and that he was out of control.

Not only was Caden calling them names, he actually put his hands on Bob! He told Bob that he was a "sissy" and that his wife wore the pants in his family. The very next day I called Caden into my office. I calmly explained to him why he couldn't call the staff names, couldn't bring into the mix someone's wife, and most especially that he could not lay his hands on anyone whatsoever. I swear that I was calm to start.

Did Caden accept this critique, apologize and tell me it wouldn't happen again? No, he blamed the workers, saying they were disorganized and that all he was doing was managing the job. I once again explained that this wasn't managing, but bullying and that it can't happen, especially on a job I needed him to remain calm on. It was apparent to me that Caden's meds were not working like they used to, and he was off a bit.

Once again, he defended his actions. It was like I was talking to a brick wall. Once again, in back to back days, I went off on a "jackpot" tangent ripping Caden for not only the job, but for not understanding the most simple, basic principles of life and business! I was furious. When I was done yelling, he went into his office and both Silas and Caden were at their desks when there was a moment of silence. I walked to the hall and thought for a moment how unfair this all was to me. Bill Gates built his great company with a pack of MIT graduates. I built my brand with two freaking jackasses, and a pack of losers including Henry, Matt and Luke. With that, I addressed both of them; a moment I will never forget.

"You know, both of you two (speaking to both Silas and Caden) think you know more than I do. Both of you think you would have no problem at all running Mr. Sandless without me. But I will tell you the truth. If either one of you was in charge of this company, it would epically fail, and do you want to know why? It is because you don't know how to work with anyone, and everyone would quit. You are both horrible bosses! You have no idea what it takes to lead someone."

I mean the entire time Silas managed my Mr. Sandless, I got nothing but complaints about him from the field techs. He was one uncaring human being and never considered what they had to do in the field. He would send them miles and miles away without consideration, set up ridiculous times for them to be at the jobs, and always overbooked work so that they were inundated daily. If this guy ran the entire company, *everyone* would quit.

Caden on the other hand believed he was the embodiment of perfection. Not only did he believe his work was perfect, he believed that his "being" was perfect because he had been clean and sober for so long. He was a "cut above the rest" because of this, so he always looked down at all the other workers. And these two are what I built the company on, a sure testament of my own management skills. I just remember wondering what the company could be like if I had normal, sane, talented people working around and with me, instead of these damaged individuals that I got stuck with.

CHAPTER **6**

Power Struggles

IT IS AMAZING how the negativity flowed from one thing to the next to the next in this company, so as to not give me a minute's peace. The very next day, I got a visit from my ex-landlord. Now this prick kicked me out of that small office with no warning. But instead of fighting this in court, I paid the SOB the next four month's rent. After I completed payment, I expected my security deposit to be returned to me in full, because the office was still in the exact shape it was in when we took it over, plus I installed an alarm system and a fire and safety system at my own expense.

When I saw him, I fully expected that he was not bringing me a check and I was correct. What he brought me was the supposed "bills" for painting and repairs that magically ate up the entire security deposit. Now at this time I was in the prime of my life: six foot one, two hundred-twenty pounds of muscle, and this guy was an out of shape old decrepit man. I could not believe he had the guts to face me to try and rob this money from me. Once again, when I saw that he was only trying to rip me off, the jackpot was triggered, and I went off—for the third day in a row! I told him that the damn office was not painted when I moved in, and that he could not charge me for a fresh coat of paint. I also had pictures of both when I took over the office and what it looked like when we left in case something like this came up.

I told him clearly that I was going to snap him in half "like a number two pencil" and told him to get out of my office before I killed him. I then had to send a letter of demand which included the pictures to prove what he was saying was false. A month later, he returned the security deposit. I know that it was only a lousy thousand dollars, but the money wasn't the issue, it was the principle. There is no law written that says I have to take crap off someone like this who is only trying to rip me off. In fact, nothing can trigger me faster than someone like this.

Okay issues like these come with the job. While they seemed to be extraordinary, I should have counted my blessings. Little did I know that I was about to be screwed in a manner the likes of which I couldn't come up with in a fiction novel. Silas Montefusco, still promoting his music career as Silas Jones, would offer to sing for people for special occasions through his website. Somehow, he booked a job to sing at a wedding of this supposed bigshot by the name of Benjamin Maypan, whose daughter was getting married. During the event, Jones and Maypan got to talking about Mr. Sandless. From what Silas told me, Maypan was bragging to Jones about his company, so Jones took to bragging about "his"; at least that is how I read it. This kind of confirmed my suspicions about Montefusco. It sure seemed to me that all he was out to do was gain control of my company.

When Silas returned to the office that Monday, he was all excited that he believed he had a sale for an entire county to Maypan who would run the business through his best friend Gary Bulb. To this point in the company, Silas had not sold a single franchise, nor did he even vet a single potential franchisee other than Doobie when I couldn't physically be there that day. Otherwise, this was solely my job at Mr. Sandless. I felt at the time that Silas was trying to prove what I said about him was wrong, and he planned on showing me this by having this guy Maypan take a large franchise with us.

Silas set up a date for Maypan and Bulb to meet with us for a one on one presentation. I remember that through most of the presentation, Maypan had his back to me, like he was listening but couldn't care less what I was showing. This guy couldn't even look at me for some strange reason which I would figure out much later. Bulb on the other hand seemed more engaged. When I was through, Maypan asked only one question.

"If this system is so great like you say, best warranty, guaranteed to stick to the floor, and green, then why do you charge half the price of sanding for it?" he asked. "Seems to me you could charge more than sanding for this."

"At some point we will," I explained. "You are free to set your prices wherever you want with your own Mr. Sandless. But for my Mr. Sandless, the goal is to completely dominate the market first, then to raise prices once I have market share. There are one hundred seventy-nine refinishers here and that is a lot of competition. A lower price and best warranty will eventually gain market share."

I was right in this thinking. Just a few years in and there were only twenty-nine refinishers left in the region, thanks to my franchise and two others I had in the suburbs. But that was all Maypan asked during the meeting and I got the sense that this guy was nothing more than a big bag of hot air; a "stuffed shirt" type with more bark than bite. But shortly after they returned home, they contacted Silas saying they wanted to move forward.

I was not convinced if I should give this guy a franchise or not. Just something about him gave me a negative feeling. I went to Silas to inquire.

"Are you *sure* about this guy Silas?" I said. "I get a really uneasy feeling about him, like he is full of crap."

"No, I can promise you he is the real thing. The wedding I was at *had* to cost a fortune. It was at a top posh country club and it had the works. So, you know he is for real," Silas told me. I had him make up the territory for Maypan and we set them up for their training week. As expected, Maypan would just be the money guy, and Bulb would train and run the business. Maypan was going to use his "connections" to quickly ramp up the business for his partner.

When it came to the Monday Bulb was to train, we had not

received their paperwork or payment yet. Silas told me that he heard that Bulb would bring the paperwork down with him on the day of training. That Monday, I was in my office early when Silas entered to tell me that Bulb did not have the paperwork or payment for the franchise.

"Then he can't train, Silas!" I told him. "We can't start to show someone these trade secrets without a signed agreement!"

"Let him go out today and I will get Benjamin on the phone to clear this up," Silas told me. He was confident that it was just an "oversight". I once again asked Silas if he was sure of this guy Maypan, and once again he gave me all the reasons why the guy "had money". I should have listened to my gut instinct which has never let me down. Who cares if the guy had money when he already wasn't playing by the rules!

"I don't care if he has money Silas!" I told him. "That isn't the point! I care that he is going to honor his word to us!"

I let Bulb train that day but told him he would need to be in my office after training so that we could get this straightened out. Silas ran downstairs to tell him like a dog fetching a bone, all excited over his first sale. He seemed *way* too enamored with Maypan in this deal.

Once I had Bulb after training that day, I made it perfectly clear that I needed a signed agreement and payment. Bulb was a slender, short man with thick black hair cut in a marine style. Maypan on the other hand was huge and looked like a four-hundred-pound peanut M&M with tiny arms and legs but a huge neck and head. His hair was jet black like he had died it himself and did a terrible job. Anyway, Bulb said he was waiting on Maypan, who Silas had spoken to earlier and that he would have the payment and paperwork by Wednesday. I agreed to allow him to train one more day if we got everything done that Wednesday.

That is when I started to hear enough rumblings that I called every one of the staff for a meeting. Apparently Maypan had taken each of them aside, including Silas, to tell them about his company and to pitch them to buy stock from him—to actually *invest* in *his* company!

Hello, this was a huge red flag to me! If you had something legitimate, why in the world wouldn't you want to talk to *me* about an investment? Why go to my staff and behind my back at that? Surely Maypan who is supposed to have been this hot shot business guy knew to go to the money with something like this? I *knew* there was something going on.

I gathered all the information I could on what Maypan told them and then I did my own investigation. Maypan owned this company that was trying to win FDA approval for a medical device they had "invented". I watched the promotional videos that were on the company's website and since I was an ace at sales, I read right through the BS sales attempt. These videos were not trying to sell the device to anyone. They were to lure investors into this contraption. What the gizmo did was take out a pint of someone's blood, run it through their machine where it was "purified" and then to put it back into the person. The goal was to cure AIDS, hepatitis and other such auto-immune diseases, even though they had no proof that this worked. The only thing they did have proof about was that it supposedly cured TMJ which is pain in the jaw. How in the world it was supposed to cure that was anyone's guess.

Not only that, I had been developing another system and was very knowledgeable about the technology they were trying to use, and I do mean "trying". They used the spectrum of light that kills bacteria to run the blood through. This "C" spectrum of light can be used to disinfect anything and is used mainly to clean water to make it drinkable after it is filtered. The issue I saw was fairly easy to see. This light won't kill just certain things in the blood. It will kill *all* things in the blood! So, they are putting back nothing of substance. My conclusion was, this was nothing but a Ponzi scheme. That would explain why he didn't want to pitch me—because I would have seen right through this.

From what I gathered, the people who invested, including Bulb, were getting returns on their investment. This company wasn't even approved to use this system, not even trials, so there was no way in the world that they could be paying dividends yet. What happens is they take other people's money for "stock" and pay a little back to the ones who already invested, so that these people can tell others that they were "already making money" so that this prick Maypan could sell more stocks to more people and keep the Ponzi scheme going. That was when I realized what I had let into my company.

That Wednesday, Bulb brought in the signed franchise agreement, but only with partial payment! Maypan sent in nine thousand dollars in cash and a six-thousand-dollar check. You would have to be a total dumb ass not to know where the cash came from. This was from people giving Maypan cash for buying stock in his company. It was also under the limit of $10K so that the bank wouldn't ask where it came from. But the worse thing about this was, Maypan and Bulb owed another *twenty-five thousand dollars* for the options they took. I asked Bulb what was going on, but he didn't have an answer. I made Silas get on the phone with Maypan who made it sound like it was no big deal.

The issue we had is that the money needed to be paid according to the agreement "at the time you purchase the franchise". In other words, Maypan and Bulb were already in breach of this agreement—right out of the starting gate! Maypan asked Silas for more time and so I had no choice but to have our lawyers draw up an addendum to the agreement to give him another thirty days to pay the rest of the money due. Believe me I contemplated just terminating the deal right then and there. But I checked with Hunter who was training Bulb, and he said that Bulb already had a full understanding of the system. If I terminated the deal, Bulb would walk away with the system free and clear. I had no choice but to hold them to the terms of the agreement.

Bulb completed training and headed back to home to prepare to open. The franchise was launched, and it earned nearly ten thousand dollars that first month. But the time came and went for them to pay the remaining money they owed to hold onto all the option territories they took. Suddenly Maypan was not taking our calls. I was totally infuriated that this guy was going to stiff us. All the signs were there.

POWER STRUGGLES

A week after the deadline to pay was gone, Maypan sent me this completely stuck-up email. He said that he only worked with "world class companies" and that we were not to his liking at all. He had the most ridiculous complaints that didn't amount to a hill of beans and most certainly didn't add up since they already made more than half their money back in the very first month. But the main issue was, not only did he say we wouldn't "get a single penny more" out of him, that he was withdrawing from the franchise altogether. He would simply be turning it over to Bulb.

The problem with that was, Maypan is the one who signed our agreement. He couldn't just walk away. There were so many problems with this deal gone bad, primarily, since they defaulted on the option payment, they would only own a small territory in a huge affluent county. If someone else purchased the rest of the county, their franchise would fail because it wasn't a large enough territory to sustain a business. Along with this, Maypan's withdrawal from the business gave me enough breaches of the agreement to be able to terminate the entire franchise.

I gave this a lot of careful consideration. First, Bulb was open and already making money. He already knew our trade secrets. Second, I felt that I could work with him to get him to pay up and continue to grow the market as they promised. Third, a termination before we were a year old into franchising could have devastating consequences on future sales. This was the most convincing item that caused me to just let it go with the hope of sorting it out with Bulb in the future. I didn't really see any other choice in the matter.

When I explained my decision to Caden and Silas, I told them that I couldn't believe Maypan stiffed us more than he paid us.

"He did the same exact thing to me," Silas said.

"What do you mean?" I asked.

"When I performed at his daughter's wedding, he was supposed to pay me fifteen hundred dollars but stiffed me," Silas answered.

"You mean *before* he came on board with us?" I asked forcefully.

"Yes, it was right when I did the performance that he promised to pay but never did," Silas said as if he was talking about tying his shoes.

"Silas, I freaking asked you point blank not once, but twice if this guy was on the up and up and you told me he was! *You told me he was!*" I screamed.

Do you believe that someone could be so unbelievably stupid as to not tell me that this guy stiffed them, especially when I asked? My heavens I was steamed. All Silas cared about was his sale, not if this guy would honor his word or not. In other words, Silas only cared about Silas, certainly not me or Mr. Sandless.

I sent an email to let Maypan know he wasn't off the hook and to answer his nonsensical charges. But I had an ace in the hole. I never endorsed his franchise agreement. I told Silas and Caden right then and there that I wasn't going to sign the agreement so that I could cancel it whenever I wanted to. When that dawned on me, I realized that if I couldn't reach a deal with Bulb, I could "terminate" in name only. I wouldn't have to disclose this, but just give them their money back and close the franchise because I never signed their deal—because they stiffed us. I felt I held all the cards at that point, which was some relief to the situation.

About a month later, Silas was to go on vacation. His stress level and negativity were really getting to me, so I was glad to see him go. I brought Willy from being a technician and moved him to the office, so that he could be an assistant to Silas and learn what he was doing to both free up Silas and have a back-up for me in case Silas cracked up. Once Silas stabbed me in the back with the Maypan deal, right after the episode with his son, it was clear that there were going to be other issues with Silas in the future. Having Willy in the office to learn all he could was my backup plan in case I had to get Silas out of my company. But along with that, he could fill in while Silas took ten days off to hopefully get his act together.

Before he left, Silas called me into the conference room. He had a bunch of franchise agreements I didn't sign, and he said he and Willy wanted to get them out before he left of vacation. There are like ten pages to sign in these things and there were two copies of each one—one for us and one for the owner. One by one, they turned the pages and I signed everything, for all the owners who we had brought in to the system to that point of the year. Shortly after that, Silas left on vacation.

Within an hour of his departure, I received an email from Silas. When I saw it, I was wondering why in the world he couldn't just go on vacation. He wanted to know if I came up with a name for a new service I wanted to add to the system. This had nothing whatsoever to do with Silas. I told him I did, told him what it was, and told him to have a great vacation. He was headed to Texas to see his parents. I had met his mother before. I won't talk bad about someone's mom other than my own, but suffice it to say that after that meeting, I understood why Silas was such a stiff. She just stared at me!

Instead of just going away, Silas saw it fit to rip into me. He said I was a control freak, that I was impatient and did things in a knee-jerk fashion. He said he "*hated*" the way I ran the company! Okay, let me see if I can explain. Silas was jealous of me. This was becoming more and more apparent. This is the company he always dreamed of having and somehow in his ridiculous mind, he thought he could weasel it away from me. That was why he pulled that power trip with his son. If I would have allowed him to get away with that, his power trip would have only continued and at greater lengths. Now he was just angry that I stopped him. Once I ended that madness, he knew whatever grip he believed he had on the company was slipping, and so he was totally lashing out. He could sense that I was trying to wrestle from him the work he was doing as well as I recognized that he was withholding everything to make it seemingly impossible for me to lose him.

I simply love it when people like this think they are smarter than me. Sure, he had much more education than I ever did and a degree as well. But I would have to be a total dumb ass to not see what was going on right in front of my face. This guy thought with his superior intellect, he could force me out of my own company.

Even given all this, I figured he would calm down after nearly two weeks away. So, all I did was respond to him to let it go and just go on his vacation. But when he wrote a couple of days later with even more anger, I knew we had reached the breaking point. I could not believe that while on vacation, Silas stopped everything to reach out to me to vent and rip me. It was clear that the issue earlier with his son was the straw that broke his back—to him. For me, it was the knowledge that his plan to "take over" my company would fail. While he focused on that event, I knew it was much more about his failed coup attempt.

The things Silas said were extremely hurtful and downright mean in that email. After all I had done for this guy, he treated me like nothing more than the first rung of a ladder of his life. He swore that I would be the end of Mr. Sandless, that he disagreed with everything I had done in the company and that if I kept it up, the company would fail. In fact, that was his prediction. But what's best is he said that he wasn't alone in this belief, and that owners in the system believed the same thing. He also said that he was the sole person keeping the company together. *Please*!

Let me answer that charge about the owners in the system. During that time, I was a cheerleader, mother, father, brother, friend and even baby-sitter to my owners. I gave them my absolute all in trying to get them to be successful. There was no way any of them would feel the way Silas said they did. No, on the contrary, they felt nothing but negative about *Silas* and were very vocal in letting me know that he was a stuck up, know-it-all prick to them! I had to constantly apologize for his behavior to them! I didn't buy that nonsense for a split second.

As for running the company into the ground, that was laughable as well. I didn't respond to any of his ranting and raving. But I did respond and asked why he was so against me suddenly and to inquire if we were not still friends.

"That's always been way more on your side than mine," he wrote back.

"What is that supposed to mean?" I replied.

"I was never your friend," he said.

All the things I did for this guy, giving him a job when he didn't even ask me for one but just showed up, the fifty thousand dollars I spent on his music career, and paying him the highest salary in the company along with financial bonuses and that amazing trip, and that was the thanks I got for all of that. There is only one way to explain how I felt and that was; knifed in the back. I was really hurt. Little did I know at that time that this was only the beginning of a long series of betrayals.

Over the next six months of 2007, we continued to add franchise owners. There were many of them who would turn into being very good with their businesses. Silas returned from vacation and I only spoke one time about the emails he sent me. I told him that if he no longer wanted to be my friend, then so be it and to just concentrate on his job. But I knew the breaking point already occurred. All I wanted to do was get Willy up to speed so that when the time came, I could boot Silas out on his ass. I didn't see any other way around it.

Meanwhile every time I had contact with Bulb, I worked him hard about Maypan; whether he was truly out, how they were going to continue with just one tiny part of the county, how Bulb was supposed to build the brand there as promised without the help and connections of Maypan and how they were going to pay us if they wanted the entire county. Every time he just played dumb and said all he wanted to do was continue with the business. But I had a decision to make before the end of the year of whether I should rip up their agreement and give them their money back or not. I needed answers.

About the only other good thing that happened that year was doing work for a very renown hospital in the city. They wanted all the benches and handrails done throughout the place but wanted to test us to see if we were truly as "green" as we said we were. I sent Caden down to demonstrate the service with all our products with him and the MSDS sheets to show the hospital staff.

They had thirty health inspectors there to see the service! It was insane. They checked out the solutions we used and watched the demonstration for about an hour before they declared that we were "safe for hospital use". Not only would this be a very large job taking our entire crew days to complete, not only would this be such a prestigious hospital that I would use the name to promote Mr. Sandless for a decade to come, they had us come back every five years like clockwork to refinish the same things. As of this writing, we have serviced them multiple times!

Toward the end of 2007, out of the blue Maypan made a claim that I "stole his franchise" out from underneath of him. Now this was the guy who told me, in writing, that he would never do another thing for the business, who I had not heard a peep out of in over six months. Suddenly he was all concerned that I was "conspiring with Bulb" to supplant him. Frankly, I was! Again, when the principle of the franchise says they are out and appears they are out, I only had two choices: to terminate the deal, or work with the guy that was running it.

Maypan demanded a $120,000 payment for stealing his franchise and if I didn't pay, he said not only would he bring me to my knees, he would bankrupt me. I responded with the truth; that he told me he was out and that he has been out. At this point, I wasn't worried one bit because I never signed his agreement. I didn't even have a contract with Maypan to worry about being sued over. But what did dawn on me was that I was totally set up. The entire deal was a setup and Bulb had been telling Maypan everything that I said. Bulb was nothing more than a puppet for Maypan, and a backstabbing jerk of an owner in my system.

I believed that Maypan took a total disliking to me from the moment he met me. Time will prove this out when I tell you more about this and you will see. It was simple and pure jealousy. I started Mr. Sandless from my home, with two workers and one truck, and in two and a half years, had grown to thirty locations with nothing but open road ahead of me. I did this on my own, with my own money, with no "investor" money, without selling anyone stocks or shares, without any input from anyone else. The entire system was created from scratch by me.

That drove Maypan crazy. He did not create the health machine his company was hawking. He did not pay for the launch himself but sold stocks to everyone he encountered and built "his" company on their backs. Now years into the development of his company, the system they were selling hadn't even been shown to work, was not being sold anywhere, and was still completely dependent on more investor money to keep it afloat. Because of these things, Maypan thought he was going to "teach me a lesson", because in his eyes, I was "arrogant", and he was the pure and real one, a total reversal of truth. I simply love it when evil sees others as evil and not themselves.

To recap this time, Silas Montefusco thought he was smarter than me and the reason the company was doing so well. Maypan thought he was a "real" CEO and that I was just a poser. Caden thought he was so much purer than me because he had been clean and sober for years and I on occasion drank, which was a disgusting thing to him. There wasn't a single person surrounding me then who brought any positive light to the company.

For Maypan, it was simple to see where he was coming from. On my stationary and on my email, I had my name, and one title, President of Mr. Sandless and that's it. As we grew larger, I changed from "President" to "CEO" of Mr. Sandless. Maypan had *seven* titles under his signature like President, Chairman, Chief Executive Office, Chief Financial Officer, Master of the Universe and all-around great guy. Remember what I said about power. If you truly are the leader or the boss, you don't have to remind people of it. They already know. Maypan was anything but a leader and if anything, he was the poser.

As evidence of his legal prowess, Maypan offered up to me proof that he could "destroy" me. Apparently, he sued the Dodge Motor Company with some trumped up charge. He represented himself in court, which as I learned is how to play this extortion game. You see, two things happen when you represent yourself in a court action. First, it doesn't cost you anything. Dodge, being a corporation, must by law be represented by counsel just as I would have to be. Just to answer a complaint without even showing up in court will cost from ten to twenty thousand dollars. A full out trial could cost hundreds of thousands of dollars and on the other side, Maypan wouldn't have to pay anything. It is just great how the law is set up to screw corporations.

Second, courts always give wickedly great latitude to someone representing themselves. Call it a "liberal" thing if you want, but the court will deem the individual almost immediately as the "victim" and the mean and nasty corporation is the "villain". The court will allow this individual to pretty much do whatever they want, even if it is not in line with code of conduct of the court, so that they cannot be charged with being "unfair" to the victim.

At that point in time, I was "all in" for Mr. Sandless. I had no money left in reserve other than my retirement funds I had saved for twenty years and my kid's college funds. Everything else had been invested into Mr. Sandless, and we had not even reached the point of being self-sufficient due to the poor performance of eighty percent of the franchise owners. I didn't have $120K to pay Maypan, nor would I even consider it at that point. I had done nothing wrong, I couldn't see how he could win any case against me because the franchise was still active, and I never took it from him—he stepped out and away from it himself. Along with that, he didn't have an endorsed agreement. It was also a simple matter of principle. I wasn't about to pay off an extortionist.

True to his word, Maypan filed suit against me and Mr. Sandless but not according to the franchise agreement. He filed suit in a lower court in his county in another state, with a judge that he had been friends with for years, and so the fix was in. When my franchise attorneys were served with the court papers, I told them I hadn't signed the franchise agreement with Maypan and so he had no case of "breach of agreement". His complaint was sheer nonsense. Where he claimed "breach", he had not a single clause of the agreement that I or Mr. Sandless breached. I mean how hard could this case be to win? This would be the only time ever in company history that an owner said that I or Mr. Sandless had breached our agreement, and this one doesn't even count. You can't claim a breach unless you can site a clause that you thought *was* breached.

The lawyers wanted a ridiculously high retainer to fight the case, and they supposedly had a seasoned "litigator" on staff to handle this. I had to take all the cash from both of my entities and pay them the retainer to answer the suit. That meant no bonuses for Caden or Silas that month. Normally I would give them a bonus based on how many sales we brought in, to keep moral high in the company and remember, I still to this point had not taken a bonus for myself nor a pay. Not only that, both Silas and Caden had company credit cards for incidentals like taking someone out to lunch, gas purchases and things like that. I couldn't have possibly done more for them.

About an hour after he received his check that Friday, Silas slammed the door of his office as he stormed out of the building. This selfish prick was angry that I didn't give him a bonus even though he got his full pay and he didn't even allow me the opportunity to explain why I was suddenly cash poor. It seemed he didn't care one bit that Maypan was suing me.

As soon as I heard that door slam, I knew something was up. By that time, I knew Willy could cover most of the things Silas did, except for one, which was our website. While I had access to the site and our server, this was not anything I could do myself. Silas knew this was my only weakness, and so immediately I tried to log into the server and the site. I was locked out! The password had been changed to intentionally lock me out!

I called the company who owned the server our website was housed on and told them that I was locked out, that I owned the company and that I needed immediate access. They were polite and said it would be no problem. All I had to do was give them the last four digits of the card used to pay for the server. Silas used his company card for this. I pulled out his credit card statement and read the last four numbers, then was able to change the password to regain control of my website. This was before Silas even made it home that day.

On his statement, I noticed another charge from this company for a "private server". Since I was on the phone with them, I inquired as to what that was all about. Our website was small at the time, and so we shared a server with other companies. A private server is just that. Whatever we have on it is ours. I asked them what was on it and they said they had no idea! Only Silas would know what was on it. I cancelled that server and told them to wipe it clean.

At that moment, I figured it all out. Silas purchased the private server, with my money, without telling me so that when he took control of the website, he could move it to that server, and then I would be locked out completely. I would not be able to have access to it. This was confirmed an hour later when I received a "ransom" email from Silas, demanding a huge payment for his "pain and suffering". He was stupid enough to state that if he didn't get paid, I wouldn't get the website back. He didn't know that I already had it back.

In one quick brush stroke, I was being extorted and sued by one guy, and extorted and blackmailed by another, both coming back to back. I responded that I already knew what he was going to do and that I already took control of the website. With that, he lashed out at me saying he was going to sue me, that I would ruin my own company and be its downfall, and that no matter what he would get what was coming to him and that without him the business would fail. I was betrayed by Matt, betrayed by Henry and now betrayed by the man I used to call my best friend. I couldn't for the life of me figure out why this business was costing me so many people.

After a discussion with my attorneys, I decided to not have Silas arrested for blackmail and extortion. Believe me, it wasn't for him. I did it for his children. We offered him a severance package, basically paying him for three months and then he would release me from all things and he accepted. I packed up his personal items from his office for him and left them outside the office for him to retrieve and I told him to leave his credit card and keys which he did. I thought his part in my business were over. I *thought*.

That was all signed and done with before I received the next blow to the gut. Maypan was able to produce a franchise agreement that I signed! I couldn't even believe it, because I *knew* I did not sign his agreement. I set it aside and told everyone that I wouldn't be signing it because Maypan and Bulb stiffed me! But there it was, clearly my signatures on the pages of his agreement.

That was when it hit me. I ran to Silas's office and began to look through everything in his desk. To my absolute horror, there in his file was the signature pages of Maypan's franchise agreement. This total back-stabbing traitor of a man must have slipped them into another agreement and had me sign them that day before his vacation when I signed all those other agreements. Then he made a copy of the signature pages, inserted them into Maypan's agreement and sent the damn thing to Maypan. Never in my wildest imagination could I come up with such a complete betrayal. He was so hell-bent on making that sale, hoping that Maypan would be the start of his attempt at controlling Mr. Sandless, that he never thought about the repercussions of this one act.

If that wasn't bad enough, Maypan started his plan of extorsion attack against me. First, he wrote an email to every single owner in Mr. Sandless to announce that he was suing me, stating that I was a "thief" and that he would bring the end of Mr. Sandless along with me going bankrupt and ending up in jail. Now imagine thirty franchise owners receiving this madness. Next, this evil prick wrote to the attorney generals of <u>all fifty states</u> stating that I committed fraud and that Mr. Sandless should not be allowed to franchise in their states!

Every day, I would receive a fax from him with some other stupid threat. "Pack your toothbrush, you are going to jail!" "I'm going to be the end of Mr. Sandless!" "I'm going to bankrupt you!" and on and on the faxes came. I had blocked his email because he was emailing the same madness each day, but I couldn't stop the faxes. This is how extortion works. File suit to cost me a lot of money, harass my business and associates, then force me to settle and pay him. His "scheme" worked like a charm with Dodge, as they walked into court and handed him a fifty-thousand-dollar check just to get rid of him. Ultimately, they knew that this would be far less costly then fighting this out in court. Unfortunately, I hadn't come to that conclusion yet and I was about to see that the worst was yet to come!

CHAPTER **7**

Mutiny Conspiracy

I COMPLETELY UNDERSTAND if you believe this book is more horror story than anything else. As I am reading through it, I remind myself why I started drinking. At this time, I urge you not to close the book and say you can't take anymore. There will be moments of shining throughout, and ultimately, the end is worth waiting for. Hang in there because I am afraid it gets much worse and I didn't want to scare you away without letting you know beforehand. The final payoff is more amazing than the amount of insanity I had to endure to get there. I promise you that!

When I saw the movie "Deadpool", right before the main character collapsed from having cancer throughout his body, which was right after he proposed to the love of his life, he made a statement about life. It was something like 'Life is just a shit-storm interrupted by brief commercial breaks of happiness". My children were with me when we were watching that in the movie and they both turned to me and said, "Dad it's you!" and as much as I hate to say it, that was true. While the entire ordeal of what I went through in this company had turned me from pure optimist into a realist, I remain very much optimistic in my approach of life. I have great stories to tell, because through all the shit storms of my life, I'm still standing. I'm still producing. I am still affecting people's lives. I am still a force in this world. Please don't let the "shit" that happened to me make you believe that there isn't hope. There is always hope for the next day.

One of the advertising and promotion venues I had not tried in the prototype test of Mr. Sandless was to display at a home show. I already figured it would be a good place to build the brand and so it was already in the company marketing plan. But still I thought it best to give it a run myself. Since we had no owners around us at the time, I took a show in a town about forty-five minutes from our offices, and in another county that we did not serve. I had some terrific floor models, candy for giveaways, and a clipboard and pad to take down the potential customer's information.

Behind me, I had pop-up displays that showed six before and after pictures of what we were capable of doing. I didn't really have any help planned for this show as I didn't expect to need any. The event was to run for three days, from Friday night until Sunday afternoon. That Friday night was somewhat slow paced. I paid two thousand dollars for the ten by ten booth. Within the first hour, I booked more than six thousand dollars in work! I was already well ahead with this event.

That next day was an absolute nightmare! As usual, the first and top question I got was how do we do the Mr. Sandless service? Within the first four hours, I must have explained how we did it three to four *hundred* times! There were so many people at my booth, I couldn't control the situation. I had to call in everyone to come help and then planned on rotations for the next day because four hours of doing this was exhausting business. From then on in, every single home show or event we did like this, we had multiple people taking "shifts" so that they wouldn't get burned out.

One of the best home shows I ever did was the following year at the same location. For the busiest shift, I took my son Mike with me. I explained to him what we were going to do, taught him the thirty second pitch and got ready for the first group of people to visit us that day. When they asked that special question of how we do it, I told them that my son and I would come to their home and dance. With that my Mike and I broke out into a little jig-like dance, to the amusement and wonderment of the people standing there watching. Then I had Mike tell them the real answer. We did this our entire shift.

The next day at the office, Cora was standing by the phones. Fifteen different people called to book; over twenty thousand in work. All of them told Cora that "her" husband and son were delightful. Cora just said "thanks" as she was not my wife, but this sale's trick worked better than I could have ever imagined. We ended up with over thirty thousand in bookings for my shift with my son.

As the company continued to grow and gain market share locally, I eventually stopped doing home shows. It seemed everyone who came to our booth already knew who we were! I would hear "You did my aunt's house, you did my uncle's house, you did my parent's house, you did my brother's house, you did my neighbor's house," and along with that, "I've seen you on TV and I see your trucks all over the place!" Once we were branded in this manner, there was no longer a need for this type of promotion.

At my last local show, when I had a potential customer, I would barely need to pitch them. That's because someone would come up and tell them how great we were! One woman was trying to decide whether to get on the schedule or not when another came up to speak to her.

"They did my floors and they came out great!" she said. "I had this one bad spot which they told me about before they started, and they thought it may be an issue, but they got it all out."

"How long ago did you have them done?" the woman who was considering asked.

"A little more than four years ago," this client replied. The potential client turned to me and said, "Put me on the schedule!" That is one thing through this entire voyage that stood tall—the system itself. It really was a thing of beauty!

One of the last customers I had at the last home show I did was a husband and wife. They walked up to me and said that I did their floor. I asked if they meant me personally. The wife responded that she thought so. I asked when the floors were refinished, and she said it was six years ago.

At that, the husband threw her a look and he asked if she was crazy. He said that it was over ten years ago! The woman then proceeded to tell me that whoever it was who did the floor talked them into getting another room done.

"*Ah* that was me then!" I replied, because I was always big on upselling customers when I did the service! She then said that there was a stain on the floor that I told her may be a problem, but that I got it out and that it never came back. I asked how the floor looked now, and they both said "great!" The service really was a thing of beauty!

Even though I stopped doing local shows, I did go on to do events across the country to promote the brand. I did a show in Los Angeles in an attempt to find a few people to take a franchise there. I could have easily booked fifty thousand dollars in work for people who stopped to talk to me and wanted to get their floors done. But not a single franchise candidate was to be found that weekend.

I did shows in Harrisburg and Lancaster, Canton and Cleveland, Dallas and Houston, Chicago and Naperville, and then took the shows international with events in London, Johannesburg and Sydney. I used the same case to cart my floor models and materials around the world, amazed that it held up going around the world twice!

I knew it was time for me to personally stop with the home shows when I could no longer take people asking me how we did it. At the very last big home show we displayed at, it was a Friday evening after a very crazy and hectic week. I was there with Caden and a few others to start the show and as usual, the first guy approached the booth.

"So how do you do it?" he asked, with his wife right by his side.

"Does it really matter?" I replied. "I mean, as long as I can do it, isn't that what really matters?" They seemed to get the logic in that, and I was able to pitch them without telling them how we did it.

The very next couple after that walked up to me, moving away from Caden and the others to talk to me.

"How do you do it without sanding?" they asked.

"If I could put a pad on his ass (pointing to Caden) and was able to drag him around your floor and somehow that made your floor look fantastic, would it really matter?" They laughed, and I booked them for a free home inspection.

The very next couple worked their way through a crowd at our booth to speak to me. I know—I am a loon magnet.

"So how do you do it?" they asked.

"If I was able to bring a bulldozer into your home, and not damage a single thing but use that to refinish your floors, would it really matter to you?" After dealing with those people, I went to the back of the booth and sat on a stool.

"I don't want to do this anymore!" I told Caden. "I can't answer that question ever again!"

I also remember several times really getting into it with certain people who were not interested in "how we do it" but *"how"* we do it, meaning, they wanted to try and figure it out, so *they* could do it. It was always a guy, never a gal, and always they thought they were intellectually superior. When their supposedly huge brain couldn't "figure out" the secret to Mr. Sandless, it was too much for them! Their heads were about to explode.

They would always ask the same, exact question: "How does it work?" Now you could read this incorrectly. They were not asking if it works well or not. They are asking a specific question for us to explain to them the "how" as in the trade secret. I remember the first joker I encountered in this and it wasn't even me they were talking to. They were talking to the other person who was doing the show with me. That person turned to me with the look of "help me" on their face, so I asked the guy he was talking to what was up.

"He won't tell me how it works!" he barked at me.

"I'm not sure why he won't tell you sir," I said very cocky, knowing this guy was another prick in the wall of pricks I encountered. "It actually works quite well as you can see!"

"That's not what I mean!" he said back angrily. "I mean, tell me how it works!"

"You mean you want me to tell you the science behind Mr. Sandless?" I asked him.

"That's exactly what I want to know!" he once again demanded.

"What are you some kind of rocket scientist or something?" I inquired.

"I'm a scientist and I create polymers for a laboratory," he replied.

"Well then sir, I hope you have a check with you and if you would write that check out to me for twenty million dollars, I will write the formula out for you!" With that, he became angry and cursed at me, and I just continued.

"Are you actually that stupid to believe that simply by asking I would tell you the science behind a multi-million-dollar concept? Really, that's what you thought Mr. Rocket Scientist?"

I had run into one of these types about once a year like clockwork. For example, any client who ever demanded to see our material safety data sheets was only trying to rip us off. Why in the world they would think that our MSDS sheets would have the trade secrets right on them is beyond me. But then again, they all thought they were smarter than me, so what do I know.

My favorite of these characters was at a large home show. Our booth that day was packed with thirty people in front of us, with three of us pitching the people in front of us. As I was speaking that day, I looked up to the back of the crowd of people at our booth. There I spied a couple working their way through the crowd to get to the front of the line. As they ping-ponged through the line, they worked their way to be right in front of me. Once there, the man presented his question.

"So how does it work?" The moment he opened his mouth, I knew he was "that guy" because of the tone of his voice. It wasn't happy and jovial, but down and denigrating. I responded with my "very well" line just to piss him off. As he sighed and rolled his eyes, like his plethora of just five words were so intellectually informative, that I should have immediately been able to recognize his genius. When he came back at me with anger for not clearly understanding him, I asked if he had a check with a lot of zeros to pay me for the information. This guy was actually yelling at me that I needed to tell him or else.

"What, are you some kind of rocket scientist or something?" I asked sarcastically.

"As a matter of fact, I am!" he replied confidently, as if *that* would get me to open up—as if I was even being serious!

"Oh, go away *please*!" I said. It was at that point he got almost violent where his significant other had to drag him away from our booth. I am telling you the truth here. People like this lose their minds because to them, there is nothing they don't know. But when they find something they can't explain, it drives them mad!

During that very first home show, someone stopped by the booth to speak to me. I wasn't there at the time, Caden was. He told her when I would be relieving him if she wanted to wait around for me. When I showed up, he brought her over to introduce her to me. She was a producer for a large local company that had a ton of national shows, and said she was at this event to find new and innovative things to showcase on a prominent national television station. Once I heard that, I lit up and saw great opportunity.

I explained to her the Mr. Sandless process and got the producer's email, where I followed up with more information including our website. It was less than a week before they offered Mr. Sandless a show, one of their new shows for the season. I was thrilled because this was for the popular cable home improvement channels, which is a perfect vehicle to get the brand name out their nationally.

The plan was that we would refinish the floors for a couple at no cost in their master bedroom that was being remodeled as the feature of this episode. I agreed to the job which would not be a problem at all. I was to meet with some associates of the show and an interior decorator who was doing the design for the new "Indonesian" bedroom. The homeowners would be there as well.

Upon arriving, I was introduced to the homeowners and shown the room. It was not very large at all, certainly under two hundred square feet. The floors were old oak, the same kind of floors we had serviced in this region for years. There was nothing at all special about this job and if anything, it would be very easy. I planned on doing the job myself with Caden to assist me, and then if they needed to film someone say running the machine, I would use Caden's brother Dominic, who I just hired. He worked at a dead-end job selling tools and was looking for an opportunity. He was probably the best-looking guy we had in the company, though rather short with shaggy blond hair, he looked more like a surfer dude than a wood floor guy. I thought it would look better with him on the show than the rest of us.

But when the interior decorator entered the mix with the associate producers, he had *way* more grand plans for the room. Along with whatever else he wanted for the room, which I didn't pay any attention to, he talked about what he wanted for the floor.

"I envision a milky white floor to accent the black trim of the inset television and new closet design," he stated, waving his hand as if he was a wizard casting a spell. We had a lot of things in our arsenal, but milky white wood stain wasn't one of them. I walked around him to speak with the homeowners and asked if this is what they "envisioned". They shook their heads as if the entire idea was foul. I took that as my cue to save them.

"Well I hate to be the spoiled egg in this show, but that isn't going to work with the floor," I stepped up and announced.

"And why pray tell won't that work for you?" the designer asked.

"This floor runs right into the hallway and the other rooms. We would have to cut a line to separate the room floor from the hallway. This one would be white, and that one will be the original color. It will look both out of place and horrendous." That is when it dawned on "sunshine" that I was right.

"Let's just make the floor look great just as it is," I said, and "I will even do the hallway as well so that they all blend together. How does that sound?" I also explained that we should be last on the work schedule because they wanted to put us first, thinking we were an invasive process like sanding. We should always be last.

Thankfully the homeowners stepped forwarded and said that sounded great, and with a quick "whatever", the designer and associates departed. I assured the owners that I would personally service their floors and let the them know they were in good hands. I had the schedule of when we were to do the work, and that was that.

But it wasn't, I was to learn. The network called the producers who then called me. Apparently, my floor system was so "scary" that the network was afraid they be inundated with calls about "how we refinish without sanding," once again with my favorite question rearing its ugly head. After kicking some ideas around to get through this, I came up with a solution.

"Why don't I just write that part of the script for the stars of the show to say to explain our service? This way they can't mess it up." The producer went back to the network, and they enthusiastically agreed. I wrote up a little bit more than our standard thirty second pitch for the two hosts of the show to explain to their viewers what Mr. Sandless was going to do.

Caden and I and a few others went to the home to service the floors. All the construction work was completed, including the painting, and we were the last piece of the job to be completed, which is how it should be when doing our type of floor refinishing. I personally went over inch by inch of that job to make sure it was perfect. I hit a nail that was sticking up out of the floor, and my finger bled a little bit.

"A little blood in the finish never hurt anyone!" I said, a line I had used for years in my janitorial company!

We put Dominic on the machine for the camera guy to film a little bit of him doing the process, not really showing anyone on film how we actually do it. I took a series of before and after pictures to show how great it came out, and we left.

Before the show aired, I got a call from the homeowners who said how magnificent the floors came out. But that wasn't the reason they were calling. They wanted to tell me the "behind the scenes" incident about this episode.

It seemed that the lead host, a master carpenter with fifteen years' experience had been given the script I wrote to use on the show. Instead of adding to his original script, he ripped it up, saying that it was impossible to refinish a wood floor without sanding. Oh, great, another non-believer! All he thought we were going to do was to ruin the floor. He bought a huge area rug that was stored in the homeowner's garage that he was going to use to cover the floor once we did ruin it. And then on the actual show, he made up what we were going to do, calling it a "chemical peel" which Sandless refinishing is anything but.

He didn't use the script because he thought we would ruin the floor and he just planned on having us completely edited out of the episode! Can you believe it? The homeowners told me that staff came and moved their furniture back into the room after we were done, and the next day the film crew and hosts came out for the "wrap up" to show how the room looked after the remodeling.

They told me that the camera was rolling when our master carpenter walked into the room, and they kept his reaction to our floor in the actual episode.

"Next, no sanding? And the floor looks brand new!" He shouted on the episode. "If I hadn't seen it with my own eyes, I wouldn't have believed it!" he stated with the same look on his face the other carpenter I told you about had. Well, well, well.

I had a producer friend of mine pull our segment out of the show, so it looked like a Mr. Sandless commercial and placed that up on our YouTube channel. That channel was a great idea as I said earlier because no other wood refinisher had ever done anything like it. I put fifteen different videos up on it and gained nearly two million views to promote the brand!

Mr. Sandless was featured several more times on this show. The master carpenter liked us so much, he kept requesting us. During that time, I was way too busy to even look to see the episodes we were featured in, but I heard that he even promoted our wood floor cleaner. Way before I launched Mr. Sandless, I had Logan come up with a special formula wood floor cleaner for us to label as a Mr. Sandless product and sell to our customers. I honestly can't say that I made a single "business" mistake in this venture. That wood cleaner has gone on to sell literally tens of thousands of bottles and once someone uses it, they continue to use it forever—because it works so well. At the same time, it promotes the brand name.

It was right around this time that I had a traditional sander want to visit with me. From just one conversation on the phone, I told him that he didn't grasp what we were doing and that I wasn't going to give him a franchise. Even saying that, he still wanted to visit, so I had him come up for a day.

When we entered the conference room where I would give him a brief franchise presentation, I had the pictures of the room and hall we did for the first television show blown up and in glossy prints on the table. He took the pictures and examined them.

"The floor sure does look good!" he said.

"Thank you, it does!" I replied.

"But I would have sanded it," he stammered.

"Why would you sand it?" I asked him.

"You see these couple of wavy boards outside the bathroom here?" he said, pointing to the one main after picture. "I could get all of that level and that's why I would have sanded this floor."

"And that is why I am not giving you a Mr. Sandless," I replied. "You aren't getting this, so let me explain. *They didn't want to sand*! Are you hearing me? This couple didn't want to go through the cost and mess of sanding when we delivered these kinds of results without sanding. So here is the punch line you are missing. At Mr. Sandless, our customer's happiness is first. We don't care if you are not happy. Do you understand what I am saying? Your happiness as a technician—as a floor guy—is irrelevant!" He never did understand.

Back to my story, with the exit of the traitor Silas, I needed someone to join the team who could do the website uploads that he used to do for us. Cora had a brother by the name of Gabriel who had worked for us for a couple of high-end IT situations we ran into, so I asked him to join the team and he did. Gabe had met Silas before and described Silas as a "stump". As it turned out, Silas was not anywhere near as good as he thought he was with the website, and Gabe had to basically re-script everything so that it could work. I also promoted Caden as the new VP of Mr. Sandless because he was the last man standing after the departure of Henry and Silas.

Meanwhile Maypan kept up his antics and attack on Mr. Sandless. He posted negative comments online to stop us from bringing in new franchisees and responded with massive nonsense if anyone asked him what his problem was with us. This attack went on as we continued to grow and expand the brand in 2008. He was absolutely relentless and assigned his secretary to constantly bombard our current owners with email and faxes.

On top of that, the district attorneys of several states wrote to me to explain the situation of how I stole this guy's money. It was maddening! The lawyers I had in a nutshell were *worthless*! Okay, they were able to get me to the point of franchising, but when it came to litigation like this, they had no real experience. They had no control over this madman as he continued to denigrate my company. My agreement with this prick had that any legal action would have to be brought in my state. Maypan filed his nonsense in a different state. My lawyers had to petition that court to move this action to high court in my state and that motion failed. Instead, it was moved to state court where Maypan filed rather than local court. But Maypan knew all the judges in state court as well! This was growing to be a nightmare of epic proportions as I was already more than one hundred thousand dollars in legal bills for this case alone. And they hadn't even done anything yet!

Two other players entered the game in 2007 by taking a franchise with us. One would be a great owner and the other turned into yet another nightmare. The first was by the name of Craig Corentine. This guy was another one of these characters who thought he knew everything, a real Silas type, who was already a successful franchise owner with another system. He was also another ginger, with deep red hair and freckles. His main shtick was to try and weasel his way into Mr. Sandless for franchise sales or support, because he was a big fish in a little pond and with his vast experience, he felt he was inevitably upwardly mobile. He took a franchise with several option territories in his state.

The second guy, Dylan, took a franchise in the same state and had options for all the next adjoining state. This guy took to Mr. Sandless like a fish to water. He had numerous properties he owned and was a contractor type who just knew this business was for him. He was the first owner to reach the level of the original Mr. Sandless, reaching the sixty-thousand-dollar level in just his ninth month. He was the first owner in company history to break the one hundred-thousand-dollar mark! I didn't have any problems with Dylan, but he is part of an interesting story I will tell you about later in this book.

That year 2008 was a blur of insanity with adding thirty-five new owners and the madness created by Maypan who continued his push to "bankrupt me". He filed multiple motions with the court that we would have to answer, bombarded my attorneys with calls, faxes and emails to simply run up my bill. In all the years I had done business, I had never been involved in a lawsuit. I had no knowledge to draw from on how this is supposed to go. I was relying *completely* on my franchise attorneys to save the day.

But they were worthless. Maypan, having done this already in representing himself, was so relentless that they wrote to the judge to have the court make him stop. But this woman judge was in Maypan's grasp and she did absolutely nothing to stop or help. Believe me, legally, there were plenty of ways to stop this guy. I had finally reached the point where I realized two things. First, this litigator from my attorney's office simply did not have the experience needed to get his hands wrapped around this. Second, he didn't really care because he wanted to milk me for as much money as possible. Before I knew it, the cost were over two hundred thousand dollars and we hadn't even seen a second of court time. Maypan was correct. If he kept doing this and I didn't pay him, he would bankrupt me.

Since my attorneys were getting nowhere with this guy, I decided to try and fix the situation myself. Of course, they were totally opposed to me contacting Maypan, but frankly I was going to do it no matter what. I am a Godly driven man and if I didn't try to make peace with this guy, who in all reality I did nothing at all to, then I wouldn't be honoring my faith and my belief. I sent Maypan an email to attempt a truce.

In it I talked about life and being, soul and purpose, in an attempt to reason with him. For all his trouble and madness, he stilled owned the franchise, which was earning decent money. I told him it only made sense for him to take all that energy he was putting into damaging the brand and instead to channel that into his franchise and make it the success that he said he would make it. It was easy to see that it would earn him far more than the $120,000 he was hoping to extort from me. It was a mix of godliness and logic that I thought would really make him think.

He responded that I was an asshole and to go f myself. But I wouldn't be me if I didn't try.

Now back to Craig Corentine who was continuing to push me to "hire" him in some capacity for Mr. Sandless. Don't get me wrong—Corentine was great at Mr. Sandless and was running neck and neck with the original site as far as earnings were concerned. But just as I was not completely fooled by Silas—only on the personal issues—I was not fooled by Corentine either. He was that transparent that he wanted to get in my company only to supplant me which was what Silas wanted to do as well. So that was never going to happen, and I told Corentine just that.

As I normally do, I wrote to him a wonderful email about life and being, soul and purpose, in an attempt to reason with him and to get through to him that God has a purpose for all of us. I pointed out all his good qualities and explained to him how I saw his role in life at this point and after my signature line I wrote "Don't shoot the messenger" so that he would know that I really wasn't interested in a nasty rebuttal. What I sent was out of caring and kindness and me being a good man and nothing more than that. He did not respond.

When it came time for Corentine to exercise his first option which is for a larger territory, he was dragging his feet. He had excuse after excuse for not sending in his new signed franchise agreement, even though I warned him that he would be losing the bulk of the territory he had been working. I couldn't understand his reluctance on continuing to develop the area he took.

He finally sent in the ten-thousand-dollar payment without the required paperwork. I went into his multi-unit option agreement and extracted the lines from it that explained what he needed to do to execute this first option. Primary on that agreement was to sign the current franchise agreement. He said he would get it to me in a couple of days.

I had a decision to make. Should I hold his check for the paperwork or should I deposit it without it? While it seemed very strange to me his desire not to sign a new franchise agreement for the *new* territory when we already had him on a franchise agreement with his *first* territory, I didn't have any other reason not to take him at his word. But I will admit this had much less to do with it than my current cash poor situation due to the Maypan suit eating up money faster than I could get it in. I decided to risk it and deposit the money. Stress makes one do stupid things.

Unknown to me, Corentine had no intention at all in signing the second agreement. He believed he was holding four aces because of something in his original agreement that I had no knowledge of. But at that time, Maypan was much more on my mind, who had Bulb call me on the phone in an attempt to get me to settle. I must be honest and say I don't remember what I said during that call, but I am sure it wasn't kind to Maypan, who had by that time been torturing me for ten months along with costing me a fortune.

Immediately after the call, I received a fax from Maypan who said he recorded the entire conversation between me and Bulb. It said that now he had the proof he needed to put me in jail for perjury or some other madness and that he wouldn't rest until I was in jail. Maypan then called all my personal friends at their homes to let them know that I was a "crook" and that I would be going to jail, and further, if they supported me in any way, he would have them in jail as well! I have copies of all the calls from their message recorders that day to prove this madness. This was way beyond out of control.

Through his connection to this woman state court judge, Maypan got permission to depose me. It was the most ridiculous thing I had ever seen of corruption because I should have been allowed to depose Maypan. But only I would be questioned, and not by an attorney, but by Maypan himself! This was to take place in state court in Maypan's state, be limited to eight hours of testimony, where I would be under oath when Maypan questioned me.

I met a lawyer that my attorneys sent to be with me during the deposition. It was just some underling who really was no help at all. I asked him what I was supposed to say about Maypan's "perjury" charge regarding talking to Bulb. He had no answer. At least he told me how a deposition was supposed to go. I was always so very quick on my feet that once I knew how to play the game, I felt very comfortable.

We were placed in a room off a court room with a conference table. My representative attorney sat at the head of the table. Maypan came in and sat to his left. To the right of Maypan was his daughter and I sat to the right of my attorney. Maypan had boxes and boxes of papers. I had absolutely nothing. I don't know what that was supposed to be, but it certainly didn't intimate me.

The attorney objected to Maypan's daughter being there as she was not a party to any of this. Maypan gave the guy some bull excuse and there was no one there from the court to help, so it wasn't going to go in our favor as she stayed.

To be dead honest, Maypan looked like "The Heat Miser" from the classic Christmas 1974 animated special "The Year Without a Santa Clause" except for the fake jet-black hair. His hair was scraggly, his face angry and crumpled, and his voice was irritating. Remember, this is the first time I was really getting a look at this guy because he wouldn't look at me directly in our first meeting. Maypan began his deposition of me.

"As you are aware, I discovered Mr. Sandless through Silas Jones who told me about this investment franchise. I worked one on one with Silas Jones who created the territory maps for me for this franchised business. Did Silas Jones show you the territory I was interested in acquiring with the franchise?" he asked.

"No," I replied.

"Silas Jones did not show you the franchise territory?" he asked perturbed.

"No," I again replied.

"Do you mean that you don't look at franchise territories before you sell them to someone?"

"That's not what I am saying at all," I answered.

"So, you do look at franchise territories?" he asked again.

"Yes," I answered.

"So, did Silas Jones show you the territory I was to purchase?" he asked, getting even more heated.

"No," I said again.

"Does Silas Jones create the territory maps for Mr. Sandless?" Maypan asked, obviously frustrated.

"No," I replied.

"Silas Jones?" he asked.

"Is that a question?" I asked.

"Does Silas Jones work for you?" Maypan asked even louder.

"No," I replied.

"Silas Jones doesn't work for you?" he asked even louder now.

"How many times do you want me to answer the same question?" I replied. "If you keep on asking the same questions this is going to go really long."

"Do you have anyone by the name of Silas who works for you?" He screamed.

"Lower your voice," my attorney said calmly. "We are actually in an open courtroom here."

"Yes," I replied.

"As you are aware, I discovered Mr. Sandless through Silas Jones who told me about this investment franchise. I worked one on one with Silas Jones who created the territory maps for me for this franchised business. Did Silas Jones show you the territory I was interested in acquiring with the franchise?" he asked.

"No," I answered.

"Silas Jones?" he asked.

"Is that a question?" I replied.

"Did you not say to me you had a Silas work for Mr. Sandless?" he pushed further.

"Yes," I answered.

"Silas Jones?" he asked.

"No," I replied.

"Silas Jones does not work for Mr. Sandless?" he asked.

"I have a Silas Montefusco," I replied. You see "Jones" was Silas's stage name. He only used it in conjunction with his music career. When he signed his emails for Mr. Sandless, he only signed them as Silas. There was no way for Maypan to know Jones was in fact Montefusco.

Every single time Maypan said the name "Jones" I answered "no" and it was driving Maypan stark raving mad! It took him forty-five minutes straight to finally ask me if Jones and Montefusco were the same person. By that time, he was lucky he didn't have a heart attack! He was completely flustered by my answers.

"Let's just cut to the chase then," Maypan announced, as he pulled out another box with more material. "When you told Bulb that he could pay for the options and own them but told the court that you had no agreement with Bulb, how was that not perjury?"

"By that time, Bulb had already breached the franchise agreement with Mr. Sandless," I said confidently. "Anything that happened after that was null and void." So much for needing lawyers. I came up with my own answer.

As I literally reclined in the seat, knowing full well that despite this guy Maypan tying up my lawyers for months on end, he was ultimately no match for me when we were one on one. He had been hiding behind the court all this time, but now he was exposed. When he heard my answer, which he had no retort to, he literally pulled his hair with both hands above his head, as if he was trying to pull his own hair out! He was that frustrated.

All that deposition did was waste more money and time for me. Maypan learned nothing in this at all and if anything, ruined his entire case against me. It was at that time I had an idea to force this total prick out of my company and honestly it was something that my lawyers should have come up with months earlier. I knew, I just knew that Bulb wanted to keep the business and that all that Maypan wanted was instant money. But Maypan certainly didn't want Bulb to lose the business. I terminated their franchise since like I told Maypan, Bulb was in breach anyway. There were clauses Maypan breached that I could terminate, such as he needed to bring any issues with the franchise to me prior to acting. He didn't honor that clause. He also breached the agreement by filing against me in his own state.

Having Bulb losing his business drove Maypan out of his mind. The faxes poured in that he was going to get me, yada, yada. The following week, I was "served" two overnight letters. By this time, I learned that I needed witnesses for everything. Because of this, several people were in my office when I opened both. Both envelopes contained blank pages. I knew that I was being set up, but there really was nothing I could do about it. Once again, my wonderful attorneys were worthless.

Three weeks after that, I was served with two counts of contempt of court: one in Maypan's state, and one in Corentine state. Both stated that there were injunction hearings scheduled against me and Mr. Sandless, that I signed and received the notices of these immediate hearings, and that I failed to show. Totally out of left field, Corentine joined forces with Maypan against me, doing this "tag team" blank serving and now having me be personally found to be in contempt of *two* courts.

Corentine apparently filed suit against me to "rescind" his original franchise agreement. That was a very serious issue. To cancel the agreement, he would have to prove that we did something very wrong when we gave it to him. That would be on my attorneys, because they alone were responsible for the agreements we used. They created them, and they filed them to the states on our behalf. If he was able to rescind, Corentine would walk away with all the knowledge we taught him, even our *trade secrets*, and he would own these things outright. There would be nothing we could do about it.

Immediately Corentine launched his version of Mr. Sandless called "Drop Dead Floor Refinishing". He had his own website; his own toll-free number and he was in constant contact with the other four owners in the region for them to leave Mr. Sandless and join him. One did join him and was on his toll-free number system to cut us out completely. This is the most scummy, despicable act I had ever seen to that point.

Let me paint the picture for you so it is clear. Corentine, as a franchisee, had to stick to his own designated territory. While he could do work in open areas around him, he could not work in the territories of the other four owners. He was effectively "blocked" from those areas by us. Without the restrictions of the franchise agreement, he could service wherever he wanted.

Now at that time, he was earning sixty thousand a month. There were four other territories, all equally impressive. If he could work them all, he would then control five areas, and it would be five times that number taking his business from making seven hundred thousand a year to well over three million. He was willing to roll the dice for that big number. If he could get the other four owners to breach their agreements with me and join him, it would be that much easier for him to take them over, just as he believed at that moment that he was taking me.

With all of this going on at the same time, I felt like everything that I had worked for was slipping away, and I honestly didn't know if I was going to be able to keep everything going without losing the company and the system. Could anyone ever imagine the evil in such men's hearts?

CHAPTER **8**

All Things End

THE ONE RULE in life that was my only salvation at that time was that "all things end". This is a double-edged sword so to speak, because both good things as well as bad do end. Nothing lasts forever. While I knew this horrible period would not last forever, given the way the first four years went, I totally expected that as one bad thing would end, five other bad things would rise to take its' place!

It was at the point of twelve months of being tortured by Maypan. For the first time in my life, I believed that I was going to compromise my principles and pay Maypan to end this madness. I figured he would accept fifty thousand like he did with Dodge. I would have to draw that money from my retirement account and pay a fine to the IRS for early withdrawal because I simply didn't have the money. I had no money left except my retirement account and my kid's college funds. But there was a problem still. Maypan wanted Bulb to remain in business. Paying this prick off and still having Bulb in the business was worthless because during a search of their business phone, I discovered that the actual line was in Maypan's house, not Bulb's. Maypan was in control of the Mr. Sandless all alone! This all made a settlement impossible.

But I was at the end of the line with my attorneys who for a year could not get this situation under control even though I had a massive franchise agreement with plenty of power that could have been used to do so. All they were doing was milking this for as long as they could, so they could screw me for more money for this fight which was now up to two hundred and fifty thousand dollars! Now I had to fight on *two* fronts—Maypan and Corentine, and with no money to do so.

I looked around for business lawyers and spoke to several. For some, this was way over their heads and the moment I told them what was going on, they ducked and ran. One total jerkoff even told me that it sounded like I was guilty before he even saw anything. I was so pissed off and the world was closing in on me and there was nothing I could do about it.

I finally spoke to one lawyer who was a specialist in trademark law, which is in the same line as franchising. Mason seemed gentle, extremely knowledgeable and he had in fact litigated before in this field. He did his best to put me at ease.

"It really doesn't matter if you did something wrong or not," he explained to me. "It's my job to get you out of it." I knew he was the guy for the job, but my only problem was, he wanted a fifteen-thousand-dollar retainer. Maypan by that time had eaten up all my available resources. Mason said, and I agreed with him, that most attorneys would ask for twenty-five thousand dollars, but that he would work with me and be fair. When things got untenable, I had no choice but to send him the retainer, drawing the money from my retirement account.

It was going to be worse than this. There was a contempt hearing set in Corentine's state in a high-level court that I had to go to. Mason of course was licensed in my state. I would have to get *another* lawyer and *another* retainer for Corentine's state to represent me. On top of that, I would have to get *another* lawyer and *another* retainer for a lawyer in Maypan's state to answer that charge! But wait there's *more!* If you buy three lawyers, you still aren't done because Corentine filed a charge against me with his state, saying I violated franchise law there. Now I would have to answer that charge as well with the district attorney of the state! This was no screwing around game. This was dead cold serious. Everything was on the line as I could have ended up in jail if this went wrong, as well as to lose Mr. Sandless.

It was a gift from God that I found Mason, who sorted through all the franchise agreements, motions, filings, injunctions and emails. He found a lawyer in Corentine's state to just kind of "sit in" for five thousand dollars, and a very big lawyer in Maypan's state to be with us at a ten-thousand-dollar retainer. I was nearing three hundred thousand dollars so far for these actions.

I knew exactly what was going on. Corentine thought I would simply release him from the franchise agreement. He knew my attorneys were inept because they couldn't get a handle on Maypan, who bragged in emails to all our owners that he was kicking my attorney's asses. Corentine thought I would not have it in me to fight. But at that point I was all in. If I lost this, I in effect lost the Mr. Sandless system and would indeed be bankrupt.

The first hearing was by Corentine's franchise area. Mason quickly put together our own injunction and filed against Corentine in court locally. Now Corentine would be in the same playing field as I was. He would have to fight on two fronts as well and he would have to get an attorney in my state to represent him. Then Caden, Mason and I were able to drive to the hearing where he was located. This would determine if I would be going to jail or not for contempt. Literally I could be thrown in jail that very day.

The judge decided he did not want to hear testimony but would accept an outline of the events by the attorneys for each side. Corentine had a real evil pistol as his attorney, a man who was friends with the district attorney of his state. The district attorney's office are the ones who approve Mr. Sandless to be able to franchise in that state or not. The fact that Corentine's lawyer was friends with the DA did not bode well for me or my company.

This lawyer read his complaints. Apparently, there was some discrepancy with the UFOC that we disclosed to Corentine. This lawyer painted a picture of an evil CEO (me) taking advantage of the poor and gullible Corentine, who risked his money on coming on board with us because he was misled and therefore should be able to be released from his franchise agreement with us. Again, I love it when the bad guys call the good guys the bad guys! But the part that really got to me was this prick, jerkoff lawyer said that I believed I "talked to God" and that I believed I was "a messenger of God" based upon the one inspirational email I sent to Corentine. I try to reach out to someone in a positive, spiritual manner, only to have it thrown back in my face. Pure freaking evil.

Mason was totally prepared and spit out how Corentine was *anything* from deceived, breaking company earning records and earning sixty thousand a month with his Mr. Sandless business. He also said that we filed for an injunction, and that we filed to combine both cases in my city, where the case belonged and that the contempt of court on me was part of a much bigger picture that needed to be fleshed out at trial.

The judge stated that he would keep the injunction on me so that I could not interfere with Corentine's "Drop Dead Floor Refinishing" business and sent the rest to the proceeding that would follow. As we exited the courtroom, Corentine stood there with his sleazy lawyer, both with smug looks on their faces, to try and lure me into punching his big fat head. Mason said to just ignore them, but I stared him down to make sure he knew that it would be over my dead body that he walked away with my system.

Next up we filed an injunction against Maypan and Bulb to force that to an immediate hearing and in high court, outside the state court where Maypan had no influence. The high court set up a schedule very quickly for us. There would be one day where both parties had to meet in high court in an attempt to settle, and then the following day would be the hearing for the injunction. I would have to show up with both Mason and the big-time lawyer, a double fee, while Maypan spent nothing representing himself. Up to that point, the state court let Maypan do whatever he pleased as he filed a dozen different motions. But this was different. This high court wasn't about to put up with this guy.

ALL THINGS END

When I showed up to court that day, me and my two attorneys, costing me a thousand dollars an hour and Maypan and Bulb met with the judge who would be our arbitrator. This judge would not be the one who would hear the case the very next day. This is so that judge hearing the real case can remain outside of hearing the details from people not under oath. This arbitration judge looked like an ex-football player. He explained to all of us that he would try to help us reach a settlement and would work with us for as long as it took.

He met with my side first and had Maypan and Bulb leave the room. The first thing he said to me is that he read the files and he thinks I did something wrong. But I read right through that! All he was trying to do was to loosen me up to settle. I believe he knew that I didn't want to settle, because I knew ultimately, I did nothing wrong. And so, he didn't want to waste his time trying to settle if I wouldn't be open to it.

I told him straight up that I was willing to settle and that was what I was there for. I also answered his charge that I did something wrong with "We'll see" and a shrug of my shoulders. He was happy that I wanted to try and settle, so he brought Maypan and Bulb back in to the meeting. I already knew exactly what Maypan wanted. He wanted me to pay him money and he wanted Bulb to keep the business. And that was all the leverage I needed, because there was no way in hell I was paying him money and keeping his good friend in my company, especially given that the business was being run from Maypan's house and that prick Bulb was recording all my calls to him!

Maypan started with his ridiculous $120K, but that ended quickly when I said that the business would be closed. He was adamant that that wouldn't happen. I asked how he thought it was reasonable for him to get paid and keep the business, and the judge agreed with me. Maypan went down to fifty thousand and they keep the business, to thirty-five thousand and they keep the business, to thirty thousand and they keep the business. I kept repeating that getting money and keeping the business was never going to work.

The judge then said he would like for us to meet individually with him. Again, he met with me and my attorneys first. I explained why I didn't terminate them right after they stiffed me what they were to pay. I explained why I tried to work with Bulb, because if they had just that one small territory, they would fail and that wouldn't do either one of us any good. Finally, I explained that Maypan can't have his cake and eat it to. I explained that they already made $120K on the business, and that realistically the maximum amount I would be willing to give them back to end this was what they paid, $19K, which is stupid because they already earned that money back. But that meant they were out of my company forever!

He said I was being very reasonable and more than fair and said he would then talk to Maypan and Bulb.

"I just want to warn you, your Honor," I said as I was about to leave the conference room. "This guy is a piece of work and you are about to see what I have been trying to deal with for over a year."

The judge met with Maypan and Bulb for over an hour and a half as I paced in the other room. The big-time lawyer said that Maypan would never cave and said that we needed to "crush him" the next day to make an example out of anyone who messes with our system. I agreed. Mason found an Appellate Court case just like mine where the offending party was kicked out of the franchise. From a legal perspective, we were positive that we would win this.

The clerk came to call us back into the conference room. I entered to find the judge with his head in his hands looking very miserable.

"That man", he said as he looked up at me, and placed his hands out as if he was strangling someone, "is a cancer!" He got nowhere with Maypan and he said exactly what my lawyer said, that this will have to go to the hearing. But I thought I was very close and nothing would please me more than to give Maypan his money back, to end this nightmare, and to kick them both the hell out of my company—on my own. I begged the judge to allow me a couple more rounds. He took a deep breath and asked how he could help. I asked him to let me talk to Maypan and Bulb one more time.

I got Maypan down to twenty-five thousand and after going back

ALL THINGS END

and forth for another hour, he agreed to shut down the business. I would eat six grand, but let's face it, the next day was going to cost me way more than that! I knew it was the best thing to do. But just as we got the judge so that he could memorialize the deal, Bulb looked over at Maypan with this sad little look on his face, so that when the judge entered the room, Maypan changed his mind and said he couldn't do it.

I told the judge that I really tried and that we couldn't settle, and he thanked me as we left to go home. As we did, Maypan and Bulb ran out to the actual court room we were exiting through. Maypan began to taunt us. The big-time lawyer went off on him in a brilliant manner, telling Maypan that he had no idea what was instore for him in real court and that we were going to crush him to teach him a lesson. Mason and I just shook our heads wondering how Maypan lived with himself.

The next day we were in the high courtroom bright and early. We were on the right side, with me in the first seat, Mason in the middle and the big-time lawyer at the end of our table. Maypan was at his table to the left by himself. He spread out boxes and boxes worth of papers across the desk, literally filling up every single space on it. All my two lawyers had was a single file between them. Caden and Jack were in the audience section as was Bulb.

When the judge entered the room, he sat up way high above everyone else. He probably wasn't more than five-foot-tall, and he was bald, but he had a booming voice that filled the room. After we were seated, the judge called out.

"*Mr. Maypan* proceed with your case." With that Maypan shuffled his papers, seemingly lost. Now here was a guy who for a year tied up an entire law firm with his motions and madness, and suddenly, at the moment of truth, he was left speechless. It was almost impossible to believe that this blowhard had no air left.

"MR. MAYPAN!" the judge screamed, "You will rise when addressed by this court!" With that, the judge ripped into Maypan for holding up the court. I had to bite down on my tongue to keep from smiling or even laughing, and I placed my hands under my legs so that I would not have any reaction. I felt like breaking out and clapping!

Maypan stuttered and stammered, and for the next hour and a half the judge repeatedly yelled at him. It was obvious that the arbitration judge from the day before who was at the settlement hearing, had told this judge that Maypan was a "cancer". When this judge had enough, he turned to us to put on our answer.

Mason stood up, asked the judge to turn to page ten of our answer, where the Appellate Court upheld kicking out an owner just like Maypan in another franchise dispute. There was high court evidence that we were right.

"I am not entertaining your motions at this time!" The judge barked at Mason.

"Yes, thank you, your Honor. Now if you turn to page ten," Mason said, continuing basically whether the judge liked it or not. He knew that the judge could not ignore what was already in law. Maypan was going to be out of my company come hell or high water!

After Mason was done, the judge dismissed Maypan's injunction, knowing again that he had no legal way to force us to leave him open, then moved to the next part of the case. Once again, Maypan didn't know where to start and once again, the judge was down his throat. It was at that moment that Maypan grabbed his chest and said he thought he was having a heart attack!

The judge had no choice but to stop the proceeding and call the paramedics. We had to sit in that courtroom for an hour and a half while they attended to Maypan, who apparently just had a rapid heartbeat. The judge came out and asked if he could continue and he said he could. Then I notice the judge tell his assistant to get a guard into his courtroom because he knew Maypan was trouble to say the least. A court guard came up and stood right next to Maypan the rest of the event.

As I looked over at him, Maypan was at his table, sobbing like a

ALL THINGS END

little school girl. I shook my head in disbelief that this SOB tortured me for a year, cost me more than three hundred thousand dollars, and he was nothing but a bunch of hot air.

"Look at the big bad wolf now," the big-time lawyer whispered to me. "I told you we needed to crush this guy to teach him a lesson."

Unfortunately for me, the day was not a total win. After a quick back and forth, with the judge knowing there was a higher court ruling on this kind of thing, he issued our side an injunction against Maypan and Bulb. I had won! After all that misery, I had won. But not really. You see, the judge called my attorneys to conference in the corner of the courtroom. When they conference like that, they turn on this white noise so that no one can hear what the judge says to the attorneys.

My lawyers came back to me as the judge now took a subdued Maypan in conference. My lawyers told me that the judge wanted me to give Maypan money to get rid of him. You see, this wasn't the actual trial. This was only the first stage. We would probably have to be several more days in court for the trail. The judge believed Maypan to be a complete loon and he didn't want to have to go through a trial with him representing himself. Therefore, he wanted me to pay him to go away. Isn't that just great? Even when I win I can't freaking win!

Of course, I said no way in hell! I already won! Why would I pay him now? When they told the judge I declined, he called them again into conference. But this time he did not speak to them directly. He spoke to me. He was looking right at me and I could hear his booming voice directed to me, even over the white noise machine. Since I am represented by counsel, he is not allowed to speak to me directly but is supposed to speak to my attorneys.

"If your boss is as smart as I think he is, if he is as smart as he thinks he is, he should pay this guy so that I never have to see him in my courtroom again!" he yelled to me. He was literally yelling at me and repeated this message multiple times. I waived to my attorneys to return to the table with me and said I would give him his franchise fee back, however, Bulb could remain open if he paid all the money he would owe me, which was $60K. The judge got Maypan to agree, and my attorneys started to write up the deal.

Maypan went to talk to Bulb and looked all happy and relieved. He totally got away with ripping me off, but at least I would make all the money back with Bulb. As we fleshed out the deal, the judge was not present. When the terms were done, my attorneys told Bulb what they would be.

"That's not the deal you gave me," Maypan announced. He was standing very close to me with just the waist-high court room partition between us.

"You mean the deal you stiffed me on?" I asked as I lunged to punch him in the freaking face. The huge guard that was next to him, yelled at me to stop, otherwise, Maypan may have died that moment, and I probably would have ended up in jail.

The judge came in and put the deal on the court record so that if Maypan acted up, we could have the court fix it rather than me. The best part of the story is right at this stage. As the judge hit the gavel to end the hearing, he could now speak directly to me.

"So how do you do it without sanding?" he asked me. I stood up and explained the service as I glanced over to look at Maypan's stupid face. It was the look of wonderment and excitement, as if Maypan was all excited the judge was asking about Mr. Sandless. *What the hell?* After I explained the service, the judge said something that made my side all laugh.

"Sounds great. I may like to get someone to do this in my home because I certainly don't want to use the dealer you have here right now!"

As we walked out of the courtroom, Maypan stayed in the hall to wait for me. He extended his hand to shake mine.

"No hard feelings," he said, as if this was about lunch money.

"Go f yourself, you piece of shit," I replied as Jack pulled me down the hall, so I wouldn't kill the prick.

A week after that, Corentine surrendered. Apparently, he had a falling out with his attorney. What I really heard was his attorney charged him a fortune for what he did so far and wanted a heck of a lot more to defend against our request for an injunction. We filed the same thing against him as we did against Maypan, knowing again, the higher court ruling would give us the win. Corentine's lawyer was a scum, but he had to know that his client was going to lose and is why he wanted all his money up front.

I made a deal to buy back all his equipment in exchange for Corentine to close his stupid floor shop and for him to agree to a non-compete. Another huge payout to get yet another wreck out of my company. Once again, I had to take out money from my retirement account. I started Mr. Sandless with half a million dollars in my accounts. Between the franchise lawyer fees to begin to franchise, the accounting fees before we made any money, the marketing fees, the litigation fees and now these settlement fees, all that remained was the money I had left in my kid's college funds. I was dead broke.

I never saw or heard from Corentine again. I also lost the other franchisee who went with him. It was a husband and wife team in the area right next to Corentine's territory. The husband sold goods at home shows and the wife ran the Mr. Sandless. She was our top franchise owner Dylan's aunt and so she had inside information of how much both Dylan and Corentine were making and that is why they took a franchise.

This wife hit on Caden several times. Seems with her old man out selling and traveling all the time, she was looking for trouble. I told Caden to not even think about it. But apparently from what I heard, Corentine may have started sleeping with her, most likely to get control of her Mr. Sandless area. Corentine was married as well. The last time I heard from the couple, they were getting a divorce and field for bankruptcy. They named Mr. Sandless as a creditor in the bankruptcy, which sparked yet another red flag with that state against me. More on that coming up.

Meanwhile, Maypan got into all types of trouble for selling stock with his company. He was accused of fraud, tax evasion, embezzlement and other offenses. He was eventually found guilty of tax evasion, but the jury was hung on the four counts of fraud that would instantly have put him in jail for five years minimum! The state grew to know what a slime this guy was, and they are going to retry the case. Their investigator called me and believe me I had plenty to tell him about Maypan. I can only hope that he finds a big jail-mate by the name of Bubba! I checked and saw that his company is still open, has reported income of just over $50,000 a year and has, drum roll please, *one* employee which would be Maypan. He is, Chairman, President, CEO and CFO of nothing. So much for his "world class company".

One interesting thing about this period was about the owner Johnny that I told you about before. He wasn't sure why he was being compelled to join Mr. Sandless as he was retired and didn't really need to work. Johnny and I became good friends and during this time, he was the only one I could really vent to about the hell I was being put through. And Johnny got it as well. He understood that I never did anything to these guys yet had to go through all this litigation simply because these pricks "said" I did something wrong! Johnny was sent to be part of Mr. Sandless to be my support network when I needed it most. When his job was complete, he sold his franchise to some people he knew. We still talk on the phone today!

If all of this wasn't bad enough, Corentine was right! It seems the UFOC that was filed with his state was not the same as the UFOC we disclosed to Corentine. Corentine had the right one—so it wasn't like what he had was incorrect. But it should have matched the one that is filed with the state—they should be identical. The footnotes on the bottom of the one filed with his state did not show that we were approved there.

Whether this was enough for Corentine to get out of his agreement is a mystery. But it does mean that my franchise attorneys totally screwed up and cost me thousands of dollars in dispatching Corentine from my company. They sent me their last bill of services, a little over forty thousand dollars. I wasn't about to pay them another dime. Mason got rid of Maypan in *two* months! *Just two months*!

These other lawyers billed me for fourteen months without any type of help or resolution whatsoever. They totally ripped me off!

When I didn't pay them, they sued me. Since this suit would take years to be heard, I agreed to arbitration. I knew that I had powerful evidence that their mistake cost me more than I owed them, and so I was more than willing to meet.

But when Mason and I went to the hearing, some underling showed up to represent their firm. I immediately pointed out to the arbitration judge that this guy was not one of the principles, that the actual litigator who drug me along for a year should be there and I inquired if this guy even had the power to make a deal. When he said he did, the arbitration could continue.

I explained in detail and with a ton of evidence the ineptitude of the litigator in handling Maypan. I had his letter to the court to tell the court to make Maypan stop. I explained that nothing was fixed or controlled for fourteen months and that once I got Mason on board, it was over in just two months. But the arbiter was an attorney himself and explained that it just came down to style of attorney's and that basically I had no case there. Shocking that one puke lawyer would defend another.

Then I presented the Corentine state's UFOC disclosures; first the one that was filed with the state that was placed in evidence by Corentine and was why I had it. The second was the one given to me by these ex-attorneys to use to disclose Corentine. They were obviously different. With something like this, the "good ole boy" network was not going to hold up and the arbiter was not too thrilled about what I was showing him. But when he asked for the underling's response to this, he said he had to call his boss! So much for him having any power.

The litigator who took me for a ride refused to come down to the hearing and face me. The arbiter took down all my information that I presented and said that the other side had thirty days to respond. They never did. They knew they were wrong. The arbiter ruled that I owed them nothing. I won again, right? No, wrong as usual.

When one thing settles, another rises. Soon after all this I found a new franchise attorney, as this was not Mason's specialty. I would retain Mason for the rest of my journey through Mr. Sandless as my litigator and business attorney. The new one I found was tens of thousands of dollars less cost than my former attorneys, he hated them and said they didn't know what they were doing (great!) and he was one of the top franchise attorneys in the country!

Now for the bad news. If there is litigation and Mr. Sandless has to pay someone money, that must be disclosed in our franchise disclosure document for *the next ten years*! For ten years, I would have to tell every single person who came on board with us about what happened! Mason wrote up all the gory details for me to insert into our franchise disclosure and made it sound as dignified as it can be. But had I known that this would haunt my company for the next ten years, I would have never paid either one of them. I am most positive had I know this and explained this to the high court judge, I could have gotten at least Maypan out of my life and company without paying him a dime. I will have to have that in my disclosure until the year 2019! Simple unreal.

Perhaps the best part of the wrap up of this time era was that Bulb wound up paying for just two option territories and defaulted on the other two, so in the end, I broke even for what I paid Maypan. It still irks me to this day that I must accept calls from Bulb for technical support after how he was in cahoots with Maypan against me. He too eventually sold his franchise and I was glad to finally close this chapter in my life.

Low and behold, to end that year's madness, I received an email from Silas of all people.

"I am starting to get contacted about various job positions and most folks want to contact my current previous employer as a reference. Basically, when they have asked me why I left I tell them that I joined a friend's startup company, we had a lot of success but that I'm looking to get back into a more technical role. Would I be able to use your name as a reference, so they have someone to talk to at Mr. Sandless?

I hope all is going well with everything...between the gas prices and the dollar the economy is in the pooper which isn't helping anyone. The Sandless website as I mentioned before looks great with the additions/updates. My only suggestion is the Products shopping cart should probably use a https:// (secure) connection...otherwise it's like having folks email their credit card information which is easily compromised.

Let me know when you can regarding the reference and once again if there is any work I can do to help earn my severance please just let me know. Thx! Silas"

I sent him a reply, first to rip this email to shreds, next to rip him to shreds. Oh yeah, right, people are starting to contact him about work? Wrong! He was looking for work because he couldn't hack it on his own. And he was looking for a more technical role? More like my plan of blackmail failed. And then to have the balls to ask for a reference? Can you imagine the nerve?

It is fortunate for all the vast number of loons, thieves, and pricks I was forced to encounter, that I answer to a higher power. I gave him the reference and he did in fact go back to a place he used to work at, where he is still working to this date. He never did make it in music and like he was shown, and he never will. Years later, he had the nerve to ask me for Mr. Sandless to buy an ad to sponsor him at a music show he was doing! Can you imagine?

CHAPTER 9

Let the Good Time Roll?

ONE WOULD THINK that moving from the backstabbing, story-making Matt, to the backstabbing cocaine addict Henry, to the user, backstabbing traitor Silas, to the evil, maniacal, extortionist Maypan, and through the corrupt Corentine, that by that point, I would be coming out of the funk and propel the company to new heights. One would *think*! But that is not how this story goes. While I was relieved that these events were all behind me, immediately new ones arose.

As we were exiting the dreadful year of 2008, I was *so* hopeful for a much better 2009. But it was not at all meant to be. In December of 2008, the housing market collapsed. Let me see if I can paint a clear picture for you of the impact of this yet-again negative event for my company. Prior to the crash, the number one customer we serviced was people moving into a new home—new to them that is. Everyone wanted to get their floors refinished before they moved in their furniture. That was the motivating factor for people to reach out to us.

You see, sanding companies cannot do move-ins. It simply takes them too long to do the service, and they are not nearly as flexible as we are with scheduling. For example, a typical sanding may take three to five days to complete. Not only that, then the customer must have the home cleaned to get all the dust out. If a sanding company is booked, they won't even entertain your call for service. They can only do just so much work per week.

LET THE GOOD TIME ROLL?

Now with Mr. Sandless, a full house for us is finished in just one day. Not only that, we can almost always fit someone in no matter what. When people called saying they were moving and needed their floors done, we told them to relax and that we had them covered. Even if they were settling in the afternoon, we would show up right after settlement to do their floors, so they could move right in that night! No sanding company could compete with us, and we owned this part of the market entirely.

Remember I told you about that day where I booked thirty-six people in a row? All those people were moving. Once the real estate market collapsed, Mr. Sandless lost that entire group of customers. No longer were people moving and in fact, we didn't get any calls that people were moving for the next *four years* straight! We lost an enormous thirty five percent of our business practically overnight! This came right on top of all the other madness I had to endure to get to that point.

It was right around this time that I took a call from the leading sanding equipment supply company in the US. They wanted to meet with me to pitch me something or other. I was immediately suspicious, so I did some research. This USA company was owned by a huge multi-billion-dollar janitorial supply company located in Denmark. I placed a call to the company headquarters to see if I could figure out what they really wanted.

I spoke with a nice gentleman with a cool accent who spoke perfect English. I expressed to him that I didn't want them sending salesmen as I didn't have the time or inclination for such a meeting. He assured me that they were sending me the two top guys in the US system to talk with me. I therefore confirmed that the head corporate office knew about the visit and were the ones pushing for it. Now I really was worried about what this was all about! All I needed was a billion-dollar company breathing down my neck.

When it came time, I met with the two guys. They were very nice and easy to get along with. They wanted to show me a machine they came up with that did "wet sanding" to see if we would be interested in buying this from them. After their pitch, I was blunt in my first question to them.

"It looks like you created this machine in order to compete with Mr. Sandless," I stated. "It that true?" They turned and looked at each other, then looked back to me but did not answer.

"I take that as a *yes* then!" I announced. I agreed to try their machine and they would send me one to play with. It was at that moment that I realized what was happening. This billion-dollar company was getting killed in the states by the growth of Mr. Sandless. The more Mr. Sandless dealers we opened, the less sanding equipment they were selling. That meant that as we grew, they were shrinking, and they were not about to let this up-start company take their market share. They figured to try and compete against us by coming up with their own version of "Sandless" refinishing via this wet sander.

The only problem was, they guessed wrong! The system doesn't have anything to do with equipment. It is a solution-based system. They mistakenly thought it was some kind of "wet sanding" and hence the creation of their wet sanding machine. I gave their machine a try when I received it and it just didn't work. Don't get me wrong, I would have loved to have this type of machine if it *did* work. It would save us a lot of time and money on the jobs. But since they were thinking "in the box" rather than outside the box, they just didn't understand enough about our system to create something that was useful to us.

I knew exactly what the design flaw was in the machine they sent me. But I wasn't about to share this with a billion-dollar company that could crush me if they figured it all out! I knew that I was in trouble anyway. I had a bullseye on my back by a company that I would never be able to compete with dollar for dollar. I knew I had to come up with some way to work with these guys to get them from being a potentially serious enemy, to become a friend instead.

Right after that I received a visit from one of our owners from an eastern state by the name of Bill Dabb. He wanted to speak with me about adding a sanding element to "Mr. Sandless". This was something I never wanted to do. Let me lay this out so that it is clear. I never

LET THE GOOD TIME ROLL?

sold Mr. Sandless as "perfection". I sold the service as a "choice". If anything, back in the day, I called it "fast food for floors" and that was the actual concept: to give people remarkably better-looking floors, in one day, with no down time, odor or cleanup and at a very reasonable price.

With all the advancements we had come up with since that time, no one could compare us to "fast food" anymore in the industry. But comparing us to food, there would be fast food joints, medium level restaurants and the high-end place. We would be the medium level restaurants of the flooring industry. Not perfection, just a great choice.

Sanding wasn't perfection either! I had seen multiple floors ruined by sanding, where it was almost impossible to ruin a floor with Mr. Sandless. Also, sanding had quite a few limitations. For example, where Mr. Sandless can refinish an engineered floor or a laminate floor, sanding could not. Where we could do all floors found in the marketplace, from concrete to real wood and everything in between, sanding could only service real wood floors and prefinished floors.

Back to this owner Dabb, who felt that adding a sanding element to his Mr. Sandless would greatly increase his income. The market he serviced was "new" compared to most of the USA. This area had increased dramatically in size thanks to the enormous growth of the United States government over the past thirty years. The floors there were predominately prefinished and that meant there were a lot of color issues with sun fading and oxidation. Dabb felt he could make a lot more money if he could sand as well as do Mr. Sandless.

Ironically, I was thinking along those same lines with my new "friends" at the equipment company. If they were not selling sanding equipment due to the growth of Mr. Sandless, what would happen if we added a sanding element to Mr. Sandless and used them as our exclusive supplier? That would make a lot of sense. First, it would get them off my back. Second, we could increase revenue in a time period where we lost significant income due to the housing market. Third, our owners should be able to make more money. It seemed like a win all the way around!

I contacted the equipment company and asked them if they had sanding equipment that could fit into the Mr. Sandless system. They sent over this "dustless" system for us to try. I had just rented an office next to Mr. Sandless to expand into sales of a new brand I developed, and this place had wood floors in need of work. So, we tried the new dustless system in a single room there. I remember the sun was shining into the window as a new guy I hired ran the big belt sander which was attached to a very well-designed vacuum system. I couldn't see a speck of dust in the sunlight! While the company said it was 99% dust free, they said we could not say it was completely dustless—even though it looked that way to me.

Between trying all the equipment to make sure it would fit in the system and working with their corporate headquarters for the best way to do this, the best prices and the easiest ordering and delivery, Caden and I put in a little over a solid month of work to put this final deal together.

The equipment company set up a special deal for our owners to purchase, under the one provision that we use just *one* of their vendors for this deal. You see, they have dealers all over the US that they would be cutting out for this special. Of course, they wanted to keep it quiet and down low as their local dealers would not be getting a commission on sales of this equipment to their markets. We sent out a company announcement that we would be adding a dustless refinishing package to the system that would be optional, not mandatory for our owners to participate in. This announcement also included that we would be using just one vendor only for the package deal, a strict warning to use just this one vendor, and instructions on how to add this to their business. I just knew that one or more of my "gerbils" would cause trouble because of these instructions.

About thirty owners added the dustless element to their Mr. Sandless, and I called the service "Mr. Sandless Dustless Refinishing". As almost predicted, within a day of sending the announcement, the boss at the equipment company called me all upset. It seemed not one, but two of our ridiculous owners went to their local dealer to inquire. When the local dealer saw the prices given to us were basically lower than what they could *ever* offer, they knew they were being cut out of this deal by the parent company. These dealers would not be making anything on these sales and they called in to voice their strong complaints. That caused the parent company to consider *not* doing this deal with us. Just great.

Why the human beings that took a business with us were so damn stupid I will never understand! While I got the one owner to stop his contact with other equipment dealers, one owner simply refused. While Sadie was the owner of this Mr. Sandless franchise in Canada, her husband was the one who ran the business. Sadie had been a franchisee before in an outdated female workout system and she sold that. She was now taking a break from working due to a new baby, but she was way "hands on" with her Mr. Sandless as well.

The easiest way to describe this woman was a female version of J.R. who I will tell you more about in coming up. While she was somewhat intelligent, she had absolutely, positively no common sense. Not a single drop! When she got the announcement, instead of reading the details, she took it upon herself to go to a local equipment guy and price out the items in our package deal. These were not cheap to say the least. You need at least six different pieces of equipment to do dustless refinishing. The package price the company gave us was $12,000. That was an incredible discount and they were able to do this by in essence making *us* the dealer and removing that profit from the equipment.

We sent a company announcement out to everyone in case any more rocket scientists came up with any additional bright ideas. Here is what we sent:

"A new announcement has been made titled 'Read this now please!'"

It is understandable-everyone loves a deal. Everyone loves to make a better deal. But every so often, attempting to get a better deal can undermine the very thing that started the entire process to start with.

CEO OF INSANITY

A few of you have taken it upon yourselves to take the prices and equipment list that Mr. Sandless® has received in good faith directly from the parent equipment company, to attempt to get those prices beaten by your local equipment dealer. While we appreciate your entrepreneurial spirit in trying to get a better deal for yourselves, you are going to cost us the deal that we already have in place. The dealers you are going to are calling their corporate entity, claiming that they are interfering in their affairs, which in turns causes grief to the people who gave us the special deal at the parent company, which in turn gives us grief and makes Dan and Caden wonder why they spent so much time negotiating this special-which by the way comes with 24/7 tech support, full training by trainers, specials on pads and a better price than you are ever going to receive from a local dealer.

Please cease this activity. The information you received, including the EXACT list of things we are going to use and the special prices we are going to receive is CONFIDENTIAL and is a breach of your agreement to share it with anyone outside the company.

Mr. Sandless Family. That means working as a family. Saving a couple of bucks is not worth killing the deal we worked so hard for. If you don't want to work with us, please just pass on this added optional service. This would be better than undermining what we have been doing for a large group rather than the individual.

Note to Canadian Owners: The equipment company will ship the product from here and your lease will include all taxes and shipping. The parent company says you will not get a better deal and your local rep will pass on ALL the taxes and increased prices to you anyway!

Stop. Please. Thanks."

This was not at all forceful or over the top, but calm, rational and informative. Despite that, I received this from Sadie who wrote to me directly even though this was a company announcement, not an email from me. She was one of the two I was told had contacted another dealer.

"I got your email. None of the guys I have spoken with have spoken with anyone. Nobody has had time to do much since I just started

speaking with them. If head office has a great deal, then it can get passed to a Canadian dealer, so we can save more than just a couple of bucks. It will be thousands we will be saving. I explained that everything more than doubles in price once it hits our doors. It is not good that a company the size of these guys with what you have negotiated with them cannot pass on the savings to your important Canadian franchise owners so that all the family can save and enjoy the benefits of your negotiations."

Now let me explain the madness of this thinking. First, she states that none of the "guys" she has spoken to have spoken to anyone else. That is completely false and proves what I mean that she had no common sense. You see how in the world could I have possibly been able to pick her out of one hundred Mr. Sandless owners and know that she reached out to some other local dealers if they didn't run to their corporate headquarters to complain? It was obvious simply by my knowledge that she did reach out to someone and that they talked! And what, they didn't have enough time for a two-minute call to their corporate headquarters to complain?

Next, the Canadian owners were getting the same exact deal as the USA owners with this equipment company! All they had to do was pay a little bit of extra shipping and that's it! She just couldn't grasp simple facts of this deal. Now remember, she received an announcement that said to not go through your local dealer and a follow up announcement that said don't go through your local dealer. Now this will be the third time I said it.

"Sadie, I don't understand. Did you not read the announcement that just went out? It asked you to stop. What does stop mean? <u>You are jeopardizing the deal we have for everyone</u>. This company is not a franchise system Sadie. They have no authority to tell their dealers what they can or can't charge. The price we are getting is UNDER what your dealer will give. Because corporate is cutting out their dealers, they could be in hot water with their dealers for doing this, and you continuing to pursue this even after I asked you to stop is simply amazing to me.

Now, imagine if instead of buying from a GM dealership a car, that GM makes a deal with Mr. Sandless to give us the cars at a bigger discount than what a dealer will give cutting out the dealer. Do you believe that if the dealerships catch wind of this--that they will be happy? You are getting a special and that includes our Canadian owners. Why, oh why must you disrupt this when I just asked for this to stop? STOP--PLEASE STOP. Is that clear enough? If you find you can't then don't add the service--but don't ruin the hard work we put into this deal. Is this clear enough?"

Sadie replied: "You said `to heck with you` to me so I did pursue it based on that you said I could do it. I have already started and have given a commitment to this guy. And he already knows the package. If you can have the equipment for me to pick it up here in Ontario, then I can do it that way. And that it is in Canadian dollars. I don`t mind but I don`t want to buy American have it shipped pay duty and end up with a bill of $30,000 Canadian for a sanding package. Business wise this is ridiculous. $12,400 for the package + $1000 for accessories+ shipping and handling and duty-usually doubles this cost to $27,000 US and then do the exchange and then add 8% PST tax on top. Do you think this is fair to the Canadians? I can see you don`t care because you are not willing to work something for us. I won't be going through the American company."

I have no idea where this woman came up with me saying 'to heck with her' because I clearly didn't say that! But my heavens, this woman's math was madness! You see, math is common sense based and since she had no common sense, she couldn't even figure out the math. The package was for twelve thousand US dollars. The accessories were things like paper, etc. that she could get anywhere. The shipping, handling and duties was fifteen hundred dollars and then the eight percent PST on the twelve thousand. The total for the special for Canadians was $14,460, not $30,000.

Now here is the kicker to all this. Canada does not manufacture anything. The dealer there would have to pay for shipment to Canada and pay the duties as well to get the product into Canada. Then on top of that, there would be a markup for that dealer. There was no way in the world that the local dealer could beat the price we were giving Sadie.

I responded to her to once again have her to simply stop the madness. It was at that time she sent me a spreadsheet she received from the local dealer for the exact dustless refinishing kit that we had put together. The total price from us directly was $14,460. The total price that the local dealer gave her for the same exact pieces was $18,360. I called her on the phone to discuss this.

I will always remember this as one of the most exasperating, frustrating conversations of my lifetime. I sent Sadie the spreadsheet from the company with the total cost to her of $14,460. Along with that, I had opened on my computer the spreadsheet she had sent me. She could not, no matter how hard I tried for more than a half hour, understand that the deal we were giving her was better than what the guy in Canada was giving her.

"The price the Canadian dealer is giving you without the PST tax is $17,000," I told her. "The price we are giving you directly without the PST is $12,000. How in the world is seventeen thousand less than twelve thousand?"

"It is, because you are not taking into consideration the duties and exchange rate!" she returned.

"With shipping, PST and duties, the total you will pay is $14,460," I replied. "The exchange rate is in your favor for heaven sakes! The Canadian dollar at this moment is higher than the US dollar by seven percent!"

"The Canadian deal is better!" she replied.

"The Canadian deal with PST is $18,360! How in the world is $18,000 less than $14,000 dollars?" I screamed.

"The Canadian deal is less money," she once again replied. I literally got down on my knees, told her I was on my knees and begged her to acknowledge that eighteen was more than fourteen, that seventeen was more than twelve, but she wouldn't.

Let me explain that I always and forever bent over backwards for my owners. This owner inadvertently sent Caden an email quote instead of a customer. Caden sent it to me because there was a boatload of mistakes in the email. I sent Sadie a very nice email to point out that she sent it to the wrong person, and that she had some issues in it to fix. For example, the quote was not personalized and had big gaps between paragraphs, a clear indication it was copied and pasted. It had no signature line, which looked cold and uncaring, and she had on it the amount of our locations which was woefully old. I also pointed out that she should have used the information I had just recently sent out to the system on bamboo floors in her response.

She replied that she didn't get the information, which is nonsense. She just didn't pay attention to it. She also said that she had no idea of the count of locations we had. I gently replied, sending her the bamboo information, directing her to our Help Desk on where to find all our announcements as they are all posted there, and directed her to the home page of our website where we post the amount of our owners for all to see. Despite the madness of her lack of common sense, I was still gentle and helpful. But this equipment issue was maddening!

The very next franchisee to get into the mix with me over this equipment package was yet another Canadian. This guy Bo had a chip on his shoulder the size of a railroad tie! He was one of these "know-it-all" characters who was so far superior in business than me, that every single communication with me had a nasty overtone, always talking down to me. Remember I told you that due to the "quality" owners I had picked in the beginning failing to make any real money with this system, that I switched to a "quantity" mentality when choosing owners? This joker was one of those in the quantity group. If things worked the way they should have, I wouldn't have given this prick the time of day, let alone a franchise.

This type of person to me is one who buys their own bullcrap. They buy their own lies! I mean if they are so damn superior to me in business, then why in the hell are they taking a franchise off me? Why don't they have their own franchise system? No, they come into *my* company so that they can tell me what I am doing wrong and feel so

LET THE GOOD TIME ROLL?

superior to me because "they know" and I don't! *Please*! But not only that, this guy Bo as well had no common sense! It is so very difficult to explain something to someone who can't grasp simple concepts!

My first run in with Bo before he "had" to throw his voice into the equipment situation, was when he asked me this question.

"I've had 2 people present me with coupons they find on line, and I've honored both. I'm not convinced that the coupons had any impact regarding the decision to have work completed. Would it be possible to have the name of the franchise, or franchise territory to which the coupons relate, included on the face of the coupons?"

There is only one line in this that irritated me. It was the "I'm not convinced" bit. Okay so his majesty was the all-seeing, all knowing Orb of life. Instead of being happy that he got two clients with an average ticket of $1,100, *he* was not convinced the coupons had anything to do with it and *his* large massive brain had to be convinced otherwise, *he* didn't see the need for coupons. But if someone found a coupon somewhere online, how would it be possible for us to get the franchise name on it? I responded to him.

"I'd like to know as well! Unfortunately, we do not have control over online coupons. The vast majority of these are placed there by the vendors that a franchisee advertises through. Some do it as a bonus and some do it as part of the ad, but ultimately, it is under their control and there are too many to try to do something like this. There is no way for corporate Mr. Sandless to try and figure out who placed what coupon online through an advertiser."

I thought this would be the end of it, but the Orb was not satisfied with my response.

"I think you should get control of the system... why are you allowing people/companies other than MS to offer discounts through coupons? Until then, however, would you entertain the notion of me charging you back for the face value of the coupons?"

Why am I allowing franchisees to use coupons in their advertising is like asking why am I allowing advertising! The coupon is to entice someone to buy. All "coupon books" do this! And why would I

153

have to pay for coupons that *he* decides to accept. No, it couldn't be peaceful, but I responded, still trying to be calm.

"A franchise places an ad with a coupon magazine. This coupon magazine takes the same coupon (Mr. Sandless, date and amount) and places it on their online system for other people to download and use. The franchise site already agreed to the date and amount on the coupon. Therefore, there is no reason for Mr. Sandless to get control of anything. It is just an extension of that franchisee's original ad. I cannot spend time and resources to make sure the many different advertisers that are used in the system be sure they place additional information on the coupon because a single location requested it, most especially when the coupon only shows up for that particular territory.

You are an independent business owner. It is your decision alone whether to accept a coupon for service. My franchise happens to gladly accept coupons, even a competitor's coupon. I do not look at this as a negative and I don't understand your issue with it. Be that as it may, if you accept it, you are responsible for it."

Do you think that settled this matter? Of course not!

"Please explain "most especially when the coupon only shows up for that particular territory" and "My franchise happens to gladly accept a competitor's coupon". The coupons are showing up as part of the "free on-line estimate process" which I thought was a corporate function... I guess I'm wrong. And the coupons are not from the competition, they are from MS. The issue is not whether or not I accept the coupons, because I'm part of an organization, I feel obligated to accept them. otherwise, don't you think we would look dysfunctional?

I don't want to get into a long debate over this; however, I do believe that a corporate initiative (web site) should have policies. Again, in my opinion, a coupon placed on a corporate site should either be a corporate initiative OR a franchise initiative. If the latter, then CORPORATE policy should stipulate the effective date(s), location, and value on the face of the coupons.

I understand you don't have the time, however, perhaps, (just my

LET THE GOOD TIME ROLL?

opinion) it's time to re-structure the corporate office. In my opinion, because you cannot be in all places at all times, nor can you see in all directions, you should hire an educated, trained director of marketing/communications. MS is on the threshold of an outstanding achievement, kudos to you, it took courage and vision. In my opinion, we need to move to the next level; the level of excellence, in all aspects of the organization. The competition will mobilize, they will borrow and enhance our technique and service; they will force our action. We don't want to be in the position where we find ourselves re-acting. We want to find ourselves in the position of pushing the threshold, we want to be the industry leaders, as such, we have to be the industry leader in all aspects. You cannot do this alone. Your focus is to build a franchise group; we (the franchise group) need a well-planned, cohesive, professional approach to the business. One of the concerns of the Canadian Group is the need for a localized manufacturer of our solutions and other products. We don't want to see our profitability victimized by the economic activities of governments and the resultant effects on the value of our dollar."

You see it is all laid out here. Bo knows things. Bo is smarter than I am. It is absolutely, positively impossible for me to have the ability to see these things listed without Bo pointing them out to me. Without Bo, I am forever lost, wandering around the business world without direction or focus. Now if anyone is to give me "kudos," it would be for my unwavering patience when dealing with blowhard Bo.

"It would have saved me a lot of time if you told me initially that you were talking about the coupons on our web site. Before placing the coupons, I checked with our legal team to make certain we were compliant with both our franchise agreement and rules. There are clear disclaimers on all the coupons offered on the web site directing the client to understand that the coupon may not be accepted at all locations. I appreciate your thoughts on the corporate office and can assure you that I am taking all the necessary steps to insure the brand of Mr. Sandless will remain the #1 brand it is today for years to come."

Could I get any more polite and professional? Did I say anything wrong here at all? Apparently, I did.

"I agree; it would have saved us both sometime if you would have assumed I was talking about the coupons on our web site. When you have time, please fill me in on the steps you are taking to maintain the brand. Have you given thought to the notion of finding a licensed manufacturer in Canada?"

After all my polite responses, he has to take a shot at me. He states that I would have saved us both time if I would have assumed what he was talking about! This is seriously insane. This from the guy who said he didn't want to get into a long debate about this? It is my fault that he has now tied me up for most of the morning with this madness and now because the Orb is not satisfied, I must tell him the steps I am taking to keep *my* company moving forward! Jackpot trigger pulled!

"No, actually, you need to be clearer when communicating with me. I read my e-mails multiple time to be sure I understand the question before I respond. You need to do the same. What you said initially to me was this: **coupons they find on line.** *There is a big difference between writing that and writing "coupons they receive from our web site." When you state below that I should have assumed you were talking about our web site--how in the world was that supposed to happen? I don't read minds my friend. Clear communication is required as to not waste time. It is also disrespectful to come back at me in this manner when it was your communication error to start with.*

Second, the best thing you can do is to concentrate on your business. You have a very large territory, and with your business prowess, I fully expect you to be a leader--the top guy--of the Canadian franchise locations. That is the best thing you can do for Mr. Sandless. I appreciate your concern for my part of this--my corporation, but to involve individual owners would be inappropriate and would send the wrong signals to the company and other owners. You have your own job ahead of you and I strongly suggest concentrating all your efforts on your part of this.

LET THE GOOD TIME ROLL?

Third, yes, I have. However, with shipping the ingredients, paying a blender, and the mark up on the Canadian side, there would be very little savings. It simply isn't worth it. Let us please move on with no more response in these matters. Thank you."

A couple of things here. I am showing you this as an example of what I had to put up with from my owners. Take this guy and multiply him by eighty and then you will understand the level and depths of the daily grief I endured in herding these gerbils. So, as I show you more from this one nut, understand I could show you eighty more examples just like this. I mean seriously, imagine getting email communications like this five to ten times in the same day! That was the norm.

All that my responses did for this situation was unleash this guy's lunacy even more! Now that I called him on his crap, it was sure to spiral downhill from there. Very shortly after this, the Orb had another problem. It seemed someone wrote to the dealer next to him for a quote and inquired as to if there was a dealer in the Orb's territory. That franchisee replied to the potential customer and said there was a dealer in that territory and that they were cc'ing him on the email so that he would have their contact information. The Orb didn't like this and wrote to Gabe to inquire *"how could this have happened?'*

It is quite simple really. Someone could go to our dealer page, click on the map, and then click on what they assumed was the nearest dealer to them. Then they fill out the quote request on *that* dealer's page instead of placing their zip or postal code into our system which would then direct them to the correct dealer. Could we have blocked people from doing that? Sure, we could! But why lose the lead just because they are on the wrong dealer's page? There is no harm or foul whatsoever in getting a lead from the location next to you. Gabe sent me the Orb's email and I responded to the Orb that this could indeed happen, explained why it could happen, and that the system was working exactly as it should. Good enough for the Orb? Not a chance.

"An interesting assumption. The system is working fine; the person couldn't identify her own province on the map. Ok."

Why this guy had to take it upon himself to throw this back in my face, is beyond me. I mean seriously, doesn't my explanation make perfect sense?

"It is not an assumption Bo. It is a fact. This has happened before. You are not the first to ask this question. I for one, have poor reading vision. If I do not have my reading glasses on, I could easily click the wrong area, and then thinking the correct area came up, fill out the form and ask, just like this person did. Be happy you got the quote!"

Given all of this above from this guy, when he received the second announcement regarding the sanding equipment deal, he just *had* to respond, not to the actual email the announcement comes to, which is our general account, but to me specifically. Please note this one important detail. The Orb had no intention whatsoever of adding a sanding element! <u>No intention at all</u>! So why say anything at all? Well, it was just to bitch and moan.

"Don't you think more information, from whom ever sources it will help you? Frankly, I would like to know the full scope of the "couple of bucks" to be saved. It's my money, and I think it would be prudent to have all the information before a decision is made. I don't understand how this equipment company would have a concern, either way the product is coming from them. OR is this simply the ranting of a salesperson who might not earn a commission? It's interesting that in this context you refer to us as a "family"; perhaps the same concerns shown here should be focused at the shipping costs for the Canadian Franchisees."

How many emails has this guy sent me so far? And now this? Although I was still trying to maintain control and a professional attitude, it was clear I was losing it!

"Thank you so much for your support Bo! I am so glad you have my back. So, let me see if I get this straight. Imagine GM dealing directly with Mr. Sandless to give us a special deal under what we can get from their licensed dealers--in essence, bypassing the dealers. You

don't think the dealers are going to be upset if they get wind of this? **<u>I am completely offended</u>** that I seriously worked on getting all the Canadian owners the best possible deal, while you think I am not focused on you. Simply great Bo. Ranting of a salesperson?? After I already told you we were working with the company that OWNS the equipment? Great. Perfect. This negative crap must end. I am not sure of the source, but I fail to see where I have done wrong with you my friend."

Would this be enough for the Orb to move on? Of course, it wouldn't!

"You have to take some time and breath before exacting a tirade. You should really re-read what I sent you. I'm simple suggesting that more info is better; it will assist you in your negotiations. In my opinion, the only negativity is from you (below), keep emotion out and stick to the point. If you can get a better deal then fine, if not, what's the harm in providing more info. I should think it would assist you. I don't think you've done me any wrong at all, I'm not certain where that sentiment came from. I'm reading information that comes across my screen, I'm not the bearer of negative news or negative sentiments, just a business person trying to make sense of this. In terms of support, I do recall a recent conversation (me phoning you), applauding you for the move in this direction. God man, you are not beyond reproach you are our business partner, put the whip away and try calm discussion."

I simply love the high road he has taken but can I ask you as the reader, is this really that hard to understand? The equipment company made us the dealer and subtracted the dealer markup to give us the best deal. Other legit dealers for them—if they found out about this arrangement—were not going to be happy because they were cut out from making profit by their own corporation! Why in the world was that so hard to grasp? "Getting more information" is madness!

"Why do I have to take a breath Bo? I mean for heaven sakes, Caden and I worked on a great deal for thirty owners for a month--a month of work, and a couple of yahoo idiots in the company look to crash the whole deal and ruin everything we have worked for. Why shouldn't I be pissed at that? Then to take grief that I am not working for the benefit of Canadian owners when that is not true whatsoever. Why shouldn't that get me upset? For some reason, some of you think I have nothing but evil and wrong intentions in the efforts that I put out, and it is flat out wrong.

Tell me this Bo, and I am being straight and honest with you and ask the same. Would you be upset if after a month of work the group you are working with calls to tell you that others who are supposed to be on your side are going behind you back and hurting everything you worked for? I know you would be upset and I have that right. This has nothing to do with partnership because you are not my business partner. I don't know where you even came up with this notion. You are an independent business owner. So, this has nothing to do with partnership and way more to do with subversion. The reason I say this is <u>fact</u>--undisputed, uncontested fact. I have not made this mandatory, right? I have not asked for a penny from anyone, right? SO why should anyone ruin a deal where nothing has been asked of them? I admit I am livid. After I sent out the announcement, I had an owner write to tell me they called their local dealer AFTER I asked not to. Can you at least consider how embarrassing it was for me and Caden to get a call like that today--to be told that the deal may end for thirty owners for this nonsense? So, on top of dealing with your madness, I am dealing with the equipment company totally upset with me because of people like you, and I am dealing with the two other owners who can't honor a simple request."

And his response continues:

"Let's look at this as adult business partners working on a common objective. Stop trying to beat people into submission, instead use them as the valuable assets they are (or are trying to be). As mentioned, I was responding to information that came across my screen, my intention is to make the BEST purchase decision, period. I'm not certain what gets you into the mindset that everyone is out to get you, I certainly don't see it that way; this seems to be more of a situation

LET THE GOOD TIME ROLL?

where people are trying to get the best possible deal for them, and, in doing so assist you in your negotiations. I don't see that as evil, nor do I see you as evil. remove the emotion from the situation. To be honest with you, I'm not certain I would be upset if someone found a potentially better deal, it would not affect my ego, rather, it would aid me in getting a better deal for all. Put another way, how do you know that the deal you and Caden have is better? What's your point of reference, other than full price? Although I thank you (both) for the time and effort involved, without information to the contrary, how do you know if your deal is better? If in your position, I would use the information gathered as a reference point and if need be, ask the company to sharpen their pencil. The comment I made regarding the salesperson and lost commission no doubt has some validity; I suspect you're being told that the deal is going south as a means of getting you pissed off (at the wrong people). Instead, just a thought, don't you think sourcing all the best potential deals will then allow you to negotiate? Again, the parent company has nothing to lose, either way they get the sale. AND yes, this would be embarrassing to them if a dealer in Canada were able to provide something better. it would be very embarrassing. In my opinion, from what I've read, this has nothing to do with 'subversion' it has to do with getting a better deal, period. So, again, try to hold the temper, hold the emotion, and work together. these people are not your subordinates, and they're not your children, they are adults, and it seems that they want to be involved with this process. If this hurts a deal, I would suggest we should shop elsewhere, they have NO business telling you or anyone else if and where you can gather information. Again, I thank you for the move in the direction of dustless sanding, let's stop the banter, think positive and move forward. With the BEST deal for all. Perhaps this should be a learning lesson, before making decisions regarding spending the monies of Franchisees, ask if they would like to be involved in the process, and then set up a task list. More info is always better."

You see what is written here? This jerk is coming from a position of zero knowledge of even why I set up the sanding deal! And

CEO OF INSANITY

what has a bug up his butt is he wants to be involved, and that he isn't is driving him crazy. The lack of common sense here is beyond imagination.

"I have no idea how you can miss the valid points that I made Bo.

1.) How is asking everyone to stop reaching out to their local dealers so that it does not ruin the incredible deal on the table "beating people into submission"? Listen Bo, I am not asking anyone to spend any money. Let me say that again. If I was telling you to spend money at this very moment, then yes, question me. No one has done that. This is OPTIONAL! What does OPTIONAL mean to you? I am not spending your money and I resent that comment.

2.) I have no idea why you cannot grasp this, but the dealers are not happy <u>not because</u> they can give us a better deal. It is because the parent company is giving us a better deal cutting out the dealer commission. Why can't you see that? Are you seriously that thick?

    Saying the parent company has nothing to lose is nonsensical. They most certainly do! They end up with pissed off dealers who should have gotten the sale. Why is that so hard to see? The norm for this company is to <u>give the sale to their local dealer</u>. Why can't you get this? That would be like us booking a commercial account in your territory and giving it to someone else to do--right. Are you getting this now?

3.) If those searching "for a better deal" trusted us, they would already know for fact that they will NOT get a better deal. Why do I know this for fact? Because we already tried to get a better deal. No dealer will beat the price we received since we got DEALER PRICE. Why is that so hard to understand? What you assume is that we are less intelligent than you, right? No, on the contrary, we are three steps ahead of your thought process.

4.) So, for a handful of owners who have a bug up their ass, who

LET THE GOOD TIME ROLL?

will not get a better deal on their own; for those couple of owners, you think it is a wise move to try and do this somewhere else and ruin it for all the others who want this deal? This isn't "gathering information" Bo. It is subverting a deal.

Thanks for the feedback and comments."

Due to the crash of the housing market, a huge billion-dollar company breathing down my neck and attempting to add a revenue stream back to the system, I added dustless refinishing to the system. I worked with the company in testing all the equipment on multiple jobs, made sure that the system was complete for our owners, and worked with the supplier for a month to get the best possible package price, way under dealer price. While not all the owners made such a ruckus, the ones that did really took the joy out of helping the system with this project.

Unfortunately, and as usual, this "good thing" I did come back to bite me in the ass in the future. No good deed goes unpunished when it comes to franchising.

CHAPTER 10

The Competition Rises

ANOTHER VENTURE TO add to Mr. Sandless as a revenue stream to make up for the thirty-five percent of work we lost with the housing market was tile refinishing. This all started in 2007 with an owner in New York who began to service the wood floors for a national restaurant chain. She started with just one location and our system worked so well for that establishment that she quickly grew to servicing five of them every six months.

Around 2008, the company approached this owner and sort of lamented that it was a "shame" she couldn't do their tile refinishing as well. They had to have a separate company for that, and they told her it would be "great" if she could do both the wood and the tile. She then contacted me to inquire.

I told her that tile refinishing was a lot easier than wood refinishing and that all there was to it was different solutions. We would use the same exact equipment we did on wood floors as we did the tile. I got her the supplies she needed, she did the work, the places loved the end product, and this was the beginning of Mr. Sandless doing tile refinishing as well as wood.

There were many times we were approached by corporate entities to service national accounts. One large entity was a women's clothing chain with seven hundred locations. They originally contacted me in 2005 about service, but I told them we were going to

THE COMPETITION RISES

franchise and to check in with us in the future. Two years later they did, and wouldn't you know it, the two locations they wanted to give us for work were in San Francisco and Houston, two places we had no franchisee yet. I flew Caden's brother Dominic down to Houston to see the two stores as we would be able to get somewhat regional owners to do the work. The bid was for thirty-six thousand dollars.

Before they pulled the trigger, I received a call from their corporate headquarters and they only had one question for me. What if someone drug a piece of furniture across the floor and scratched it? How were we able to address that situation? I told them that basically they would be out of luck because the nearest dealer was eight hours away. They wanted local accountability and so they passed on us doing the work.

But as we grew, others became clients. One particular clothing store had real wood floors, laminate floors, bamboo floors, tile floors and concrete floors. Every location they gave us was different but fortunately the Mr. Sandless service could do them all. Once we landed that account, I added tile refinishing to all of Mr. Sandless as an additional revenue stream; anything to try and keep the revenue propped up due to the housing crash!

I even went ahead and launched my next franchise system called Dr. DecknFence. Only a year after creating the Mr. Sandless system I was outside of my house in the Spring. It was the time of the year to refinish my deck. Every year after the harsh winters where I lived, I would have to power wash the deck and then re-stain it.

This time, I had my new indoor refinishing system, I thought to myself, why don't I try this for outdoors as well? With that I went into my garage lab and created a concoction to use on the deck after I power washed it. It looked amazing! That old deck was splintering and breaking apart, but with the new stuff I created, the splintering completely stopped! The kicker was this lasted an incredible five years on my deck! Five years of not having to have to power wash and stain again. I knew I had to bring this to market.

I had Logan work in his lab to come up with the formula to use for the outside decks based upon what I discovered. When he sent me a pail of the sealer which we would mix our outdoor colors with, I had Caden build a deck in the back lot so that we could test it out. We ran the entire process that I designed for outdoor wood and when the deck was dry, we coated it with the color and sealer. The boards we use for the deck were thrown out by someone who was replacing their old deck, so they were very worn. But they looked brand new after the service.

I wanted to test the durability of the product. So, we poured full strength, heavy duty stripper on the deck, waited ten minutes, and then power washed it. The color wouldn't come out of the board! That was another light bulb moment for me. I instructed Logan that there was no reason we couldn't use this product indoors as well. He tweaked the formula and then worked on the colors for indoor wood, and within a short period of time, Mr. Sandless had a massive arsenal of products to choose from for working on floors. We now had sealer to go with our finish, as well as eleven different colors.

I had built into the system for owners to pay a transparent administration fee for the products they got through us. Many franchise systems build huge markups into their product line, then don't really disclose this to their systems. I felt that was deceitful and so having a transparent administration fee of just ten percent was more than fair, as other systems marked their product lines up well over one hundred percent!

Now I could take this money and do what I wanted with it, but instead I reinvested it into Mr. Sandless. We used the money to be able to pay for a chemist to work on all these new products for both Mr. Sandless and Dr. DecknFence. Without that money from the owners, there would have been no way to afford the chemist. I reinvested the funds for six years and didn't stop until we reached all the products we needed to have in the system. This would eventually include the first non-toxic satin finish in the USA, a matte finish, and a completely new finish line I called "top coat" which was a urethane hybrid finish for more durability. We tested all these products in double blind lab

THE COMPETITION RISES

tests against the best products available to sanding companies and beat them all!

I originally hired Caden's brother Dominic to be a trainer in Mr. Sandless. But with the new franchise system to run, I put him in charge of Dr. DecknFence. He would run the original Dr. DecknFence for the counties I serviced, as well as to offer franchises to others who came on board. Having a multi-brand system was the way to go I thought. This way, owners in rural areas could add a Dr. DecknFence franchise to their Mr. Sandless and be able to service both indoor and outdoor wood. For an ever so brief moment, I thought that I had finally set the table for great and strong growth of the company.

Now when I launched Mr. Sandless, I launched with a slogan that explained what we did in six simple words. This slogan was on our advertising and website for the first two years. I kept trying to play around with those words to make it flow better during that time. In November of 2006 I made a change to the slogan based upon what our customers were saying to me over the phone. Where I had "no fuss" in it, no one seemed to care about that, but people wanted to know if the system had odor. Since we had no odor, I made that word set change; keeping the main feel of the slogan.

By October of 2007, I made another change. Our customers didn't care that we didn't sand, they already knew that. They wanted to know if there was any dust. So, I made the change to incorporate that into the slogan as well. Finally, in 2008, I made the change that I knew was a winner. Our customers wanted to know if there was any mess and since there wasn't, the slogan was then complete with the three main words that customers used to ask about our service.

That slogan worked great! In 2008, Mr. Sandless used that slogan on every ad that went out for the company for the entire year. Completely out of right field, before the end of the year, I was served papers for yet another lawsuit claiming that Mr. Sandless was illegally using a trademark owned by a company called "SxBoost". Their trademark was my exact slogan that I had come up with, which they filed to protect after we had been using it for some time.

I had never even heard of this company SxBoost. Apparently when I went to their website, I was shocked to see they were a painting company. I did some research on them. It was owned by the world's largest service company. They were losing market share throughout the 80's and 90's so they thought about doing something with painting.

They found a guy out west who was doing this "revolutionary" system and purchased it off him. Then they took it to franchise just as I did with Mr. Sandless and just as they did with their enormous service system.

SxBoost was a horrible name! It is like some kind of male enhancement gimmick so much so that when you searched for the company online, you would only find male enhancement treatments! Their name was no match for Mr. Sandless. Seriously, who would pick that for a name of a painting company?

On their website, they had some very limited before and after pictures, so it was hard to tell what they really did.

Unfortunately, they instantly surpassed Mr. Sandless in franchise sales. They sold the system to their current service owners and since they had literally thousands of them, they were able to have two hundred franchise units up and running without batting an eye. They were also so much more well-funded than I was.

Now SxBoost somehow went ahead and took my words and got a trademark for them! I couldn't even believe they were granted a trademark on such generic words, because a trademark is not supposed to be descriptive words, which this clearly was! We tried prior to get these words as a trademark and were turned down because they were "descriptive." I also looked at their website home page. They launched in September of 2004, *after* Mr. Sandless. On our home page at that time had the beginning stage of my slogan and on their site, the slogan was nowhere to be found.

But another lawsuit and at that time, when I was still trying to recover from all the other litigation, when I still was trying to get our owners to make more money, when I was still trying to replace the work we lost during the housing crash would have been the straw that broke my bank account for certain. On the intellectual side, I felt I could win with the evidence I had. On the mental side, I couldn't bring myself to fight these a-holes. Through Mason, we agreed to never use this slogan ever again. While it pissed me off that I had to relinquish using words that should have never been given as a "trademark," along with the fact that I had been using it since the inception of Mr. Sandless and prior to SxBoost, I really made what I thought was the best decision. We sent out a company directive that the slogan could no longer be used.

If this were the only issue I had to deal with, that would be one thing. But thanks to the "appearance" of success with Mr. Sandless, many more were to come into the mix. The first up that I had to deal with within the first year of business was a company called StratumAble who launched in 2004, just like Mr. Sandless. What in the world are the chances that two alternatives to sanding floors would launch at the same time? It was like it was a conspiracy against me. It is almost unimaginable!

I found StratumAble from a local advertisement they put out. They were headquartered just seventeen miles from my offices! What are the chances? They were way too detailed on how they did their service on their website, so it was easy for me to figure their system out. They ran over the floor with a machine that was more like a carpet cleaner and probably used some type of alcohol as a prep solution. Then they applied a layer of glue to the floor that took five to six hours to set up. Then they would apply a single coat of oil-based urethane that would then stick to the glue.

Let me be perfectly clear. This was a brilliant idea and concept! But it is just the beginning stage of a quality service. There were many holes that were apparent in this system that needed to be addressed. As I learned, the owner had an ego that was monumental, so much so that he thought his "creation" was already perfection. It was anything *but* perfection and what it really needed was much more research and development to make it something great. This guy rushed to market with a system that wasn't ready, where I had spent four years developing mine and he rushed to market because he discovered Mr. Sandless.

My first run-in with StratumAble is too unbelievable to even fathom. I saw on this guy's website in his "FAQ" section an anti-Mr. Sandless remark. Let me state that many competitors and knock-offs of my company would copy what I had on my website. When I launched my website, only Mr. Sandless had an FAQ section. Within months, both SxBoost and StratumAble had FAQ sections remarkably like my own! Mason said there wasn't anything I could do about it, and reminded me that when you are number one, you have a bulls-eye on your back for the rest of the pack to come after. For me, there is nothing worse than someone plagiarizing my written work!

Now in the StratumAble FAQ, there was a question that said something like this: "Should I use Mr. Sandless for my floor refinishing?" The answer they gave was "No, their finish is junk and will not hold up!"

The first issue with this was the use of our trademark name without authority and without designating that it was indeed a registered trademark. The second issue was this disparaging remark without any real knowledge. Once again, I had to spend money on attorney fees to have Mason reach out and tell this jerk at StratumAble to remove our trademark from his site.

StratumAble's owner Dick sent Mason a response, stating that he had evidence that a "real customer" of ours contacted him and told him our finish was indeed junk and didn't hold up. Mason asked Dick to prove that and Dick sent us a copy of the email he received from this "client." I couldn't believe what I was seeing.

"Mr. Sandless is junk. The floors didn't hold up at all" the email stated. That wasn't the shocking part. The writer and person who sent StratumAble this email was none other than Drusilla, Henry's wife! This total bitch of a woman who I never did a damn thing to except give her spineless weasel of a cocaine addicted husband a job took it upon herself to start trouble for me. Fortunately, once I revealed to

Dick of StratumAble that this was not a client but a disgruntled family member, he removed that section of his FAQ without legal action.

This would not be the end of my dealings with StratumAble, but just the beginning. This guy Dick was going to become a thorn in my side for a long time running. I had franchise interest from a supposed oil executive "big-wig" in Dallas by the name of Austin who wanted to take the entire state of Texas for a franchise. This is normally known as becoming a "master franchise" where the person would hold the state and franchise out to others just in that state. They would collect a royalty as would we, and many systems do this to quickly establish the brand in each state. While I didn't have this in my disclosure document, it would be easy enough to add, but that wasn't my main consideration. The fact was, Austin would have to pay two hundred and fifty thousand dollars for the master franchise rights for the state of Texas, and I desperately needed the cash.

Austin flew in with his wife to meet with me regarding this deal. I took him out to see a job, and then took him and his wife, with my wife, Caden and his girlfriend to a ridiculously expensive dinner on a boat restaurant that was on a river. The dinner for six of us cost me seven hundred fifty dollars before the tip! But I wanted to impress this guy and make the deal happen, which would be a game changer for my company.

But shortly after his return to Dallas, things soured. It was obvious to me that this guy was nothing more than a bag of hot air. He had no funding of any kind to put into this venture, and within a week, he went from taking the entire state of Texas, to taking a single franchise location in Dallas and he couldn't even afford that. I finally told him that he was not qualified and that was that.

Another guy from Canada approached me for a franchise in a similar fashion for the entire Toronto region. His name was Apollo, an Indian who was now a citizen of Canada. His goal was to franchise the Toronto region for us. It was going to be a very lucrative market as The Greater Toronto Area (GTA) had the highest number of online searches for what we did than any other market I had ever seen.

Apollo visited with me, but since this deal was smaller, it was just Caden and I that took him out to dinner.

He too returned home, came up with excuse after excuse for not moving forward and finally he declined to come on board. As a master salesman, I read right through this guy's nonsense. He simply didn't have the money to open a business.

The next thing I knew, there was a new Houston StratumAble owned by none other than Austin and a GTA StratumAble owned by Apollo! Since Dick couldn't compete with Mr. Sandless head to head, he began to "give" his system away, saying "try it for free" and if you "like it", then you can pay for the franchise. I don't know how in the world he was able to get away with this, but it was a very bad idea to give someone your system for free, most especially when I turned them down for very good reason. If you have no money, you shouldn't launch *any* business no matter what it is!

Austin serviced a job at a Dallas downtown bar with the StratumAble system and Dick posted the before and after picture on his website for the world to see. He was so proud for that moment. A month later, Austin's StratumAble was out of business, having serviced just that single job! Dick kept the picture on his site for at least a year, even though it was done by a failed owner. To the best of my knowledge, Apollo never even got off the ground and closed his StratumAble with very little fanfare.

Now how in the world was I able to know when these sites closed? Dick was silly enough to have a list of his owners on his website. Every time one of them closed, he would replace their name and number with *his* name and number, so he could keep up the illusion that he had more locations than he really did! This pattern continued for several more years, where I would turn a guy down, Dick would give them his system, they would promptly fail, and Dick would take over their site. Before long, it seemed Dick was serving from Maine to St. Louis, and all the way to Vancouver Island, British Columbia Canada! It was a joke.

I was to run into Dick and StratumAble at a home show we both

THE COMPETITION RISES

displayed at. Everyone who came to our booth who had visited his booth told me he had nothing but horrible things to say about Mr. Sandless. This from the guy who couldn't find his own franchisees but palmed off my rejects and who had a failed franchise system! He was telling everyone that our finish was "junk." I was furious.

I went back to my office, sanded a wood floor model and applied stain on the entire piece, then finished one half with Mr. Sandless products, and the other half with top of the line sanding products. I called my video producer to get over to the back of our Dr. DecknFence office to create a new video. I poured full strength floor stripper over the model, then power washed it, then showed that the Mr. Sandless side held its color and look while the sanding product side came right off. I ended the piece by saying "Now, what do you want on your wood floors?" and posted it on our YouTube channel to shut this guy Dick up. We received ninety thousand views on this video alone!

On top of this, I sent Dick an email and explained that if people inquired about his system with my team, that we invited them to simply visit with him at his booth to inquire. We did not bad mouth him. Then I asked why he insisted on bad-mouthing my company. Of course, he was nothing but excuses in his reply, but my favorite thing was this part he wrote me.

"Competition is a good thing! It makes more people aware that there are alternatives to sanding. We are like Frazier and Ali battling it out!"

Let me make this clear. This was no "Frazier and Ali". By that time, Mr. Sandless had fifty locations and StratumAble had two. This was a little, beat up Chihuahua nipping at my pant leg and this guy Dick knew damn right well his system was failing. By that time, we had twelve trucks in the region working every day through three franchise locations, including my own—right in StratumAble's market, where he was lucky to have a single job per month! He couldn't even compete with us in his own market.

That led my boy Dick to become so frustrated that he started to advertise *as* Mr. Sandless. His online ads would say "Mr. Sandless" and then when clicked, they would go to his StratumAble website. He had "Mr. Sandless" with just about every state name, anything to palm off our customers. I wrote to him again and told him to stop and he refused. Once again, more legal fees as Mason had to send this guy a cease and desist letter for trademark violation.

It was right around that time that I received a call from a guy who was calling under the guise of taking a franchise with Mr. Sandless. During my conversation with him, he made a strange statement. He said that he already did what we did. When I inquired what in the world that meant, he said that he was already doing Sandless refinishing and that he was already successful with it. I said that if he was already doing this and was already successful at it, then why in the world would he be on the phone with me to take a franchise? That was when he gave me his website to check out which was floordeminators.com. Apparently, he wasn't very good at spelling!

When I clicked on the site as we were still having our discussion, I noticed that this knucklehead had used all my copyright protected words: what else was new. His before and after pictures were excellent though—some *really* great work. The only problem was, he didn't do these floors—*I did*! He not only stole pictures to use on his site, he stole my *personal* floor pictures! Let me give you an example of what thieves like this do. Here is what I had on my site at the time:

"Mr. Sandless makes refinishing wood floors quick, affordable and painless! There is no mess to clean up, no odors, and service is complete in just hours. We are always less expensive than sanding, and everything we use is kid and pet safe. There is no better way for your wood floor refinishing needs!"

His Floor Deminator website stated this:

"Floor Deminators makes refinishing wood floors quick, affordable and painless! There is no mess to clean up, no odors, and service is complete in just 3 hours. Our system is less expensive than sanding, and everything we use is pet and people safe. There is no better way to bring life back in your floors."

That was blatant copyright infringement.

Since I had him on the phone, I told him right out that he stole both my words and my pictures and told him by law he had to remove them. He told me that he would not and that he had every right to use them. Again, in a long stream of legal actions, I had to have a lawyer send this guy a cease and desist letter. It blows my mind completely that when you catch someone blatantly stealing your words and pictures and they refuse to take them down.

Immediately following that *I* received a cease and desist letter. Apparently yet another knock-off company was launched, liked the one slogan that Mr. Sandless used, and they filed and received trademark protection for it, then threatened to sue me for my system using my own words yet again! I know this sounds like I am making this crap up, but I am not. The slogan was so benign, like "Have a nice day!" and now this crappy little company was going to sue me if Mr. Sandless used "their" slogan. We already *had* been using it! I mean for heaven sakes, why can't a floor refinishing company tell someone to have a nice day? It is pure nonsense!

When I checked out this company, they were another "Floor Deminator" system. Apparently, some company came up with a way to slap a cheap acrylic finish on the floor for ninety-nine cents a square foot and made it sound as good as Mr. Sandless, so they could compete with us. I know it was the same exact system because the picture on this guy's website was the exact same stock picture as the first guy I encountered. I immediately knew what they were doing. But this guy was a bit more sophisticated. He infiltrated my system, watched my franchise presentation, got my disclosure, then modeled everything in his system after ours including the way he decaled his vehicles. They were a *true* knock off company! Once again, more legal fees to tell this thief that we would no longer ask anyone to have a nice day. Can you freaking imagine?

If this isn't enough, I started to get calls from my own owners that they were being approached by a franchise system to leave Mr. Sandless and join them! Yet another knockoff company called "Wood Savior" infiltrated my system as well, used my fifty-thousand-dollar disclosure to model theirs off, and launched their system. Once again, they had some magnificent pictures on their site, once again they were floors that I personally serviced, once again they refused to take them down and once again I had to pay lawyer fees to get them to stop. The woman who ran this company was a real piece of work. After infiltrating my franchise presentation, she threatened to report me to the Federal Trade Commission that I was breaking the disclosure laws with what I said in my franchise presentation. I was not, and I told her to shove it.

All these systems turned into nothing special. I even had one of the Floor Deminators in my market and after about a year, they were out of business as they couldn't compete with my Mr. Sandless. Several other knockoffs popped up as well, some even growing as large as twenty-five locations. But I heard from potential franchise owners from our system that they reached out to these companies and were not at all impressed with their earnings, training or support. Although I unleashed a monster, it didn't seem to be that much effect to me, other than the continued legal fees. There were twenty-four times a company used my pictures as their own, twenty-four times where they refused to remove them and twenty-four times where it cost me legal fees to get them to stop! By the time I finished this book, the number was up to fifty!

During all the competitor madness, I had another serious issue to deal with. You see when Corentine filed his complaint against me and Mr. Sandless with the attorney general of his state and the attorney general and Corentine's lawyer were friends, that put me high on the target list for franchising. This complaint was assigned to an assistant district attorney by the name of Annabelle. Even though my legal matters with Corentine were over, even though Corentine was only out to steal my floor concept out from underneath of me, Annabelle treated me like a complete criminal!

This witch of a woman ordered me to do a full audit for the state. That meant anything and everything that we had done to be compliant with state law she wanted to see. That would include receipts for disclosures for anyone who got one in that state whether they took a franchise or not, and every single paper trail for anyone who did come on board with us in that state. Fortunately, I kept extremely detailed records—that wasn't the issue. The issue was simple ballbusting. This Annabelle wanted everything reproduced and mailed to her for review. It took me a full week to have everything printed and boxed up for her—two full file boxes of everything which I sent certified to her at the District Attorney's office. Along with that was the massive costs to reproduce everything.

I totally got what she was doing. On top of busting my balls over this nonsense that I could have emailed to her electronically, she was hoping to find something where I broke the law and so she could have me charged. I included a letter to her with the truth of exactly what happened with Corentine to show that *he* was the bad actor in all of this, not me as he purported me to be.

That didn't help me at all. After her lengthy review, Mr. Sandless was then not allowed to offer franchises in that state. On top of this, she sent me a long list of questions to answer. Annabelle thought she was *so* smart that she could twist things to catch me doing something wrong. I answered the questions and returned the information to her, expecting that this would be over. There was no way she could find anything that I did that broke the law!

But no, Annabelle was not satisfied as if anything I ever did really worked. She ordered me to do *another* printed audit, this time not concentrating on anything for her state, but on our franchising overall, and she created new specific questions in an attempt to catch me yet again. She wanted to know what I told people about earnings before they came on, she wanted our business plan to see if that contained anything she could use against me, and dozens more questions. This was not a state audit, but a complete audit of my entire franchise system. Once again, two full boxes of printed materials were sent down to her for review.

Annabelle was probably furious that she couldn't find a single thing done incorrectly with the franchising of Mr. Sandless. So, to keep me from franchising, she ordered a *legal* audit. She wanted to see every single file and filing for both the Corentine case as well as the Maypan case, which was totally irrelevant to anything in there. This was all just to put ridiculous pressure on me so that I would quit trying to franchise in that state. This witch would not accept electronic copies but insisted on printed copies and I would have to pay Mason to produce all these things! I was so pissed off, I considered suing the state. But my franchise attorney told me to stay the course and get registered there again, then to sue if I wanted to. Mason said the same thing.

I felt bad for Mason's assistant Betty, who had the ridiculous task of reproducing literally hundreds of pages of madness from the Corentine and Maypan filings! I felt bad for me because I had to pay for all of this! Once she got it, there was nothing left for Annabelle to torture me over. So instead of going direct, she went after my franchise attorney and tried her best to keep us from being approved that way. Annabelle questioned ever single solitary item in our disclosure!

The only way to deal with this was to make a separate disclosure for that state alone. I had to agree with stripping out the disclosure to practically nothing so that it would basically tell a franchise candidate from there nothing whatsoever! Annabelle hoped that this new strategy would prevent Mr. Sandless from ever opening again in that state, even though one of our owners there, Dylan, was making a fortune and setting company records! It was so unfair, but I had no choice. She even questioned the word "is" like Bill Clinton did!

Just as I was getting over that, another knockoff company showed up in yet another state. The company was called "Mr. StratumAble", apparently because this prick of a man liked both the Mr. Sandless name and the StratumAble name. Dick from StratumAble gave this guy *his* system to try. This jerk found out that StratumAble was not registered for franchising in New York. So, our new Mr. StratumAble was able to keep the StratumAble system for free and there was nothing Dick could do about it.

I wrote to Dick to inform him that one of his protégés was

THE COMPETITION RISES

now rogue. By this time, I was nearing one hundred locations and StratumAble had five. Dick confirmed the situation but refused to accept any responsibility for creating this new Frankenstein. My issue was simple. Mr. StratumAble launched five Mr. Sandless URL's to drive traffic to his Mr. StratumAble website, a clear violation of our trademark. When I contacted this jerk to remove those URLs he refused (and again what else was new) and I had to hire an attorney in that state to sue him to get him to stop using our trademark.

Meanwhile I responded to Dick with a taunt.

"You remember the time you said we were like Frazier and Ali?" I asked. "What are you now, Tony Tubbs?" Tubbs was a boxer who came close to fame but always seemed to fall back down to earth. I thought it fit well with StratumAble.

It cost me thirty-one thousand dollars to finally be able to get the Mr. StratumAble guy into court. When he finally showed up, he cried "poor mouth" to the judge. This liberal judge said that instead of paying my attorney fees as required, he could pay me "whatever he could". The jerk paid me a lousy dollar and turned over all the URLs to Mr. Sandless and that was the last I heard from him. I don't know how anyone can look themselves in the mirror when they are such blatant thieves.

Along with all the above going on, losing the slogan in our advertising did not sit well with my owners. Why in the world I would expect support from my own owners? As usual in franchising, I took nothing but grief from them for deciding not to fight losing the use of certain words. That was easy for them to say as they didn't have to live through Matt, Henry, my mother, Silas Jones, Corentine and Maypan. I sent out another company announcement to explain the decision:

"I have heard some rumblings that a few of you are blaming Corporate for the loss of those words. I truly feel this is unfair. Mr. Sandless owns and has protected numerous trademarks. However, when we first tried to get our slogans trademarked, we were told by the Patent office that they would not accept slogans that were "descriptive" and rejected our applications. The corporate attorneys who

represented Mr. Sandless at the time simply were not good enough in this department, even though we paid them boatloads of money. Therefore, there were ways around this that we simply didn't know. You must understand that Mr. Sandless has been franchising for 3 years, and SxBoost has been franchising for 35 years. They have a little more juice in this regard than Mr. Sandless.

Did we use these words before them? I would say yes. However, to continue to use the words would take a long and costly legal battle, costing at or above $100K. Litigation is a hideous proposition for both sides where the only true winners will be the attorneys. Also, anything can happen. I have learned a valuable lesson over the past two years that I can share with you, and you can write this in stone. Where litigation is concerned, there is no such thing as "fighting for principle". Fighting for principle means that you are 100% certain, beyond any doubt you are right. Litigating because you are right-even if in fact you ARE right-is like cutting off your arm to save your brain. The wiser choice is to get out with your entire body intact.

I really want you all to understand this, so I will give you a great example. I just found a knock off guy who took both my words and photos from the MS web site for his own site. What I mean by photos and words that are "mine" is in the exact. The floors he is using were floors I personally serviced, the photos he is using are photos I personally took, and the words he printed are the exact words I wrote. It is a total violation of law and it is theft of my work, copyright, and trade dress. I am 100% in the right and did nothing wrong, and he is 100% in the wrong, and what he is doing is against the law-illegal. If the FBI wasn't busy with other more important things, they would arrest this guy for me. But that is not going to happen-it is too small and too simple for them to get involved with. So, my other recourse is to sue him, right? That would be fighting for principle, and ultimately cutting my own arm off. You see, I've tried this before and only one person loses-that would be the good guy. I sued a guy for calling himself Mr. Sandless in five different URLs. He came to court and cried poor mouth to the judge. The judge said I was the bad guy for beating *up on him, got him to turn the infringing materials over to me, and he paid a dollar for the trouble. It cost me $31,000. I fought for principle. In litigation, that is a mistake.*

So, are we correct and right with this slogan? I believe we had a very good PRINCIPLE in this. Is it worth cutting an arm off to do battle with them over words? I don't think it is worth it. It is a wiser choice to let them have it, change our words, and ignore them. If they catch you using the words, they could sue you directly-and for that I can't help you. Welcome to my world!"

Two announcements went out to warn my owners not to use the slogan, then we created a "use and don't use' document for advertising that included this and the other slogans we couldn't use and sent that out to the system. No one would be foolish enough to use it after all this, *right*?

CHAPTER **11**

Ending the Bad Run

SINCE WE WERE just about to reach one hundred locations, and given my run-ins with all these slogan stealers, I decided to create slogans and have Mason register them as trademarks for Mr. Sandless. These included:

Refinishing the world, one customer, one floor at a time! ®
The quick no sanding solution to beautiful wood floors! ®
Quick, Clean, & Certified Green! ®

I didn't want to take a chance on some other stupid company stealing any more of the slogans we used, so I had them all trademarked. Of course, this cost even more attorney fees to accomplish!

Along with that, I was fortunate enough to find a great company to handle a national toll-free number for us! When someone called that number, they would be prompted to enter their zip or postal code and be directed to the nearest Mr. Sandless dealer. This way, we could mass produce advertisements using one number for every location.

Along with that, I purchased two great numbers to use: 877-WOOD-360 and 877-TILE-360. This new toll-free number system wasn't cheap but divided by all the owners that were in the system at this time, it was only going to cost twelve dollars per month per location for this great tool. We sent out a company announcement on how this would all work and our plans for using the number to the system. But the biggest part of this was, I made it optional! While

ENDING THE BAD RUN

our agreement with our owners was clear that we could add toll free numbers and charge them for this, I was hopeful that the concept would be unanimously accepted by all.

Wouldn't you know that owners complained about the lousy twelve bucks! Imagine other franchise systems club their owners over the head for every tiny thing, but once again I was the bad guy for trying to move the system forward. One owner who flat out refused to use the numbers was the sound and logical Sadie! Another dissenter was none other than the Orb himself, Bo, who sent me an email, once again talking down to me.

"I'm assuming you're asking for my opinion, so, I feel obligate to acquiesce. I understand the premise behind the national # and I've read all the supporting info you've provided, so, no need to re-iterate. Despite the fact that all Canadian Franchisees have their own ph #'s and marketing plans, which include, but are not limited to: yellow pages, tv ads, print, decals on vehicles, business cards, mailers etc.., and given that all of the above will have to be changed (additional cost to Franchisees), in order to communicate the new #; and, in addition, for some of us, there is the new Sanding equipment, extra vehicle, insurance, maintenance, sanding personnel etc...I'm certain you're taken these (near term) looming incremental costs into consideration.

Kindly detail the marketing plans of MSLLC in terms of how a national # will be advertised in Canada by MSLLC so that potential customers will readily use it as a go to source."

Yet again, this character missed the point of the number completely. There was no need for any owner to change anything they were doing for heaven sakes! Our number would be a way for us to advertise nationally in both the USA and Canada for all owners to enjoy and the calls that we garnered from the national numbers would ring right on their own phones! They didn't have to do a damn thing! On top of that, it is a year later, and the Orb was *still* complaining about the sanding addition—*even though he didn't do it*!

This guy had been a sword in my side ever since he came on

board. Every single solitary time something went out from this company, he had something negative and nasty to say about it. He 'assumes I am asking for his opinion'. What a pompous airbag! I had reached a breaking point with him and hence my very wise but lengthy response to try one more time to turn him from the dark side.

"Bo, I have to tell you that out of all the owners, you are my undisputed #1 non-conformist. It certainly seems that everything I do, say, write, add, or move to--that you have a problem with it, a negative reaction to it, or are flat out against it. I know you believe otherwise-that your thoughts are good ones, and that the positive things you say outbalance the negative. I have saved everything you have written to me, and the negative outweighs the positive-that's my opinion, and I am not trying to talk you out of yours. I am simply pointing this out to you. That is my perception of how you have been doing business with me. And so, this response is to attempt to get you to see things from my perspective. You may be shocked and think that I am overly sensitive or taking this way out of proportion. I don't have to prove to you that I am not, and heck, I could very well be over-sensitive and taking this out of proportion. That is irrelevant. Sometimes in life we inadvertently step on someone's toes. We may not mean to do it. We may not even know we are doing it. But when we are told we are-even if we don't think it is warranted, it is vital to change to stop stepping on their toes. So, if you find in this you do not believe you are out of bounds that's fine, because what is important is I feel you are.

Out of the entire system, only two franchise owners said no to the new toll-free number. You should know that the second objector is the #2 non-conformist in the system. I doubt that I will ever get either of you to be agreeable to a franchise system simply because it doesn't seem to fit your style and you are not willing to let someone else drive the bus. That is unfortunate, as it is required in a franchise system. But I think to become a happy owner in this system you are going to have to learn to do this. And I want you to be a happy and successful owner.

I will tell you exactly what I told that other owner, in the hopes that you will begin the process of trusting me. This is the most important part Bo. So, I am kindly and respectfully requesting that you read this twice, to be sure it is understood and clear.

According to our agreement, Mr. Sandless can make adding the new service mandatory, make everyone in the system purchase the new dustless refinishing kit, make everyone purchase that kit directly from Mr. Sandless, make you send someone to the states to train in the system--all at your expense. That is exactly what Mr. Sandless can do and furthermore, it is exactly what <u>you agreed to do</u> already. This isn't anything new. I have your signature on a contract that says you agreed to these things.

Instead of that, I have made everything in this new additional service optional. Please stop and re-read this entire section. You have accused me before of "beating people into submission". Can you see why I believe that is so very much unfair to me? Here is what you wrote today: there is the new Sanding equipment, extra vehicle, insurance, maintenance, sanding personnel etc...I'm certain you're taken these (near term) looming incremental costs into consideration.

This statement by you has both truth and falsehood in it. Yes, I have indeed taken these costs into consideration and that is why they are **optional** for everyone. However, the falsehood is that you lump these costs in with an e-mail about your monthly fees, where I do not see sanding equipment, extra vehicle, insurance, maintenance, or personnel listed. Your e-mails to me always take shots at me and I am telling you this in the most honest way I can-I feel they are unwarranted. No one Bo-no one has said you had to do any of the above things that you wrote.

You must stop Bo. Before you send anything to me in the future, you must ask a couple of questions. First, can you not figure this out on your own, or at least find the silver lining in what you perceive is bad? Second, is what you are going to send productive and positive, or whiney and bitchy? If you can figure it out on your own-even if you don't have it confirmed by me, then you should not send it to me. If it is productive and positive, yes, send it along. If you need your bottom powdered, then don't. My powder doesn't seem to appease you-unless of course it is service or client related, and then yes, lean on me for that because my powder is very effective.

Now, regarding the national toll-free number. It took a lot of work to find the right company. That means making certain it was a good price and best service we could get, and that it would be all inclusive. I am not asking for thanks for doing things I am not required to do-I'm just pointing it out. Looking back over all your e-mails to me, I believe I see the key. You want to be the franchisor. You honestly do not like not knowing where we are going as a company, and that probably drives you a little bit crazy. So, I have to point out that I am not required anywhere in our agreement to provide you with a business plan on where I am taking Mr. Sandless. Conversely, the only thing required in the agreement is for you to tell Mr. Sandless where you are taking your business-not the other way around. Again, for clarity sake, I am merely pointing out to you that this is what you already agreed to.

When you send me things like this-for me to spell out my plans for the company, you should know that it is not required that I tell you and in fact, I don't even think it is necessary for you to know. The reason for that is I started this company with one truck in 2004. My leadership of my company has been most stellar and award winning. On top of that, on occasion when I do in fact release to the system where I am taking the company, it winds up being released to the world. Take for example the dustless refinishing. Thanks to one of our owners, StratumAble now knows exactly what we are adding and the exact equipment that we will be using. Brilliant, however, this is proof positive why I do NOT want to tell any more than I have to. If for whatever reason you cannot understand this, then there is nothing I can do for you. Your understanding is not required.

I hope that you can be honest with yourself in saying that you believe you know better than I do-which means you trust your own instincts and business skills over mine. That means you would like to be the driver of the bus-the franchisor-because you feel you know better. I do understand that is how you are, and I am OK with that understanding, however, this is my bus and I am the driver and most importantly, you knew that when you came on with me. This is a franchise system where we do the leading, and you do the following. Your sole job in this is to take what we know works and make your location a winning location-not to be worried about the direction of Mr. Sandless, which is my job. Let me say this clearly. If you don't trust my direction, then you should immediately consider getting off the bus. I am not saying that to be mean. I just know that if you can't trust me, then you can't, and you should depart quickly.

Having said that however, you should know that it is perfectly acceptable to me if you feel you have street smarts, business knowledge and vision that are better than mine. I don't for a second have a problem with that and in fact, that is the reason I wanted you in Mr. Sandless. You may very well be better than me in all those categories. However, as it stands so far, it is all talk. You have plenty to say to me about how I run my part in this, yet your part in it so far has been horrendous to say the least-not only as a business owner but most certainly as a franchisee. Why?

Right now, you are in breach of your franchise agreement for failure to pay the required ad fund fee. You find plenty of time to respond to me but have ignored two Enforcement notices about the breach--which is in turn another breach of your agreement. Your database is a mess. You have 41 service dates in October, where you serviced only 4 jobs. Why are there 41 service dates? All those additional clients you did not book should have the service date removed, and instead a call back date applied to those you need to call again. You need to learn to use the call back feature to track when you should contact these clients again. Your reports are all off and inaccurate because of the incorrect service dates which skews the entire company records as well as your own. You booked 10% in October; 53% under company average and perhaps the worst booking percentage in the system. If you would have booked the company average, you would have serviced 23 jobs and earned nearly $27,000 since your average job is a very good $1,164. Of course, I had to use a calculator to figure that out since your reports are completely skewed. I saw that you battled with Enforcement when you were asked to correct your database. I see that your number one source of leads is "television". If this is in fact true, you are again in breach of your franchise agreement-multiple breaches-for failure to have whatever you are running approved prior to use as you agreed to do. Do not get angry with me for your breach, but I will be turning this over to Enforcement and you will be getting a notice that will require you to submit the television commercial immediately for approval.

Clearly this shows that so far, you are a bust. I say this to you to get you off the high horse you are on, and to join me down in the dirt. You need to hear this loud and clear. **It is in fact possible, that despite your street smarts, business knowledge and vision, that perhaps, just perhaps in this particular business I in fact know more than you do.**

I am here and available to help you. First, we will go through your database and clean it all up. Next, we can review every client that didn't book to discuss the reasons and to come up with a plan of action to get them to book. You can send in the payment you owe and submit your advertising materials so that you can become compliant again. Then you can move to a more productive Mr. Sandless business. Tell me a time that we can review these material issues and we'll set it up. Or not. That is your choice, but what I am clearly showing you here is that what you joined is a franchise system. You must learn to accept conformity. I have to be honest with you that I don't accept non-conformity from my top owners. It simply makes management unbearable. But it makes it even worse when you are in breach of your agreement and come back to me with <u>anything</u>. Can you understand that? As it stands right now, you are in multiple breaches of your contract with me, and you want me to explain the company toll free number? See what I am saying?"

This may sound as if I was losing my mind, but I didn't put the fifty other emails I received from this guy in this book! Every single time an announcement went out he was on me and I couldn't take it any

ENDING THE BAD RUN

longer. Not only that, how many CEO's of International Companies allow idiots like this guy to even directly contact them? *None*! But it gets better. There he was bitching at me once again, while his franchise was in default! On top of that, this moron Orb sent in to us the television advertising he was using in his market to *now* get approval for it after he had been using it for <u>months</u>. Wouldn't you know it, but this idiot had in the commercial the slogan that we are not to use! This was found in November. So please allow me to re-cap so that you see why my level of frustration was so high with this guy.

In July, Mr. Sandless issued a notice to the system that SxBoost had trademarked this slogan and sent in a "cease and desist" letter to us. In the beginning of August, Mr. Sandless reported that SxBoost did in fact own the trademark and had a team of lawyers who were going to defend it. In Mid-August, we announced that we had learned about a lawsuit filed against Mr. Sandless <u>and all our franchisees</u> for using this slogan by SxBoost. In late August, Mr. Sandless sent out a system wide notice that all sites were being sued by SxBoost for using the slogan, to stop using the slogan, and to check with their business insurance policy about coverage for the lawsuit.

In early September, Mr. Sandless announced that instead of a long and expensive legal battle, which would include all sites, that it would be best to stop using this slogan altogether, and to come up with something else to use. The very next day in September, another announcement went out to be certain no further advertising was done using the slogan, and for everyone who had a television commercial, to stop using it *immediately* and that the commercials would be replaced, and for everyone to replace advertising that had the slogan.

In early October, two more announcements were sent out including an FAQ answers, where I explained in vivid detail why we could no longer use the slogan and that to avoid any litigation, especially to all our owners, why we were going to settle with SxBoost to never use it again.

Do you see my point? After all of this, why in the world would the Orb go ahead and use an unapproved commercial containing this very slogan in November? Why would he risk a lawsuit? Why would he want to blow the agreement I had received and paid the legal fees for by continuing to use their slogan? Why would he risk bringing a lawsuit down on every other single owner in the system?

There was a very successful man I ran into years before Mr. Sandless. He was a big believer in eliminating negative people from your life as soon as they showed themselves to be negative and even if you believed they would be difficult to be replaced. Thankfully, the Orb didn't last much longer in Mr. Sandless after this event. I let him sign back the franchise to us and walk away without penalty. He was not only not suited for a franchise system, but he was a blowhard, know-it-all who really when it came down to it was a blatant idiot. I was so very glad to get this negative human being out of my company because as this successful man said, what he brought to the table of Mr. Sandless was just merely his negativity.

Speaking of the perfect example of this, at the end of that year, I received an email from great and powerful Silas Montefusco...*again*! As you may recall, I invested a ton of money into his music, thought we were best friends, accept him at a high position in my company when he made the decision to join me without asking me, made him the highest paid in the company, thought he was my best friend (had to say this twice), only to have him attempt to blackmail me, and then to end up having the balls to ask me for a reference so that he could get a job. Now why in the world would I want to hear from this guy ever again? Not only that, I blocked his main email and he knew it.

Silas wrote to me through his music website email instead about issues he thought our website was having. Now as I said, Gabe was so much better than Silas at the website scripting. All I did was forward the Silas email to Gabe, who then wrote to Silas to inform him that no, there were no problems on our end. The problems were on Silas's end! Would that make Silas go away? Of course not! All this email was about was to try to "pretend" that nothing transpired between us, to ease his guilty conscious. You will note his "praising" of my accomplishments sound exactly like the Orb.

"Hey Dan...thanks for having Gabe get back to me yesterday...I didn't realize the script debugger was on for my browser which made those JavaScript errors fatal (not something your average consumer would experience). I guess there's still a bit of "chicken little" inside of me with the sky is falling...still working on that part of me:) Btw all 4 websites you have running now look great...Gabe is doing a superb job and I'm really glad you were able to hook up with him.

I see you're about to pass the 20,000th floor mark and have gotten the Green seal...congrats on both they are quite an accomplishment. There was a press section on the website that's probably due for an update and once you do you may want to link it from the home page bottom links. For me things are going as well as I could hope for on my new job situation. I survived a layoff just 3 weeks after I started (I think they were getting rid of some dead wood). It's a good job, good people and I'm extremely happy to have somewhere to belong and contribute again, and taking all my lessons learned about what not to do. So I'll definitely stop sending ya notes about the website but I'll still be checking occasionally to see how you all are doing. I hope you and everyone at Mr. Sandless have a good Christmas and New Years...hopefully will be a great year for all."

Why did Silas feel the need to write even in the first place? It was for him to tell me that he was still so much smarter and wiser than me and that he was a hero for pointing out that there were errors on our website. He wrote the second email to cover his own ass. He *knew* Gabe would tell me that Silas was a "stump" and was full of baloney about the website. So, Silas tried to cover his own stupidity with a "ho-ho-he-he-hah-hah" explanation of what went wrong. Just laugh it off instead of eating crow. How perfectly Silas of him. Was this supposed to make me believe that he had changed? Not a chance! Once a back-stabbing traitor, always a back-stabbing traitor! It was exasperating that I even had to see an email from a guy I blocked and for good reason, so I responded quite clearly.

"Silas honest to God, you have to move on. I cannot tell you how much I do not want to hear from you. I am trying not to hurt you, because that is not my way, but I have already made this clear to you, and nothing has changed in this regard. When I hear from you, I think back to the hurt you have caused me. The problem is easy to understand. Since things went SO bad, I take any good that I got from you, and it has been replaced with the bad. I take the love I had for you as my friend as nothing more than a mirror reflection of how I felt-that nothing, repeat NOTHING came from you-I was just seeing my own reflection. I think back and remember how you sent your demand/blackmail e-mail to me and the company attorneys and will never forget how mortified I was that my friend was doing this to me. I think back of how my friend changed the password to the company web site so that he could extort me. I think back of how my best friend thought he was irreplaceable, how he thought he knew so much more than me, and how he believed he could do anything without me, and that I couldn't achieve "ONE TENTH OF WHAT WAS ACCOMPLISHED" without him. I think back where my best friend told me he didn't trust me when it came to business, and numerous other things my best friend found negative in me. It is impossible to repair the damage done. You should know since you caused it all. I put you above Maypan in the nasty column because at least Maypan wasn't my friend. Et tu, Brute? Get it? I've got news for you friend. I have sold more franchises in this period without you, than at any other time in company history. We are opening three new locations a month without you, a fifty percent increase because there is no longer negativity in my company from you. And the top franchise magazine in the country has Mr. Sandless listed as #1 home improvement franchise for this year. Everything I said to you has come to pass-all of it as if it was written in stone. You need to go away and stop reminding me of the pain. "The knife is still in my back."*

That line I had in quotations was exactly what Silas said to me; that I would not be able to achieve one tenth of what was accomplished while he was with me. Honestly, had it not been for Silas, I wouldn't have had one tenth of the issues I had in the company. I would not have had Maypan as Silas was totally responsible for that entire fiasco. Corentine only acted up because he saw that my attorneys were so bad that they couldn't control Maypan. No Maypan, no Corentine issues, no three hundred thousand in legal fees, no distracting me for a year and a half and much less pain in my life. That is what Silas Montefusco brought to the table.

As what seems will be my curse, just about everyone I started with at Mr. Sandless was faltering, starting with Caden's brother Dominic. This guy had worked at Mr. Sandless for a few years as a trainer in the system before I moved him to run Dr. DecknFence. Now at the end of the year, the outdoor worked stopped completely. The year before, he sat over in his office in the other building I leased and for four months did absolutely nothing! Of course, with me fighting Maypan and Corentine, and dealing with Sadie and Bo and Silas, I was overburdened and quite frankly while I knew it was happening, I just turned a blind eye to it.

But this next year as the smoke of the litigation had passed, I went to Dominic at the close of the season for Dr. DecknFence and asked him what he was planning on doing the next four months. His response was "the same as last year." I pushed harder and asked him to explain exactly what that was, how it was moving the business forward and how it was bringing in income. He had no real answer.

It was then that I told him that he should move over to my Mr. Sandless and start to go out on estimates for us. He refused me! Now let me explain this a bit further. Again, due to the madness of the company at the time he took over the Dr. DecknFence business for me, I was too wrapped up into the other things that were more pressing at the time. But let me say that it didn't go unnoticed that he was not earning very much money with the business, that he really didn't like what he was doing, and that he was negative and grousing most of the time about his job.

"Let me put it this way Dominic," I responded with to his refusal to do estimates. "You either get over there and start to work those estimates, or you are laid off as of today!" He reluctantly agreed but over the course of the next four months, was surly and negative about his new assignment. I knew there was going to be a reckoning with him in the future.

Meanwhile his brother Caden was really starting to fail as well. Prior to 2009, I had a full company paid, top of the line health insurance plan. It was the best plan money could buy. Obamacare kicked in and our rates went through the roof. The company didn't have the money to pay all those lawyer fees and so the insurance lapsed. Instead of seeking coverage elsewhere with the ninety-five thousand a year I paid him, Caden did nothing, and then wasn't able to renew the medication that kept him balanced. That was the first issue—he was off his meds.

Next, once I moved him from the field to the office, he started to get a "country club" attitude about work. He started to come and go as he pleased—like he was the owner. Instead of doing the one job that was at the top of his list, which was making sure each owner I brought in was properly trained, we had to rely on the likes of Hunter and Ken to do it. I will tell you about these two "brain-trusts" coming up later. That meant the training was not being done like it should have been. On top of that, during October, Caden took the entire month off to work on this neighborhood "haunted house' for Halloween. I have to say that this more than anything really pissed me off. He put so much time, effort and love into something that would be used literally for a handful of hours while ignoring the job I was paying him to do. If he had put that kind of effort into his job, I wouldn't have had to do nearly as much.

When he finally did return to work, all he did was bitch and moan about his workload. To make things better, I took from him the tech support calls for people in the field—without even telling him I did. At the end of this year, I exploded on him. He came at me bitching that he didn't have his meds and basically blaming me on that, along with saying his workload was too much. When I told him that he should have stepped up and dealt with it like I have had to do, he screamed and hollered that how would I know with all the money I had! It was like all the prior years of misery and legal fees eluded him completely.

The next day I told him that he had it easy. All he had to do in the company was email quotes, customer relations and tech support. He would spend an hour on the phone every day with just three owners, each getting an hour, to talk more like school girls than professional business owners. He basically powdered their asses every day. I told him that he should have never stopped training but that he did and if anything, his workload decreased, not increased. Then I told him I took over the tech calls from him without him even noticing.

I told Caden that he should be grateful for the cushy job he now enjoyed and that instead of looking at it as a burden, he should look at it as a blessing. I told him that if the company failed, he would just go and get another job and I would be bankrupt. He responded by telling me that he was worth more than what I paid him and that he wanted more. I reminded him that I still had not taken any pay and that he was the highest paid employee at that time. I told him straight up that with the limited amount of work he did for the company that he wasn't worth more money, saying my plate looked like a twelve-course meal and his looked like a light salad. Then I ended by telling him if he thought he was so unappreciated and that he was worth so much more, than he was free to move on. I simply didn't have the energy to fight someone like this, another user, who I had given such a great opportunity to.

I knew that the writing was on the wall with both Caden and Dominic. They were excellent workers when they were in the field. But placing them in management was never going to work, as they were not self-motivated enough to not take advantage of the situation. Even though we were right at the threshold of one hundred locations, the company still was not to the point of viability, especially with the downturn in the economy from the housing crash. But there was a glimmer of hope at the end of that year! I received a huge amount of franchise interest from abroad.

My plan for the USA and Canada went from a quality model to a quantity model due to the inability of my owners to come close to the earnings of the original model. But only twenty out of the hundred owners were doing well. The clear majority or eighty percent did very little. But with an international expansion, I saw a possible light at the end of the tunnel. If I could launch three, four or five other countries, and they all started selling franchises, that extra income that I didn't even have to work for after the initial training period would be the company's salvation! If I could grow to ten or more countries, the income from both franchise sales and my percentage of royalty should propel Mr. Sandless to become a powerhouse as I envisioned and get me out from under the years of struggles I had endured to this point. Would you think by now this plan would work? Just wait until I tell you about this part of the adventure!

CHAPTER **12**

International Salvation (or so it seemed)

IF MATT, HENRY, Drusilla and my mother, Montefusco, Maypan and Corentine, SxBoost, Dick and StratumAble, the Orb and Sadie and pour performing owners were not enough for one human being to take, from the time I launched Mr. Sandless until late 2009, I had serious marital problems. That entire time I was estranged from my wife in my own home. I lived upstairs, and she lived downstairs with our two children.

It would be so very easy to assume that this was my fault, after all, it may appear that all I did was work during this time. But that wasn't true at all. I sacrificed sleep for my family. Since this is an important part of the story, I have to give you some background. I won't be going into all the gory details as that is reserved for another book. I need you to know at least the basics, and at the same time, none of this was my fault. I gave my wife and children the world and every drop of me that I could.

It was years earlier when I was a professional musician performing at a night club. One night this woman walked across the floor in front of the stage as I was preparing to play. It was love at first site for me! I romanced this woman, getting her name and address from my band's mailing list. I sent her poetry that I wrote to her and signed my name "Rumpelstiltskin", the fairy tale character who said: 'you will never know my name.' The entire one-year time frame between when I saw her that first night and when I married her is chronicled in my book "Once Upon a Lifetime: How I Romanced the Woman of My Dreams" published in 2011 (Xlibris).

I didn't just love this woman. I absolutely adored her, and I did everything I could to provide an incredible life for her and our children. Now jump ahead to 2004, the year I launched Mr. Sandless. She had bouts of depression, especially post-partum depression after the births of our two children, self-esteem issues and general anxiety issues. After the loss of her parents nearly back to back, she checked out of the marriage completely. I needed to get at least four hours of sleep and the kids being young stayed up fairly late. I had to move upstairs in my home. My wife remained downstairs with the kids and refused to join me in my bed.

This arrangement went on for five brutal years, all while I went through all this other madness in Mr. Sandless. It was so difficult because she wasn't interested in the least of what I was going through as I couldn't talk to her. I really am a big believer that behind all great men is a great woman, and I didn't have that. So not having anyone at home to support me really took its toll. I hung in there with the marriage solely for my children. Not only was I lonely, the physical part of these years was torturous. To not have sex for that long wore heavily on me.

It would have been quite easy for me to have cheated. Cora was single back then and very available to me. It was so very easy to read that I was miserable with my home life. It was written all over my face. I was desperate for adult companionship and conversation. Even so there was no way I could cheat. For me, cheating is not about the other person but about one's self. I would be breaking vows I took and would go from what I considered being an honorable man, to one with no honor. I would never be able to look myself in the mirror again. And that is why cheating was out of the question, even though I very much doubted my wife would have cared one bit. I don't think she cared if I lived or died during this period.

INTERNATIONAL SALVATION (OR SO IT SEEMED)

For five years we lived like this. We would go out to dinners, to the movies, and on vacations and there was a distance between us the entire time. If it wasn't for the kids, I would have never been able to make it. But in 2009, I overheard my wife talking to her sister. The way she talked about me was shocking, basically painting a picture to her sister that *I* was a piece of crap! A *total* piece of crap! I couldn't believe it. This woman didn't want for *anything*! She didn't have to clean as I had a weekly cleaning service. She didn't have to get groceries because I ordered them online and had them delivered. I did my own laundry, cooked my own breakfast and dinner, and packed my own lunch every day. She had money to spend, a new car to drive and didn't have to work. She would go to breakfast with her friends, lunches with her sisters, dinner with her friends and even out to night clubs with her friends. Then there were dinners with me and the kids, movies and vacations. What the hell else could anyone want?

It was then that I considered that perhaps she was cheating on me. She seemed happy and I didn't know how under those conditions anyone could truly be happy. As I started to think about her cheating on me, my heart started to break. At that moment, I realized that I still very much loved her and that I was miserable because I didn't have her. Since I couldn't speak to her, I wrote her an email and ripped her for talking so poorly about me. I also told her straight up that this was her fault and if she wanted to fix things, to get into my bed again and be my wife.

We had a short fight after that, and she finally came up to my room. She cried that first night, which while I thought was ridiculous, I didn't say anything or force her into anything. I figured to make it a gradual reconciliation. But shortly after that, things turned around and I had what I had always wanted with this woman—a great marriage. Yes, she still didn't cook or clean or do laundry or go grocery shopping. But at least she talked to me and we were intimate again. I am a giver and need very little to be happy. She absolutely could have done so much more, but I was happy with what little I had.

Once this oppressive situation with my home life was cleared,

I began to flourish at work. 2010 would go on to be the best franchise year ever with Mr. Sandless. We reached the incredible mark of one hundred thirty-five owners in the system, and from 2010 to the half way point of 2011, I brought the system to *eight more countries!* What an amazing testament to the power of love. All I needed was someone to love and I unleashed an unstoppable power onto my system. Mr. Sandless was ranked #3 fastest growing franchise in the world and #1 in our category.

While I franchised Canada myself, the first real international country to come on board was New Guinea. I really appreciated the entrepreneurial spirit of anyone who wanted to become the master franchise for us in another country, as it was a rather daring thing to do. This first guy by the name of Libby Smith decided to take the master franchise for New Guinea. I remember when he first showed up very late at night over a weekend to prepare for his training to start on a Monday. His eyes were glowing and blood-shot from the wickedly long airplane trip!

Libby was a bit of a scatter brain, but I did attribute some of that to massive jet lag. You see, it is like being twelve hours ahead on your time schedule. It can take at least a week to even feel somewhat normal! He completed his two weeks of training and went back to New Guinea to prepare for opening. It took him nearly a month before he had his equipment figured out and to order his supplies. Then another six weeks before he would get his supplies shipped from Logan to New Guinea. By that time, Libby was a bit nervous about starting up because it had been so long. I would have to get someone out there to make sure his first week really worked. If I had success with him, I knew I could get many more countries opened. This first master franchise was vital!

Since I was on an epic roll that year, I asked Caden to go to New Guinea and work five days with Libby to make certain he was ready with the system. At first, he agreed, and I booked the trip that cost over four thousand dollars for him. He was with me when I booked it, so he could pick his seats and other details of the trip. But the weekend before he was to go, he wrote me a bullshit email that he thought he was getting sick and couldn't go. I knew it wasn't health, but that his heart was not into it. Once he had stopped training, he didn't want to go back to doing it. I had to send the big jerk worker I had Ken to do the training and the airline wouldn't let me switch the tickets, so I had to eat the four thousand!

Of course, the training failed and over the course of the next three months, I had to constantly baby Libby to get him to figure everything out. I must have sent him two hundred emails to get him on the right course. Eventually it took, and he started working without crying to me every two minutes. I was not at all happy with Caden, who as I said was doing very little in the company. He should have been the one to go and I told him that straight up. If I could no longer depend on him, what good was he to me?

The next country I sold was Ireland, to a guy very similar in background to Libby Smith, by the name of Crispin. Both guys were "worker" types who moved to the owner level. Both were hands on in the construction field, and so I was hopeful their background would work as well as mine did toward their success. Prior to coming on board, Crispin wanted to see the service first hand. He arranged to fly over to spend two days with us to witness the service himself.

The first floor we showed him and even allowed him to work on was in the building I leased for Dr. DecknFence. We were going to do a training for coloring in the system for our USA owners and I needed a floor to work on. We pulled up the carpet in one large office in this building and we let Crispin do that floor with the service, knowing that if he screwed it up, we could fix it. The second day he went out on a typical customer's floor in the city. We met in my office when he returned the second day.

"What do you think Crispin?" I asked of his two days with us.

"To be honest, I thought you set me up the first day!" he announced.

"How in the world could we have set you up?" I countered. "I mean you saw the floor before, and you are the one who did the work. How could that be staged?"

"It came out so well, that I thought it was some kind of gimmick," he answered. "But when the second floor came out just as well, I knew it was for real. I'm in!"

With that we had a deal for Ireland. What happens with these master franchisors is they get to open their own Mr. Sandless, just like I had my own. Once they proved that they could be a success, they could franchise to others. I didn't take any more money for a master franchise than I did for a standard franchise, which at that time was just fifteen thousand dollars. Many franchise systems charge a fortune for the master franchise rights of another country and I get that. What they want to be sure of is if the person coming on board has enough "skin" in the game to be serious about what they are going to do.

To that point with Mr. Sandless, we had no master franchise owners who were successful yet. If I had asked for a ton of money upfront from these guys, chances are I would have lost the deals as well as if I did, I would hurt their ability to invest into their business to get it up and running. Initially they all got a great deal. The real earnings would flow when they started to franchise, as it was set up that Mr. Sandless would receive fifty percent of their earnings in this regard.

The other interesting thing about master franchising was that I needed to have a lawyer in every country we opened. Their job would be to be sure I was compliant with that country's laws regarding franchising. By the end of that year, I would have eleven lawyers on retainer: Mason, my USA franchise lawyer, my Canadian franchise lawyer, and a lawyer for the other eight countries. It was totally insane.

Instead of relying on Caden to do any training abroad, I went to Ireland to train myself. I took my family with me and Jack and his wife Missy and two of their kids, as Jack would be my helper for the trip. This would mark the third country that I did Sandless refinishing in. The trip was excellent! We got to see all of London and took a train ride to Paris as well. Jack and I worked several jobs with Crispin and we felt he really had the hang of it before we left. Ireland is loaded with wood, and so I felt this was going to be a very strong market for us.

INTERNATIONAL SALVATION (OR SO IT SEEMED)

Following Crispin was a much more organized business man from Mexico by the name of Roberto. He and a member of his family visited to decide if they wanted to come on board with us or not. They had purchased a ridiculously expensive non-franchise system for cleaning concrete tiles that cost them over one hundred twenty thousand dollars. They had two trucks, two of these systems, and were considering adding wood floors to the mix to make more money. Roberto already owned other businesses in Mexico including a successful pawn shop. I thought that if anyone could make a go of it there with our service, it would be him.

After training with us, Jack and I went to Mexico to work one on one with their team to get them up and running. We stayed in an historic hotel in a town called Santiago de Querétaro where Roberto's team was stationed. It was about an hour and a half away from Mexico City. This hotel had antique furniture that was beyond belief! As the story goes, a Spanish Conquistador had landed in the city and fell in love with a nun there. To impress her and get her to come live with him, he built this wonderful place which was now the hotel we stayed at. She wasn't impressed, told him that the city needed water and that if he provided water to the city, she would move in with him in his place.

This guy went and built an aqueduct system that went from the city to the mountains to bring water in. This monumental structure was miles long, thirty to forty feet high and still stands today, hundreds of years later. Since it worked well to bring water to the town, the nun agreed to move in with the Conquistador, but that didn't work out, as his wife arrived from Spain and put an end to the romance. She took possession of the place he built for the nun!

The first thing I did was drink the water! They had this special drink for guests to quench their thirsts when they were checking in, and Roberto poured me some. I felt obliged to drink. It was then we got into a discussion about "drinking the water" in Mexico. Roberto said it was impossible that it was bacteria because no one is immune to bacteria and so they would all be sick all the time. What he believed it was, was a combination of the spicy food mixed with alcohol like tequila. Most visitors are not used to either things and he believes that is what caused "Montezuma's Revenge", better known as gastral intestinal issues!

Spicy food it was! We all sat down in the town square for a wonderful dinner. I had enchiladas with this sauce on them that looked hot just by the color. After a couple of bites, I was really sweating, but looked over at Roberto's brother in law who joined us for dinner; an Argentinian, who had the same thing I had, and he was sweating too! Then I didn't feel bad about my condition.

The street was filled with performers including a full mariachi band. One street performer came over and did her act, and I went to tip her. She spoke to me in Spanish. I had practiced up on my Spanish for this trip and had the roll of the tongue and accent down pat. But it is spoken too fast for me to have been able to converse in real life. Roberto asked her to speak English, then told me what she said in Spanish back to him. It seems he wasn't too happy she wasn't able to speak English to me. She explained that she neglected her studies and she apologized for insulting him. It seemed to me that Roberto has some weight and status in the town and I know he was trying to impress me with his people. Believe me, it was a wonderful experience and I was very impressed! It couldn't have been a more pristine town!

Mexico is a tipping culture, so when I went to tip her, Roberto wouldn't let me give her more than two pesos. That is like twenty cents US currency. It is an interesting scenario when it comes to money there. The only thing that is cost effective is labor. The average worker may make four to six hundred dollars a month. But the costs it seemed to me were equal to the states. For example, there was a pizza franchise in the US that had a "two for ten" dollar special. The same franchise in Mexico had "two for one hundred" pesos, just a little bit better deal than the states if you did the currency exchange.

Jack and I serviced many places with Roberto and his team while we were there, adding yet another country where I did the Mr. Sandless service. The hotel we stayed at was top of the line and I had

INTERNATIONAL SALVATION (OR SO IT SEEMED)

a tenderloin steak there that was the best I had ever had to that point in my life. It was wrapped in bacon and covered in a sauce with mushrooms. All the meals came with beans and while I don't think they are very good for you, they were amazing in Mexico. I even had real tacos! I remember when Roberto visited me in the states, he stopped at a taco place and couldn't believe that the tacos were "hard shelled". That just flipped him out. Everything in Mexico is a soft wrap.

About the only thing bad on this trip was the coffee. It seems the coffee in Mexico is terrible and I couldn't find a good cup anywhere. The service though is the best I have ever seen, and I returned there to visit with Roberto two more times in the future. He asked me after the first trip what I felt about Mexico now that I experienced it.

"It is completely different from what we think!" I told him. I could tell he really lit up when I said this. There is a great sense of pride for the Mexican people about their country. I have never seen a more cleanly people. Every single day they wipe down everything. It is really something to behold. When we visited the pyramids, I was stunned to find that they had no guards on duty and the exhibits were within hands reach. When I inquired of this to Roberto, he told me that Mexican people would deem it a disgrace to dishonor their heritage and is why they never had to worry about that kind of thing. I was very impressed and was one of my favorite trips that I had ever taken.

After Roberto came another owner who was in the same mold as both Crispin and Libby named Oliver, who was looking to take the master franchise in Australia. Although he was a displaced Kiwi (New Zealander) Oliver had a very successful tile company in Malaysia. He was planning on moving to Western Australia and wanted to open a new project there with Mr. Sandless.

To this day, Oliver is the most interesting person I have ever encountered in my life! He has traveled the world so much so that the word "worldly" doesn't do him justice. He can spot a person and by their look, know where they originated from, or hear just a word or two and immediately recognize their dialect. During his training, he and I sat in my office just talking about life, beliefs, family and business; arguably one of the best conversations I have ever had. When we were finished, we sat in silence for a moment, after talking about our beliefs in reincarnation. Oliver was heavily influenced by Asian culture, and so he leaned toward believing it was possible.

"You know Dan," he said with his lovely accent. "If reincarnation is true, I think you are at the end of the road."

"I think you are right, Oliver," I replied, knowing this was one of the best complements I had ever received.

Once again, when it came time for Oliver to open, I went for his special week of training yet again. Once again Jack went with me. It was a brutal plane ride. We had to take a plane from my city to San Francisco, from San Fran to Sydney, and then from Sydney to Western Australia, a thirty-six-hour jaunt. I looked over about half way through the flight and saw Jack's face and told myself that this would be the last trip I would take him on.

Oliver had a vehicle he had to pick up on his way from the airport after getting us. So, either Jack or I would have to drive the extra vehicle and of course, I didn't trust Jack to do this, who immediately bailed on the idea anyway. You see, you drive on the other side of the car and road as you do in the US. I didn't have any problem at all following Oliver until we turned onto a street with no lines. Then I was freaked out a bit on where I should be. But we made it there without any real problems.

We stayed with Oliver at his new home in Australia as his wife did not come over yet from Malaysia. It was just the three of us. In the back yard of the property was an enormous lemon tree. These lemons were the size of grapefruits and I am not even joking. I went out to retrieve a couple to make some fresh lemonade.

"Oh Dan," Oliver yelled to me. "Be careful in the garden. There are spiders here that can kill you!"

"Oh, that's great news Oliver!" I responded, now very worried about the lemons I had in my hands!

I soon learned that Oliver had many other quirky characteristics.

INTERNATIONAL SALVATION (OR SO IT SEEMED)

To start with, he was a horrible driver. Jack and I would be forced to sit in this very strange van with no seat belts and our faces nearly pressed up to the windshield. Meanwhile, Oliver was all over the road to get us to the first job. We were right behind this massive truck that was carrying huge logs that stuck well out from the back of it, and Oliver pulled so close, I thought we would be turned into Shish Ka Bob! I almost kissed the ground when we got out.

Oliver was also beyond cheap. I noticed that he reused absolutely everything. He hated throwing anything out! When I reached for a trash bag on the first job we did with him, it had holes in it. Same with the gloves I reached for. We were servicing the floors in a one and a half million-dollar home that sat on the Indian Ocean. This would add another country to my growing list of international services. During the job, Oliver was out front, pulling dust and debris from a vacuum cleaner bag instead of just changing the bag. He planned on getting as much out of the bag as he could through the little hole where it attached to the vacuum, putting that into a used trash bag, then taking that back to his house to empty the bag in the trash "bin" so he could reuse both the trash bag and the cleaner bag!

While he did this, he was engulfed in a plume of dust and just as he was, the homeowner turned the corner and saw what he was doing. The look on her face was priceless! She had a look as if he had a head coming out of his ass! I just shook my head in disbelief, and then later I spoke with Oliver about this. I told him that it didn't look professional at all and that he should just change the damn bag and save all the nonsense. He told me that he was brought up this way and that he would have a very hard time changing.

It was so bad that Oliver wore the same exact pair of socks every day. He was so sloppy with applying finish that he often got the liquid on his socks, so much so that they now stood up on their own when he took them off. I am not even close to kidding! They looked more like shoes. When we pulled up to his house in his driveway, he came within an inch of smashing into the house! I asked him why all the glass on the house by the driveway was broken and he told me he had a few "slip ups" with the van and the house colliding. I got out and walked around the van and noticed way too many bumps to count. I just hoped to live through the week with him driving every day!

Oliver couldn't find the keys to the front door of his home, and fortunately he hid a small key container in the grass. But he couldn't find that either, and he started violently routing through the lawn to find it.

"Oliver, my God, what about the damn spiders?" I yelled to him. All he did was chuckle every time I said something that seemed obvious to me! He was such a good-natured fellow!

That week, Jack and I did five floors. The one job on a Wednesday was the absolute worst. It was sixty years old and had been under carpet all that time. It was raw, still had mill marks in the wood, had tons of lead paint splatters that are extremely difficult to get out of a raw floor, had huge areas of tape stuck to the floor and massive colors issues. We scraped for four hours straight. Remember, the time is nearly backwards. By two o'clock in the afternoon, it was like two o'clock in the morning our time! I was really dragging on this job as the jet lag started to set in.

There was one section that was in the corner of the living room where a few boards were missing. There was a similar section in one of the bedrooms that the owner was going to carpet. I took the boards from that area to use to fill the missing ones in the living room. As I removed two boards, I dropped a third into the hole and reached to retrieve it. As I did, a bug crawled out from the stone wall underneath the floor the likes I have never seen! It was black and big as my fist and had huge eyeballs. It gave me a look that said, "I wouldn't put your hand down this hole to get that board if I were you!" I agreed with the bug and skipped the last board.

That floor killed us! It took ten hours to complete and I threw everything but the kitchen sink at it to get it done. When the home owner came in, he almost fainted with how good it looked. I patched a big gap in the floor with a trick of mine and added color to blend

INTERNATIONAL SALVATION (OR SO IT SEEMED)

it all out, and it was truly amazing from how bad it was when we started. Oliver learned all my tricks on that one!

The next two days, Oliver left me and Jack to do the work while he ran around on estimates and calls for work. His phone was blowing up with calls, so I knew this was going to be a very viable market for Mr. Sandless. His pitch on the phone was dreadful and I had to really get on him about that. When asked how we did it, he would respond: "we washy-wash the floor". I told him, "I'll washy-wash you if you don't start using the script!"

The job on Thursday was huge! It was a loft apartment and they wanted the color to be darker. Oliver had found equipment locally to use in his Mr. Sandless business that were more like something you would see in a Barbie play house! That made this large job go even slower. While we are on this job and knowing that we were booked for the next day as well, Oliver took a call. The person was inquiring if we could squeeze in a job that week, and Oliver immediately started to say we could! I was going to kill him. Between being overworked that week and the massive backwards jet lag, I started losing my mind.

"Hey Boo-Boo," I said in the voice of Yogi Bear. "There's another pic-a-nic basket! I think we can grab that one up too!" With that I yelled "Oliver, there is no way we are adding another job this week! On top of that, your cheap ass is buying me a steak tonight!" The owners of that place said it was a "million-dollar job" when they looked at the floor that Jack and I did. Oliver charged then eight thousand dollars!

That Saturday, Oliver and his daughter took Jack and I to the mall. We had a blast buying souvenirs and shopping before we were to depart. Oliver's daughter picked out a sixty-dollar dress she wanted him to buy for her, but he wouldn't. So, I bought it for her! Oliver was losing his mind, saying that she didn't need it. The more he complained, the more I wanted to spend! Then because of the physically brutal week, I took all of us to get a massage. When we were done, I tipped all the masseuses and once again Oliver cringed with my actions. No one tips in Australia as the minimum wage is twenty-five dollars an hour!

It was a great trip and I was thrilled that I had Mr. Sandless in six countries! Our domestic sales were excellent as was our international sales. I finally felt like I was coming out of such a very long funk since I launched this business.

Country number seven would be South Africa with a smart business guy who had been in the wood flooring business for several years by the name of Lincoln. He was looking to add a refinishing system to his business and was looking at a bunch of competitor systems that were not nearly as good as Mr. Sandless. Once particular company was rather kind to us and told him that we were not as good as they were because of the machine they used. Believe me that was being kind! On the contrary, their machine didn't work and that is why we didn't use it. I told Lincoln that there would be nothing at all to stop us from using the same machine, but that we didn't because it wasn't effective. There was a technical reason why it wasn't going to work, but I didn't share that with him in case he decided not to come on board with us.

He did sign on and I was off on my next adventure to Johannesburg South Africa and my seventh country to refinish wood floors in. I did a job with his team the very first day I was there. They were having difficulties with a woman where they had pulled up the carpet from the floor for and were going to do her floors. Those floors were under carpet for many years, and they had a horrible smell to them! I knew that once we processed them and sealed them, that not only would they look great, but the odor would be gone as well.

The surly woman greeted me at the door and I told her to relax, that the "A" team was there and that I was going to make her happy. With that she left us to go to work. Lincoln's two main guys were miffed over the incident, so I tried to put them at ease.

"That's not the floor that smells like that," I told them. "That's the old lady's ass you're smelling!" They never expected this CEO guy from America to land that day and make fun of a client they were

INTERNATIONAL SALVATION (OR SO IT SEEMED)

having problems with! That broke the ice and I immediately had two new friends.

I have to say it is an interesting culture there. For example, I was told that if you got a flat tire, to keep on driving, because "they" would create the flat so that they could shoot you and steal your car! The "they" is all the people who flooded into Joburg after the end of white rule and the rise of black leadership. There were tens of thousands of them and they had no place to live. So, they set up these townships to house them, and it was poverty like I had never seen before. Lincoln took me by one of these places to show me. Unemployment was like at 65% and most were living in cardboard shacks. The crime rate was through the roof as well.

Most of the homes in the region had electric fences or high walls to keep out buglers. Other than that, it was a beautiful city. There was a thunderstorm one night and the lightning was ridiculously violent. Even the two guys I worked with that week were talking about it. There were also birds that woke me up every morning. These were not your typical sparrow type bird, but more like giant vulture things that was their version of a sparrow!

The hotel I stayed in was gated with guards. I had been there four days before I noticed a posting on the bureau in the room. You know that many hotels have a post that they are not responsible for your lost or stolen goods? This place had that, but it also added extra details.

"Not responsible for you lost or stolen goods, or your life, even at the hands of our employees."

From that moment on, I started to pay way more attention to my surroundings in the actual hotel courtyard. Up to that point, I assumed I was safe there. It wasn't like I was worried. I have never been a fearful person and traveled to all these places with no anxiety of any kind. On top of that, I was three times the size of the average "they" and so they would need a group to take me on.

The cost of living in South Africa was the best I had seen in the world! I took a group of eight of us out to a five-star restaurant located inside a large casino in Johannesburg. We all had steaks, drinks and dessert and it cost me just one hundred dollars US. I left the trip there believing that this as well would be a good market for Mr. Sandless except for the exchange rate. At that time, it was very favorable to the South African rand. But if the US dollar grew in strength, this was going to put a lot of pressure on our owner there to be able to import products.

The exchange rate was a big factor in opening in other countries, period. While Europe and the euro were very strong, most other countries failed in comparison. For example, I had a guy who wanted a franchise in Indonesia. The exchange rate was like nine thousand of their dollars to just one of ours! They could never afford our products. We had a guy come out who wanted a franchise in Jamaica. He expected to be able to offer our services to all the hotels there and this would have been a great market for us. But the exchange rate was terrible. I was basically going to give him the franchise if he could get a full franchise equipment and supply kit, which I would mark up and make our money that way. While he signed on and came out and trained, in the end he could not come up with the funds and we terminated his franchise a year later.

Just through email, I signed up a Malaysian lawyer and his Singaporean partner for the master franchise in Malaysia. The lawyer seemed smart and had a lot of strong connections and even said he would take Singapore if it worked out in Malaysia. The partner, not so sharp and would be more of the "grunt" type worker; running the business and doing the service. This was the first team who wanted to train in their own country as he was not able to make the trip to the US. Personally, I was worn out with training abroad, so I asked Caden to step up for a change and do this training himself. I would also pay for him to take one of my personnel from my Mr. Sandless with him. He decided to take Emma, a gal who was a very good worker for my franchise. I was going to go to the beach for a week to take a break with my family.

The trip was planned and booked, with the partner having five jobs for them to work on to train him. On the day they were supposed

INTERNATIONAL SALVATION (OR SO IT SEEMED)

to be there, I received a call from Cora who told me that something happened that they got separated. How in the world could that happen, I thought? It turned out that Emma had carry-on that they made her check, and in her one carry-on was her purse, money and passport. Now that is brilliant to check those things. It seemed that she was hung up in Hong Kong after a brief layover, because she couldn't get her bags off the plane to show her passport.

Instead of waiting with her, Caden left her there and departed for Malaysia! The simplest task was too difficult. By that time, I had been all over the world without a single incident with Jack. The moment I turn it over to someone else, it is calamity! It turned out that Emma made it there a few days later and the training somehow was miraculously completed.

After that, I went and did shows for franchising in Sydney, and in London. The London show did nothing for franchise sales in the UK. There were a ton of tire kickers there. But I did have a couple come from Denmark who after speaking with Crispin, decided to come on board. They were game to train in the USA because of the shopping deals they could get here. Jeans are like two hundred dollars in Denmark, so they showed up for training with empty suitcases and packed them with the things they bought here.

Jorggen was a professional chef in Denmark with the strange inclination not to like food. I don't know how in the world someone could be a chef and not like food, but that's what it was. I took Jorggen and his wife out to dinner in London and he refused to eat. I didn't know how this was going to pan out as both people were in their late middle age. The physical element of the service I thought would be too much. But they left training and opened in Denmark, becoming our ninth country.

The other visitor I had in London was an Indian who lived and worked in Qatar. He was very interested in taking a master franchise for Qatar. His name was Parth, a very well-spoken man, who explained that he had a floor installation company in Qatar and that adding refinishing, especially with all his past clients, would really work out for him. Crispin and I took him down to Soho for some entertainment, but he didn't seem interested in the street shows, but wanted a bit more action. So, we took him to a popular London strip club which was where he said he wanted to go. I bought him a dance with a very attractive blond, and before I knew it, he was on board! Too easy. There are no blondes in India, and so this really set him off!

Parth wanted us to train in Qatar. Since I didn't trust anyone to do this but myself after the last screw up with training abroad, I told Caden that he would be going with me. I wrote to Parth six times with the rules, that he must have at least five jobs for us to be able to train on. He picked a week for us to be there, saying that everything was in place. At the same time, he was going to be displaying at the Domotex in Qatar; this giant flooring event, and he hope to land interest in Mr. Sandless there. I booked our flights to do the training and the event.

When we got there, we were picked up by a guy who spoke no English. This is a very strange country. You have the upper class, which separates themselves from the other classes with the Arab custom clothing they wore. It was very easy to spot this class. The next layer was the manager class. They aspired to be the upper class although through birth they never would be. But that didn't stop them for pretending they were. They did very little work and just bossed around the worker class. There were some four million worker class people living in the Qatar, mainly from India and Pakistan. They worked like dogs in extreme conditions and for very little wage, but a better wage than they could get in their own countries.

This driver took us to a warehouse where the equipment and supplies were stored. To my absolute horror, they didn't even unpack anything from what it was shipped in, and we were going to be doing a floor at the Domotex show that very night. We were going to start the training at the show by doing a floor that their workers installed for the show.

Parth was nowhere to be seen and no one in this dusty, heat-soaked warehouse spoke English. So Caden and I had the unenviable task of unpacking all the boxes and loading up the van, in temperatures that exceeded one hundred and twenty degrees. But don't worry, it was a dry heat. No really, that is so stupid! One twenty is one twenty, humidity or not! It was like a freaking oven!

Once we got loaded up, we went to our hotel to shower and change, then directed a group of twenty or so Indians on bringing in all the equipment to the booth where we would start the training.

So here is the scene. Parth was there with his two manager types who didn't want to do a damn thing. Along with them were the twenty or so Indians who were uneducated and spoke no English. And we were supposed to teach these guys the system? Caden and I had to do the work in the hopes they would catch on. We did half the floor they installed and refinished just half, so that people coming by could see the massive difference. All the while, Parth and his two mangers laughed at us. You see, work was beneath them. So here was the CEO of Mr. Sandless and his vice-president working and they thought that was the funniest thing. I wanted to freaking kill all three of them as this attitude toward work would never lead to success in anything.

The next day there was no jobs as was promised. I was so pissed off, because I knew this training would be a total bust. I felt I was totally wasting my time. Instead of doing nothing, Caden and I worked the booth at the Domotex. I met a gym floor manufacturer from Canada who said that no one could coat their floors and she wondered if we could. Their product had nine coats of urethane sprayed on it, so nothing would stick to it. I knew we could get adhesion, so I asked her to send me some sample boards to the states and I would refinish it and get it back to her. Other than that, the day was uneventful.

The following day was the same thing. No jobs to train on as promised, so we once again worked the Domotex. It was then that I caught onto what was really happening. Parth was nowhere to be seen for those two days. Apparently, he got a big installation job in a high-rise outside of Dubai right after he told us to pick that week for training. So, all his guys were on that job, making training that week impossible.

That night he did have a job for us at a clothing store in the biggest mall in Dubai. We had our twenty non-English speaking Indians to work with to do this massive store. First, all the clothing racks had to be moved. They were so heavy that it took ten people to move each one. Then we had to get them to work in unison to get the job done. Caden imploded as his manic-depressive behavior kicked into full gear. He was running around the clothing store basically screaming at everyone, who couldn't understand a single thing he was yelling about!

I finally calmed him down and got him to focus on just one part of the job. Then I divided the Indians into groups and showed each group what to do like I was working with a group of kindergarteners! But it worked and before long, we got the job completed and moved all the furniture back. It was much easier working overnight as that was my real time zone. I was thankful I was able to get Caden under control as well.

The next day, there were no jobs. I told Parth that he really screwed up and told him that I knew about his big job that week that he was hiding from me. He admitted the job but took no responsibility for the training screw up. I told him I would not pass anyone for the training and that he would have to send someone to the states to train— someone who could speak English and understand the service, so that person could train and return to train others for him. He agreed this would happen.

That Thursday, Parth left us again to go work his big install job, and the driver he put us with spoke a bit of English. He was a Frenchman who worked for a local Sheik. This Sheik wanted to meet with me as he was intrigued by Mr. Sandless. Parth believed this was the way for him to really jump start the business in Qatar. You see, to do business in Qatar, you must have an Arab partner. You may be able to get one for thirty five percent of your business, but you don't really want that guy. You want the guy who will take fifty percent of your business because he will light you up with connections. Just a few of these high-rises there could be worth millions in floor business. Parth was hoping this guy would come on board with him for this new venture.

INTERNATIONAL SALVATION (OR SO IT SEEMED)

This arrangement may seem strange to people in the US. But they had no taxes—this is how they made their money. Think about it this way. I too have a partner called "Uncle Sam" who takes a huge chunk of my profit. The only difference is this uncle doesn't do anything for the money. The Arab deal makes more sense to me!

The French guy drove us to one of those giant high rises that the Sheik owned in Qatar and we took the elevator to his office on the billionth floor. Between the broken English I really didn't know what to expect and from what I gathered, all we were going to do was meet the Sheik's manager, who was also French. But as we were ushered into the plush office, it was the Sheik himself waiting to greet me.

After the introductions, with this billionaire in his white garb, I sat directly across from him and studied the details of his face. He was the darkest man I had ever seen. I don't mean that by skin color, but in details. He literally had black eyes, black hair and black beard and mustache, the darkest black you could imagine. I leaned in to really get a good look at him. I don't think he really knew what to make of me, but he spoke decent English.

After I explained the service and that we were now in ten countries, he lit up, spoke French to his driver, and then we proceeded out of the building and to follow his Mercedes around Qatar where he showed me all his properties. It was quite boring to be honest and at that point I would have rather just cut to the chase and this Sheik to tell me what he had in mind.

Three hours of this and we stopped at his final retail establishment, where he spoke French to his driver. His driver spoke French to my driver, who then explained to me that the Sheik would like to give me a "lunch" in my honor. I inquired as to what that meant. Basically, he would slaughter a lamb in front of me and they would cook it right there, while we drank. And of course, there would be belly dancers. The goal was for him to loosen me up so that then he could make his proposition and "steal" Mr. Sandless, or whatever his real goal was. I was told this was a "great honor".

Now remember I took Parth to the strip club in London and got him to come on board? Well this was exactly what the Sheik was going to attempt with me! I know how the game is played and to be honest, at that time I wasn't interested in playing. I instructed my driver to tell them that I appreciated the offer but wasn't interested.

The look on the Sheik's face when I turned him down was beyond description. He was shocked and incredulous that I dared to turn down his offer. You must understand that in this culture, no one turns down these guys! I remember the one day driving to the Domotex, and a Mercedes cut off the guy driving Caden and I to the event. Our driver started cursing and honking until we pulled alongside of the car where he could clearly see four upper class individuals in their white clothing. At that sight, he immediately began to apologize and bowed to them several times. That is the culture we are talking about.

The next day, since we had nothing better to do, Caden and I worked on a large stone walkway for one of the Sheik's new buildings at the behest of Parth who still wanted to get in bed with this guy. It was the most brutal working conditions I have ever faced. I had to take a bunch of rags and create a headpiece to keep the sun off me. It was upwards of one hundred twenty out, as Caden and I took turns going back to the car to sit in air conditioning so that we could make it through the job. I have the pictures to prove it as we transformed that stone. I heard later that the Sheik didn't like it, which I took as yet another ploy to get a better deal. But I didn't hear a peep from him after I returned home.

The Canadian company did send a box of their product for us to test if we could coat it. At the same time, another board manufacturer stopped by our offices with some sample product he said no one could coat as well. We ran the process on both and had no issues at all with our products adhering to their floors. The system really is a thing of beauty!

In a year and a half, I brought the company from two countries to ten in an amazing, epic run! I was on fire and felt like I had finally broken through the madness to see the light at the end of the tunnel. This was the first year I took a pay from the company and even so,

INTERNATIONAL SALVATION (OR SO IT SEEMED)

we ended the year with a profit of over four hundred thousand dollars. This was the first year in seven that I had some peace in both my business and my life. But would it continue? That was the question that weighed heavily on me. I just knew that something was coming around the corner to hit me yet again.

CHAPTER **13**

Shattering of a Dream

ONE YEAR OUT of seven in Mr. Sandless I had peace and success. You could easily look at this writing as a depressive jump off a cliff, or as I choose to look at it, a triumph of the human spirit. I just happen to be that particular human spirit in the story. From a spiritual standpoint, I wondered if I was being tortured for completing the Silas Jones song thing I was compelled to do. Was this event *so* important to warrant me being tortured for having completed it? Ultimately, you the reader can make this determination as you see what is to follow.

Around this time, I got a call from a local number that I did not recognize. Normally I don't answer numbers that I don't have logged into my cell. But since it was local, I thought it may have something to do with my home or business.

When I answered, the person on the other end started to immediately rail against me. I had to stop them and ask who the heck it was as I didn't recognize the voice. It was Henry! When I found that out, I told him to calm down and tell me what his problem was with me. It is too much to fathom how these people who did me wrong kept coming back into my life. You will see this pattern repeated over and over again!

"Why are you talking shit about me?" he asked angrily. "My stepdaughter came in tonight with tears in her eyes, saying that she ran into somebody at the park who said they worked for you and that he had nothing but bad things to say about me."

Now let's talk about this sweet, innocent step-daughter first. This would be Drusilla's kid who she had out of wedlock prior to marrying Henry. This is the step-daughter who posted on her Social Media page after Henry quit Mr. Sandless the following: "Henry is a loser and a spineless asshole!" This kid had no love for Henry, so I wasn't buying the "tears in her eyes" BS.

I went on to tell Henry that I have never spoken about him to the staff after he departed. I explained that it would make no sense at all for me to even mention him, as he brought absolutely nothing to the table in Mr. Sandless. He wasn't even a footnote in the company history. I also told him that if I ever heard from him again, I would rip his black soul out and show it to him.

A little while after that, I heard some more rumblings coming my way from him and I had it. I wrote him an epic email and ripped him to shreds. It is absurd that he blamed me for his drug habit as if I held the straw to his nose and forced him to do it. He had been doing drugs for ten years before I had anything to do with him and that was the truth. He later told Caden that I really hurt his feelings with the email. Truth can be painful; poor baby. Maybe he should think about the hurt he caused me.

As if this "blast from the past" wasn't enough, I received a letter in the mail from none other than Matt! Another lying loser trying to weasel his way back into my life? Yes, that is exactly what it was. In the letter, he detailed that he cleaned himself up, that he had a wonderful girlfriend he would love for me to meet, and oh yes, by the way he saw how big Mr. Sandless had grown and was wondering if I would consider taking him back. Can you imagine the balls of this guy; without even apologizing for the lie that cost me so many people?

Once again, I sent an epic response of how if there was a bridge that used to be between us, it was not only destroyed by his actions, but the foundation was gone as well. There was nothing left to ever be built upon.

Just to wrap up the story of these two wonderful former employees and human beings, Matt eventually got this girl pregnant, only to leave her with a baby and nothing else. He continues to be nothing more than a user and a liar and goes from one job to the next just for beer and drug money. He was then and is now a total waste of life. This guy could have had the world and I would have handed it right to him, but no, drinking and drugs were a better offer.

Same is true for Henry, who basically has fallen off the face of the earth. I heard Drusilla made him get another job about an hour away, and probably so she could keep him out of her hair. The company stock she owned went public and she is probably worth well over ten million dollars. She enjoys her life with her family and friends, never mentioning Henry at all.

Then, out of the blue, Drusilla contacted several family members to "see how they were doing" when they hadn't spoken to her in years. They, or course, asked me what I thought was going on, and I said point blank that she was trying to determine if they had heard anything about her and Henry. My bet was she was going to divorce him, and she was trying to see if he reached out to any family to tell them what was going on.

Damn if I wasn't right! A few months later, friends showed me pictures of the dear and wonderful Drusilla, on a Social Media "hook up" site. Seems her and Henry had been "separated" for some time and now Drusilla was out to have some fun. Paybacks are a bitch for sure.

As it seems in my life, all good things come to an end much sooner than I would want, but why after all I went through did the hot streak have to end in such an abrupt manner is beyond me. I was about to face the worst event and the worst person I have ever encountered in my life and I very much doubt I will ever face another like this.

I was at work and got a call from my wife. She was in the grocery store with my daughter, walked over a wet rug, which was literally pulled out from under her and she crashed to the floor, hitting her head. I couldn't figure out what she was even doing in the grocery store since as I said, I ordered our groceries and they were delivered to our home. There was no reason for her to be in the grocery store, and I couldn't even tell you the last time she was in one! Why was she even in the grocery store that day? But she was, and she slipped and now her head hurt.

I called my son and asked him to look at his mother—to make sure she had color. If she didn't, I would have called for an ambulance. But he said she had plenty of color, so I rushed home to take her to the hospital. On the way to the hospital, I called the grocery store from my cell, yelling at them that they should have called an ambulance. They told me something like 'she said she was fine' to which I yelled, "she hit her head, you idiots!"

At the hospital, I had her seen right away. She handed me her purse as they took her up for a CAT scan, and I went out to lock the purse in my SUV. I noticed her cell phone was still in the purse and figured she would want to text our daughter—who was very worried. I grabbed her cell from her purse to bring to her. As I walked to the hospital, I looked at the phone and it was off. That was very curious to me as she was *always* using it. Why would she turn her phone off when she *knew* that our daughter would be texting her to see how she was?

I turned the phone on, figuring I would check if my daughter did text her, and I would simply send a quick text that everything was fine. But what I saw immediately was a missed call from a *guy*! She had the same exact phone as I did—a Blackberry. The guy's name came right up on the front screen as a missed call, and his name was logged into her phone: "Dirk". I didn't know a *Dirk*! I didn't know *she* knew a Dirk!

"*Who the hell is this*?" I mumbled to myself. I clicked the name. On the Blackberry, when you click a name, the entire history can open right up, and well, it did.

Immediately came up sex texts between them. I scrolled to the first one of the day—that very same day. It was from my wife to him:

"Good morning lover, I'm horny! Come f*** me over my kitchen table!"

I collapsed in the parking lot as I couldn't catch my breath. It was like I was punched in the gut. I immediately knew that what I had believed was so right, was so very imperfect. What I had believed could never happen, had indeed happened. The woman who I was married to for twenty-two years, who I loved and adored, was in fact, a liar and cheater.

The rest of the gory details I put in another book I wrote, so there is no reason to rehash it all here. Let me just say that none of this made any sense to me. The year before this unfortunate discovery we did the training trip to the UK and Paris, we had our yearly convention in San Diego, we did Disney and three weeks at the beach. She was cheating on me the entire time and it was with more than one guy. After discovering the second guy, I stopped looking, so who knows how many there really were.

This was more than a mid-life crisis. This was a need and desire for attention. It had nothing at all to do with sex. We had an incredible sex life. This was about her need and addiction for attention. The more attention she got from other men, the more she craved. Throughout my entire life to that point, I had been a rock. I was the strength where others failed. I was the captain of my ship, the master of my world, the leader and the boss. This one act of betrayal in a word, shattered me. I was devastated that the person I held as the most important to me betrayed me in such a horrific manner.

This was in July of 2011. That entire month is nothing more than a blur. I could barely function. From that month until November, my dear, sweat precious love of my life wife tortured me. She had no remorse whatsoever for her actions, and if anything, she was angry because I had found out and interrupted her fun and games. Even worse, she continued with her antics no matter how hurt I was. She set herself up on an online dating site as "divorced" and wrote, "men find me to be sexy and wild". She did everything she could to rub my face in her infidelity. She also had unprotected sex, putting my life and health at risk.

My business stopped completely—dead in the water. Here I had remained faithful through five years of putting up with my wife checking out of the marriage, to hang in there to what I thought was better times, only to find out this was a total charade. I did everything I could to try and save the marriage, because I thought it was worth saving. But when I knew there was no way I could, I calmly asked for a divorce. My wife cursed at me, dialed 911 on her phone and told the dispatcher that I was trying to kill her. I, the victim in all of this, was forced to leave my own house.

She went on to get a protection order against me, refused to allow me to get any personal items, stole my things and sold them including my coin collection which I had since I was a kid. I was not allowed to contact her in any way, but she texted me every single day with taunts to try and get me to break the order. She was awarded my house before I even filed for divorce. She sold my things at a yard sale. I set up an apartment in the building I leased for Dr. DecknFence, and both of my kids came to live with me and away from her. Meanwhile, I was forced to pay her four thousand dollars a month in "support" even though I had the kids!

She even went so far as to contact Henry and Drusilla who were more than happy to insert themselves into my marital issues and convince my wife that I was indeed a drug kingpin and user. My lovely, wonderful and supportive wife was more than happy to share this new-found information with my children. She also told them that I really did try to kill her the night I asked for a divorce.

At that time, I stood six feet one and weighed two hundred twenty-five pounds of muscle. I sat my kids in the kitchen of my new crappy apartment and asked them if they believed her. They both said that they knew she was lying. I balled up my fist and said that if I ever hit their mother, it would only take one blow and she would be dead. I then said it was impossible that I was physical against her that night because if I was, how in the world was she able to stop me?

"Unless she is Sponge Bob and my blows bounced right off her, it would be impossible for me to have hit her without leaving damage behind!" I told them. It was vital to me that my kids knew that what their mother was saying was nothing but lies.

While there are so many horrific things that happened during this time that I am not going to list, it unfortunately got worse. The rest of 2011 and moving well into 2012, I did not sell a single franchise! The franchise company was not in the position yet of being self-sustaining, so I had to open several large credit lines to keep the company afloat. The franchise system started to collapse with the loss of twenty-four owners in 2012. The quantity over quality system had failed as poor owners who should have never been given a franchise lost their footing completely.

Another reason for this was the training they were receiving. I had warned Caden countless times to get out in the field and oversee the training which was being done at that time by Hunter and Ken who I will tell you about coming up. But he simply refused. If I yelled loud enough, he would go out for a day, and by Wednesday of that week he would tell me that the training was going fine, and they didn't need him. Well that was a crock. These owners trained during those three years were not strong enough in the system to be able to sustain growth. These also included idiots like Sadie and the Orb who refused to follow the franchise system. They would answer their business line "hello", sounded like morons when they didn't follow the script, didn't ask for the sale, didn't follow up and didn't use their company database. The entire system was out of control.

If the economy had stayed like it was pre-2008 and the housing crash, these owners would have been able to sustain. But with the full effect of the housing crash, a serious recession, Obamacare strains, and a very weak economy, all made it that only the best were going to survive. That was why we lost so many in 2012.

Not only that, the "brilliant" international expansion I had would fail as well. I could see the ump yelling "You're out" with my third strike in a row. I struck out on my marriage, I struck out on the domestic quantity model, and I struck out on the international owners being able to franchise this amazing system. Mighty Casey struck out.

SHATTERING OF A DREAM

The first to falter was Jorggen from Denmark. Despite an abundance of wood floors, they never really got off the ground. It seemed he and his wife were having marital issues as well and he ceased operations without any notice or explanation. To the best of my knowledge, they had completed just one job with the system there, making this a total bust.

Following that was the idiot Parth from Qatar, who claimed he could not send anyone to the States to train as he was afraid they would "take off" once they got here. I told him that in no way would he be allowed to do anything with floors until someone there passed training. He screwed around for another year, then threatened to both sue me if we terminated his franchise and to take me to some sort of international board to press charges that I ripped him off. The guy was full of hot air. He lied to me that he was prepared for training. He lied to me that he would send someone here to train. He lied when he told me he would be able to make it work. Once we terminated him, we never heard from him again.

Crispin was the next to go. While he did work on occasion, it was never anything spectacular. It is much more difficult to advertise in Ireland than in the states, and so he found it hard to get footing. Right before he took the master franchise for Ireland, he purchased a run-down home in a nice section in a small city. He spent most of his time rehabbing that home. When it was complete, he sold it for substantial earnings, then purchased his next home to rehab and do it all over again. Somewhere in between that, he lost interest in his Mr. Sandless business, and he disappeared with no real notice or explanation.

Following Ireland closing was Mexico. Parth, Jorggen and Crispin were all weak owners and not real business types that could have made a franchise system successful. But Roberto was different and if he couldn't make it there, no one could. The problem in Mexico was the labor. It was so inexpensive that Roberto could not compete using Mr. Sandless. First, people in Mexico simply didn't care if sanding was toxic and Mr. Sandless was not. Second, if there were any potential customers who were concerned, Roberto couldn't get them to find him as Internet use in Mexico is very low. Third, these people could just sand for the same exact price they would pay for Mr. Sandless. So, they just sanded.

I had no ill toward him and if anything, I was kind of sick to my stomach that he tried so hard and didn't have success with it. This was the first time where I had an owner who was truly deserving of success with the system, a guy who really wanted to be the race car driver, but the market just did not allow for that to happen. Unlike the other three, he sent a very detailed notice that he had to shut it down and although it was a bad moment, we have remained friends ever since. I have nothing but the utmost respect for him.

Another total loser was the Malaysia franchise. This guy couldn't sell his way out of a plastic bag and did very little work with his franchise. The Malaysian lawyer withdrew from the franchise after he realized his partner wasn't a good choice. This left the business to meander for another year until finally he signed it back over to us and exited. That meant we failed in Jamaica, Malaysia, Mexico, Ireland, Qatar and Denmark; all this while I lived in a make-shift apartment in a leased business building with my two kids, while the business was being consumed in more and more debt, and as my soon to be ex-wife ran up even more debt by maxing out the company credit accounts and filing motion after motion in the divorce court against me. Was this the lowest point I was going to reach? No, unfortunately not yet!

I want to say for the record that all the terrible human beings that I encountered during this part of my life and business were nothing compared to my wife. Matt, Henry, Drusilla, Maypan, Montefusco, Corentine all paled in comparison to the vile evil creature that woman had become. It is totally unimaginable to me that the person I held in my life as the highest would fall to become the worst of them all. She continued to torture me by opening a Facebook page to announce to the world that even though I didn't hit her, she was abused by me nonetheless. I guess if having money and taking trips, going to dinners and movies, not having to have to go grocery shopping, cook, clean or do laundry, and sleeping in every day was abuse, then okay, I was an abuser. I will never understand how a woman who had everything including a man who adored her—how that was not enough. When is everything not enough? I suppose in the end, I was not enough.

Out of the other international countries still open, only Lincoln had success with franchising in South Africa. He grew to six franchise locations, which is astounding that a third world country was having better success than places like the Ireland. That was a testament to his business savvy. I went to a business expo there with Lincoln and his family to show my support for his success.

Oliver tried but was more "worker type" than franchisor. He sold one franchise for Sydney which failed less than a year later. The problem with Australia is that it is very easy to go and work in the mines with no experience and make ninety thousand a year. The guys who took Sydney abandoned the business to go work in the mines as it was easier than running their own business. As for Oliver, he did very well with his local Mr. Sandless and is the leading refinisher in that market. We awarded him franchise of the year for his years of success with his own Mr. Sandless.

Meanwhile in the last remaining international location of New Guinea, for the nearly two years Libby was open, he reported very little earnings to us. He was constantly complaining that the business was failing and that he was having a hard time keeping his head above water. I did everything I could to support him, including not accepting anything in the way of royalty to try and help him out. I sent him numerous franchise leads from some excellent people and Libby could not close on a single one of them.

He finally had success opening a franchise with a couple from the end of the island by the names of Charlie and Amelia. Since Libby had so many issues with the system at his outset, the very last thing I wanted him to do was to train these guys himself. I told Libby to put together a week of jobs and that I would come to Guinea and train Charlie and Amelia myself. He readily agreed.

When I got there, Libby and his girlfriend had a room for me to stay in their home since they had a spare bedroom. Libby picked me up from the airport in his Mr. Sandless vehicle. We started training Charlie and Amelia the very next day.

The first thing I noticed was Libby's cell phone. He couldn't and didn't help with the training whatsoever the entire week and it was left just to me. His cell phone rang constantly with calls for the Mr. Sandless service. Along with that, he had a ton of estimates to go on. I didn't really see him the entire training! That was the first red flag that what he told me about his struggling with his business may not have actually been true.

Charlie and Amelia were lovely people! They had both worked in the corporate world before and seemed to be very sharp business people. They took to the system decently, although not all the jobs Libby set up for us would wind up working out. I enjoyed their company as we visited a casino in Guinea, they took us out to a wonderful dinner, and we went shopping and sightseeing.

One of the jobs we trained on was three rooms for a catering center in the main city there. I had a guy who was very interested on taking a franchise from Libby for part of the city, and so I arranged to have him show up to this job to both meet with me and see the service first hand. I found that Libby really blew the sale of this job. He made a deal for all three rooms, but what he should have done was to make a deal for just one of the rooms of the catering facility. Then once we serviced that room, the guy would have to pay full price to get the other two rooms done, because our floors looked so much better. It was a mistake to give the guy the immediate discount on all three rooms and I told Libby that.

Now when the franchise candidate came to visit, he told me straight up that he was very impressed with the service and that he would like to come on board. But then he told me that Libby most certainly did *not* want to share the city with him! If anything, Libby was badmouthing the service to this guy, once again going with this "struggling" story. But I believed this guy who had no reason to lie to me. It seemed to me that Libby was only trying to hold onto and control the city because he *was* having great success. Second red flag raised. Let's face it. If you were not doing well yourself, you would welcome selling part of it! The last thing you would do would be to fight to hold onto it!

When I returned from training, I decided to keep an eye on Libby's activities. I assumed he was working "under the radar" and taking cash for jobs with the thinking that we were never going to find out. After a couple of months when Charlie and Amelia were up and running and already surpassing the earnings of Libby, they wrote to me saying they could no longer stand by and watch me get ripped off. It seems they were not too keen on Libby's activities as well or with Libby himself for that matter.

Charlie and Amelia told me that Libby taught them how to steal from Mr. Sandless. Isn't that just so precious of him? He called his hidden work "cashies", where he would offer his client no GST tax if they paid cash. Then he wouldn't have to pay us royalty either. He told them that he had no problem keeping this from "the home office" and that we were so far away we would never know. He also admitted to doing at least "one to two" jobs every week this way, although I suspected it was an awful lot more. That meant over the two years he was open, Libby hid from us one hundred twenty-five to two hundred fifty thousand dollars in work, all the while crying poor mouth to me.

Of course, I needed to confirm this before acting. The first thing I did was look closely at Libby's customer database system. To my horror, I discovered that he was so brazen as to not report a single job being completed for the entire week I was there training! He actually hid all those jobs from his sales report. He was a thief and a dumb ass as well. We sent him an enforcement notice and for him to send us a copy of all invoices for jobs he serviced since he started. He sent us two invoices and ironically or stupidly, whichever the case may be, both jobs were not reported to us! We immediately terminated his franchise and gave the master franchise rights to Charlie and Amelia, who have held them ever since.

This was the first time that I ran into someone who stole from me for one simple reason only: greed. Pure, unadulterated greed. You see, the royalty he owed us was only two and a half percent! Just two and a half cents on the dollar and this guy was so greedy as to not want to pay us our proper share. For a lousy two and a half cents, this guy lost his lucrative business. I will never understand the insanity of that or how he could be so damned stupid telling Charlie and Amelia he was stealing from us. But in the process, he seriously hurt my international expansion. If he reported all his earnings, they would have been substantial enough to entice others to come on board with us. But with the pathetic numbers he did report; it did nothing but hurt my brand.

Libby Smith would not go away and remained open for nearly a year and a half after being terminated. Just to have a New Guinea lawyer send him a single cease and desist letter cost me five thousand dollars. Nothing would have pleased me more if I had the funds than to file suit against this thief and kick his butt in court. But with the system failing and my marital issues, the money just wasn't there. I had to bend and receive instead until he finally went away. It is hard to sell the service with no website and company brand to use, so it was just a matter of time before his work dried up.

Let me explain the failure of these master franchise owners this way. In what is the strangest turn of events, my own humility is what blinded me to the truth. I was speaking with a guy from Germany about coming on board with Mr. Sandless in Europe. This guy was a wealth of insight and information about the market there, having spent twenty-five years in the flooring industry. He knew exactly where the best markets would be for our service.

After much consideration and due diligence, he decided to pass on the opportunity. His reason really got me thinking. He said that in his opinion, being a master franchisor for just one country was too much for one person to be able to handle. This seemed shocking to me, as I was the master franchisor for *two* countries already by myself! I didn't think this was hard at all, but there is the rub. I am not sure how you view me at this point, but it should be clear that I was not arrogant at all. Only a humble man would get down on his knees to train someone when he had the title of CEO of an international company.

The problem was my humility. I didn't think it was any big deal to run my own Mr. Sandless. I didn't think it was any big deal to be the master franchisor of two countries. But I was wrong—completely wrong. Over the course of Mr. Sandless, less than five owners beat the earnings of my own Mr. Sandless. As for expanding the brand in another country, no master franchisor even came close, in fact, no one even came close to what I was able to do in Canada. While I thought it was no big deal, it was in fact a big deal. It seemed I should not have been humble, because what I was able to do was turning out to be one of a kind—an anomaly. I was way better at both the individual business as well as franchising than anyone I had encountered, especially abroad.

Right after this realization, I had to stand before a judge in court to be released from the order of protection my loving wife falsely had against me. If I didn't fight it, I would have had a criminal record for doing nothing! It was despicable that I had to be in that courtroom like I was a criminal anyway. At the last minute, my attorney told me that my wife was going to say that I did not comply with the terms of the protection order by breaking into her email account; which was a total lie. I told my attorney to tell her that if she wanted to play this way, I would introduce to the court that she stole the identity of a woman so that she could stalk one of her lover's wives! She backed down after that and while I stood there facing the judge, with my loving wife next to me, listening to the judge warn me of any further incidents, I felt like turning to her and punching her in the face right then and there. By that point, I was sick to death of all these people coming at me when I did nothing at all to them.

The business continued to shrink, the economy continued to be bad, and I continued to have a hard time finding my footing with all that was going on in my life. I guess by that time I just expected it to get worse until I finally hit rock bottom. But I wasn't one to simply roll over and die, not after I had come this far, not after all I went through. I bought a book written by a CEO of a famous franchise system and read it to see if he could inspire me to take this company out of the massive funk it was in. He had inherited the job of a floundering system as well and was able to turn it around in an epic fashion.

I used some concepts from this guy's book to attempt to bring my company back "online" as it were. I had to stop the decay of the franchise system and felt the staff I had in corporate Mr. Sandless was a big part of the problem. I designed an incredible retreat where I would take everyone to the park for the day for a retreat and lunch. I explained what each staff member could do to better the company overall and laid out a plan to get back on track.

I also created the new awards for the system called the "Big Oak Awards." These would be given out to any owner who did something extraordinary during the year and it was a real piece of oak board, finished the Mr. Sandless way, with a decal for the number and award they received. I created the "Big Maple Awards" for our Canadian owners as well. This was to promote the system and make the owners want to reach higher than what they were currently doing.

Primary of all these things was Caden and his brother Dominic who were the absolute least productive in the company. In fact, the only real bread winner in the franchise system was me. If I didn't produce, then we had no growth at all. I wanted Caden to do two new things. First was to oversee all trainings that came in to the system. Second was to help me sell franchises. Many people who came to us for a franchise were somewhat fearful of talking directly to the CEO and creator of the system. They found me to be intimidating without ever having spoken to me. These people would be way more accepting of Caden reaching out to them.

For Dominic, it was to concentrate on the current owners. I told him to reach out to every owner once a month to find out how they are doing, what we could do to help them succeed, and what if any issues they are facing. This way, instead of continuing to lose owners, we could get to them and help them instead to stop the bleeding. Not only that, I explained that they all knew what the deal was with the company by then and it was time they stepped up with their own plans on moving the company forward. Up to that point, every single tiny thing came from me!

The retreat at first was approached with skepticism. But once everyone saw the way it played out, I believed I hit a nerve and could actually turn things around. But that was just my optimism. I have since moved from being optimistic to be a realist who leans to optimism. The reason was; nothing I did ever seemed to work.

Dominic called maybe a dozen owners that first month and then announce, "I'm not doing this," and stopped altogether. He was yet another one who I was hoping would step up and lead, but just didn't have the pedigree for it. Instead of training like he should have, Caden threw himself into a project he called "Most Wanted". The best way I can describe this is in two parts. Part one was Caden's manic side trying to show that he was as artistic and creative as I was. In other words, he was becoming another Silas Jones trying to prove his worth to the company. The second part of this was supposed to be some type of positive feedback from owners on how we could help them— I believe that was the original premise of this program. But what it turned into was a forum for our owners to bitch and moan about corporate, rather than to focus on their all-too-many shortcomings!

I stayed completely out of the mix of this Most Wanted program while Caden's depressive side screamed and hollered at the rest of the staff to help him finish it. When it was completed, the entire staff came to me and exclaimed with exasperation that we could not send it out. I looked at this beastly creation and the way it was supposedly finished and was horrified. It was, the ramblings of a mad-man. You would have to either be completely drugged to be able to understand it, or crazy enough yourself to understand the lunacy of it. Nothing in the entire piece was cohesive or constructive.

Believe it or not, in order to save Caden from massive embarrassment, I had to take over *his* project. He was already shooting his mouth off to the system that this "incredible" program was on its way to them. I had to start completely from scratch, reach out to all the crying, whining owners who had sent him their tears, and somehow turn a monstrosity of negativity into something positive and productive. I changed his questions from negative on us; to negative on these horrible owners.

"What else can we do to help your business?" was one of his questions. Mine was "What prevents you from answering your phone when it rings?" Instead of "How do you feel your Mr. Sandless business is doing?" I had "What keeps you from using your company provided database on a regular basis?" This way I could attack the real issue, not give these lousy performing owners an "open season" to shift their weakness back onto us.

I even had to go so far as to change the cover photo of the program. Caden had the entire staff's faces superimposed on a cowboy type-outlaw setting. I didn't even get the idea of the "Most Wanted" name although I was stuck with it. His idea, I *think*, was to expose the bad owners, when all he did was shift the blame for them being bad onto us. We released it when I finished it; to no fanfare at all in the company. It made no effect at all and I worked on it for a month straight to fix the damn thing. So much for Caden's wonderful contribution.

Occasionally, I would reach one of these bad owners. I had what I called a "Canadian Conference" around that time to try and reach our Canadian owners about stepping up. I listened to and responded to their questions and thoughts in a meeting we had in Toronto, as all were in attendance. Then I told them exactly what they were doing wrong in a step by step manner. None of them, not even one, was following the business system like they should.

One group of owners were to my direct right and I caught them nodding approval for each thing I said. When I was finished, I asked them what they were thinking and why they were nodding, because they were not doing anything like they should. They told me that they knew these things and were kicking themselves for not following the system like they knew they should. They returned home after that and quadrupled their income and have been the top franchise location in Canada ever since. Why all the owners couldn't do that still eludes me to this day.

The next "one-two" punch to my gut was a killer for me. The second punch of this combo; I saw that coming down the road. But the first punch was totally unexpected. One of our few successful owners, Dylan, who had won "franchise of the year" three years running, ran his business on his personal credit card. This is the credit card company that loans you the money for a month, and each month you must pay the balance off in full. Dylan paid everything through this card, because they had a great rewards program; it was easy to manage cash flow this way, as well as it was super convenient.

After the housing crash, this company wanted to become a bank, and I suppose they felt the need to review how much credit they were giving out monthly with this program. I don't understand this because they were making big money on this with high fees when the card was used. Apparently, Dylan, who as I told you earlier had a bunch of properties, had one fall behind on its mortgage during this downturn. This credit card company caught wind of this, and immediately cut off all his credit! Now at that time, no company was offering anyone credit, especially business credit. There would be no way Dylan could get an instant fifty thousand dollars in credit to keep running his business, and he couldn't use his available cash because they cut his credit where he owed that much money. He would need to pay them and then have no cash to continue his business!

In just four months, he went from earning seventy thousand a month, to being bankrupt. This one credit card company bankrupted him, and he lost his business and took from us our top earner. That second punch I mentioned? I did the same exact thing with this credit card company! I knew it would be a matter of time before they cut my credit as well.

A short time after that, I received a very rude call from a representative of this credit card company who said that it had been a long time since they reviewed my account. Now I had just come off a great 2010 and had the audited financials of 2010 and 2011 to show them. I proudly offered these up, told him that in the eight years I used the card I had never once been late with a payment, and that I was a very good customer because we accept this card from all our locations for our service; which was way worth what they gave me for credit. Despite all that, on a Friday afternoon, these chicken shits sent me an email to wipe out my credit with them, when I owed them thirty-five thousand dollars. If I paid them, I would not have been able to pay any other bills the following month. They forced me to the brink of bankruptcy just like they did my top owner and they cancelled my credit for both the franchisor company as well as my own franchise.

With another year of declining sales and losing more owners, I had to dig deep into my credit to keep things moving. Before long I was up to three hundred fifty thousand in debt, when I started this venture having more than a half million dollars in cash. I knew I couldn't sustain this any longer and had to make some very big decisions. Either I laid people off, or I went into a debt management program so that I could restructure my debt and keep everyone working. I told the staff what I was going to have to do and told them this was their last chance to step up.

The debt management company had a huge track record for other corporations and told us to not take any calls from my creditors and to pass all of them onto them to negotiate with. That was a huge mistake, in fact, the entire deal was a mistake. Several creditors sued me personally, including that POS credit card company that started my wicked decline in the first place. My credit was instantly ruined, going from 810 to the 590 range, and I was loaded with bad remarks. On top of all this, my loving, precious wife, moving toward becoming my ex-wife, stopped paying the home mortgage despite her four-thousand-dollar monthly support payment, and put the house into foreclosure. My name was still on the mortgage. Since the court awarded her the house (thinking erroneously that she had the kids) there was nothing I could do to prevent this. If I paid the mortgage, she would continue to take that money and the support payment. I had to play "chicken" with this to see if I could get her to relinquish the house.

What does Caden decide he was going to do during this time? He decided he was going to extend his country club benefits by coming in to the office at ten thirty every morning and leaving by two every afternoon. I mean, there was nothing pressing going on anyway. It wasn't like I was watching myself slip into bankruptcy and bleeding from every possible avenue while living in an office building that I converted into an apartment with my poor kids having to have to endure this with me.

Dominic was also no help at all. By the end of this next year, he wasn't doing a damn thing that I should have been paying him for. The retreat failed to inspire either of them. Going into debt management failed to inspire them even though they knew this was a last-ditch attempt to save their jobs. Instead, Caden just stopped coming in all together. This went on for three weeks while my patience was nearing its end.

When he finally did show up, I asked him what he was doing. During his absence, several owners showed up at our office and all of them remarked "I guess Caden isn't in again?" Even our owners knew he was checking out. He told me that he got "more work done at home" than he did at the office. I inquired what exact work that was since the real work was in the office. He had no answer, because the truth was, the only work he did at home was his own. It got to the point where my cash was gone, and I had no choice but to lay everyone off—the entire staff of the franchise system.

Willy and Gabe were kind enough to stay and work. At least there were a few that would stay on the sinking ship with me. The rest rolled out, way more concerned about their own affairs than the affairs of the company. After only a month, I told Caden and Dominic that I would not be recalling them. I replaced them both by taking a new trainer I had in my Mr. Sandless by the name of Tony and promoting him to management. He replaced both without missing a beat. They brought that little to the table.

Even so, I gave them both an offer that most other people would have jumped on in an instant. I offered to give them a franchise in the area where Dylan was number one in the company, along with a service vehicle, and a full set of equipment and supplies, so that they could have their own business. Caden didn't even respond to the offer. Dominic wrote to me an email, ripping the offer as a "joke" because "Caden is so talented that he doesn't need any help" from me. Dominic then opened a carpet cleaning company, and Caden opened a tile and grout company.

Instead of doing this "on his own" and with his "own talents" Caden used the Mr. Sandless business address to set up and launch his tile and grout company. Not only that, he was offering wood floor refinishing. So was Dominic. I had to call Caden and tell him that he had to change his business address because I wasn't about to allow him to palm off my customers to his new business. No good deed goes unpunished.

I got out of 2012 wondering when or if the bloodshed would stop. The only saving grace that year was my kids. I put together a wonderful Christmas program, trying desperately to distract them that instead of spending Christmas in our home, we would be spending it in an office building. We started around 8 P.M. on Christmas Eve where they could open one large gift each hour and in between I had all these games and crazy things for us to do until the wee hours of Christmas morning. Both kids said it was the best Christmas ever! Thinking back on it now, I guess I was just blessed that it turned out that way, because my heart really at the time was broken.

I was so glad it was great for them, and while I loved being with them and being their father and care-giver, I couldn't believe how far I had fallen. Would it all come down to "last man standing" with just me running the entire franchise system? It was beginning to look like I was not going to be able to hold this company afloat any longer.

CHAPTER **14**

More of the Less

NEVER IN THE first ten years of Mr. Sandless was there a time of real "peace". Instead it was always one thing, on top of another, on top of another and on and on. When I would clear on issue, two more would crop up. And nothing was ever really clear anyway! It seemed every single person or company or competitor I had an issue with came back to haunt me yet again. Coming out of 2012 was no different as two more major events shook the company to its core.

To start with, one of my owners sent me via email an anti-Mr. Sandless advertisement flyer. There was no name on it as to who created the piece, but he claimed that a customer gave it to him and that customer said they got it from yet another competitor. Here we go again!

The flyer was very well done—professionally done—not something that was just thrown together. In it were four "tests" that showed the difference between this competitor's finish, our Mr. Sandless finish, and two over-the-counter products. According to the test results, our finish was not even as good as some cheap over the counter product, and of course, their finish was the gold standard. Now we had already done multiple third-party tests, double blind tests by top of the line labs, and against oil-based urethane and beat them. So, my first problem with these so-called tests was that they would have to know our system to use our products. Unless they totally infiltrated our franchise, this would not be possible. None of these tests could therefore accurately portray the results of our system.

The next issue I had was the tests themselves. Two of them were totally made up! Not only that, the one that was legitimate was presented backwards to make their finish look that much more impressive. I had to learn more about this and confirm if in fact it was this competitor, who must remain nameless, who were the ones responsible for this or if it was just one of their owners who created it themselves. I also need to know if they had actual Mr. Sandless products and if they did, how they got them, and if these tests were faked as I thought. I sent the ad to Mason who would craft a letter to the attorneys of this company to inquire what this all may mean.

Meanwhile, I received a notice that Bill Dabb wanted to sell his Mr. Sandless business. This was the guy as you may recall who first came to me years earlier to add a sanding element to his Mr. Sandless business. He won franchise of the year two years later and I got to know him a little better. He was a real blowhard, trumpeting his prowess to the other guys in the system, claiming he had four trucks on the road doing the service. With everything else going on at the time, I didn't pay that much attention to it. But this guy seemed to me to have a screw loose somewhere. Dabb told me a story of where his father made him fight a neighborhood kid until they were both bloodied and bruised, and it seemed to me the old man was as screwed up as he made his son.

Ever since Dabb added the sanding element, he was a real "Debbie Downer" on Mr. Sandless. Every single time he wrote to me it was to talk down to me, like he had a bug up his butt. In other words, been there, done that with that jerk guy the Orb and many others. Dabb took the Orb's place in this department. If we sent out an announcement, Dabb would respond to me personally with some sort of shot. When he was contacted about some issue with his site, he was always surly and negative. He never had a good thing to say about Mr. Sandless.

After two years of his crap, I had enough, and I sent Tony down to one of Dabb's job sites to investigate and see what this guy was using on the floors. Dabb's team at the job Tony visited were all illegals doing the work, and they readily showed the urethane they were given to use; certainly not our product. All of this was recorded on both pictures and video. Dabb heard from his guys that we inspected him and basically said "bring it" if we wanted to come after him. I was *very* happy to see he was going to sell out and move on.

We had a five-thousand-dollar transfer fee at Mr. Sandless at the time per franchise. While it was clearly in his Agreement with us, this drove Dabb crazy as he didn't want to pay it. The transfer fee was earned, believe me. I would spend more time on a person buying an existing Mr. Sandless than a new owner coming on board, usually five times as much time! On top of that, we had to train the new owner and then spend time after training to make sure they were up to speed with everything.

Of course, Dabb was a real jerk about his sale with his "holier than thou" approach to me. It seemed to me this guy had a real dislike of me on a personal level, and I had no idea why. I allowed him to sand when he requested it, it made him a lot of money. I personally congratulated him on being franchise of the year and gave him an award and allowed him to speak at the event. Any time he had a problem I always responded quickly and professionally. I had no idea what was in his head to have such disdain for me.

The first person he found to sell his business to, I spent an enormous amount of time with—way more time than I should have spent because I wanted to get Dabb out of my company. Despite my best efforts and my belief that this new owner would light up that market, he bailed on the purchase. Dabb of course, in his usual manner, blamed *me* for the loss of the sale! No one worked harder on that sale than I did, so that was a total crock. It was shocking to me that the guy didn't move forward as well.

After his first sale fell through, Dabb grew to be much more of a pain in the ass. We had to move the entire website to a new private server and there was some issue in the transition. On occasion, some

CEO OF INSANITY

things didn't work right. But after about three weeks, we got everything functioning, when I received a bizarre email from Dabb. This is so you can see how this jerk treated me. Now remember, this email was sent totally out of the wild blue yonder and you will notice how much this is like the Orb.

"*How's that database working for you*" It said. That's it. No preface. No grammar. No punctuation. No explanation as to what this is referring to. This, after being blamed for the loss of his sale pushed me to respond in this manner.

"*Are you drinking or something Bill? Because I don't mind read and I would have to in order to understand what exactly this email is about or refers to. If you are having trouble with your database, you have to send a notification to support for help. As of the last announcement to go out two weeks ago, there were three owners still having difficulty logging on, and all three were fixed two weeks ago. So, if this is to ask me if everything is working well, then yes, thanks for asking, it is. Now is there anything else I can help you with? Next time, you can invite me to happy hour with you.*"

This was sent to me after 5 P.M. on a Friday. I believed my assumption could have been correct, especially with the follow up email he sent.

"*Almost as incoherent as your last notification.*" What that was supposed to mean, I had no idea, other than my explanation in that announcement that shit happens when it comes to cloud access to our website. I waited until the next day to respond to this "incoherent" response.

"*Bill: My books are hosted on a third-party server that I pay for each month, and they are a very reputable online server. There are many times throughout each month where we can't get on. It happens in the land of the internet all the time. It isn't just us.*

As for your comment regarding my last notification, I would tread very lightly if I were you. As you know, we have inspected your jobs and have both pictures and video of urethane being used—not our urethane. We videoed your "guys" telling us they use urethane. Want to give me any more smart remarks now Bill? I have been hoping and praying for you to sell your franchise and will support any valid candidate who comes along to purchase your business, and I have even sent guys to look at it for sale. That is your only hope and why I don't terminate with extreme prejudice. Now perhaps you should go back and read that notice once again with this in mind.

I am sick of your attitude with me when you are breaking both the law and our Agreement completely. You want out? I want you out. So, let's be civil until that happens and with both of us working to exit you out of Mr. Sandless, I'm sure we can accomplish that."

And of course, a nasty response.

"Dan, A little sensitive, are you? My first line was to ask if you knew the database was down, as CEO I figured you would, I was wrong. My second response was letting you know politely that your last announcement was illegible, the font was so large that all the sentences overlapped. But I could make out a bit of what you were trying to say.

Now I just got back from my morning run, 10 miles in 1:16:32, not bad after sitting in happy hour all night pondering your reply. So, I am pretty clear right now.

For you to think I did not know your guys visited one of my jobs is alarming, I know exactly what went on, and so do my attorneys, who by the way state I am not acting illegally in any regard, and we are willing to defend it at all cost, and we know this could get very expensive for both of us, fortunately I am in a very good position to back this fight if it comes about, are you?

It is hard to follow a CEO that cannot even satisfy a client to the point that the client posts a terrible review on rip off reports, hurting everyone, then the same CEO turns around and asks us to tell prospective franchisees that all is great, did you really want us to lie for you as well. Many of us do feel that we were sold a bill of goods, how many of us have invested our life savings in your dream to fall flat on our faces while you continue down the same path without regard to the lives you have negatively impacted. Or maybe your personal life has been affected by poor decision making, only you know that answer. Regardless I am still trying to sale this franchise as it may have some value, if not it is not a financial gain for me any longer and I will allow my employees to continue operating the Sandless only operations, don't worry, we will meet our minimums, and then shut it down at the end of the agreement. I can remain civil until this sell, but if this is the time for dick measuring, I am all in. Bill"

Let me take a moment to explain why I wanted to strangle this guy after getting this. Sure, I was a little "sensitive". This total prick was using a toxic urethane on his sanding jobs when we are a green company. He was lying to our customers. On top of that, he was using illegal aliens as his workforce, which no matter what his "attorneys" said was against the freaking law. So yeah, rightly so I was concerned!

In no way could he stretch his explanation of what he sent me further than he did. How was "How's that database working out for you?" mean that he was asking if I knew if the database was down? It wasn't down; he just was having his own computer issues of which we have no control. Then he wanted to say that "almost as incoherent as your last notification" was supposed to tell me that the last announcement wasn't legible because the font was too large? What was I, some kind of mind reader? No, he was a prick and now he was trying to backpedal away from being a prick and make it seem like it is all on me. You will also notice the shots about my personal life and my financial standing. And this was a top owner in my system?

Then he was going to remind me of his physical prowess by running ten miles in an hour and a quarter. This was "Napoleonic Complex" as this jerk was five foot nothing and on top of that, he was another Corentine who thought that just because I was in a poor financial state, that I couldn't fight his insurrection. He ripped me for a seriously insane client I will tell you about later, and you can clearly see he had a "power" issue with me over being CEO of my own international company. Then he bemoaned the "bill of goods" he was sold when this prick was making $700K a year with his Mr. Sandless—for buying in at a lousy $15K. Yeah, right, some bill of goods I sold him.

And a wrap up with some idle threat about shutting down and his wonderful and impressive "dick measuring" contest. *He's all in*? We will see. I took on Maypan, I took on Silas Jones, I took on Corentine and this guy wasn't even in their league—he just thought he was!

Meanwhile, that competitor responded to Mason's inquiry admitting that they did create the flyer, that they sent it to their system franchisees to use if their clients asked about us, and that they did in fact have our products. Well, all that did was open a can of worms that I needed to know way more about! Did I have a rat in my company who gave them our products? How did they acquire them without my knowledge? I had a leak somewhere, so I had no choice but to have Mason file suit against them. They immediately filed a counter-suit against Mr. Sandless and me personally for some nonsense.

To turn the heat *way* up on this, Mason, filed another case against them in a different court. Yes, I knew this was going to cost literally tens of thousands of dollars. I also knew that I was broke and headed for bankruptcy. But you know what? The hell with it! If I was going to go out, I was going to go out fighting! I could not allow these assholes to screw me over like they were.

Back to Dabb, who I was thrilled to hear had another buyer for his franchise. Unfortunately, this character with a last name very close to sounding like "Dumbass", was *nowhere* near the caliber of the first guy Dabb had on the hook. I would be taking someone who really was a dumbass as a franchisee to replace the successful and belligerent Dabb. It was worth the trade, because at least this Dumbass guy was nice and respectful.

I spent about a month with this guy in doing a one on one webinar with him, answering his multiple questions and guiding him to the sale. He finally sent me an agreement of sale as well as an equipment list on what he was getting. I was rather shocked at what he was supposedly buying. Dabb had just the Sandless refinishing part of his business listed as far as equipment, vehicles and trucks were concerned. Missing completely were the dustless sanding equipment and vans that Dabb bragged about having.

I placed a call to Dumbass and asked if he even knew what exactly he was buying. He said to that point, he hadn't even seen the system! He went on a couple of estimates with Dabb and that's about it. So, he wasn't aware that Dabb offered both Sandless and dustless refinishing. My heavens, he didn't even know what the service was that he was going to buy! The price was a quarter of a million dollars, so I told him he had every right to see both services before he came on board. He had that right, even though Dabb was trying to say he didn't.

Just as I got off the phone with Dumbass, Dabb sent me the same bill of sale. I responded with letting him know that Dumbass had sent it to me as well, to ask why he was not listing all the sanding equipment and vans in the sale, and to remind him that once he sold, he would have a two year non-compete with Mr. Sandless. That means he would be out of the flooring business. It seemed obvious to me that Dabb would sell his "Sandless" part of the business to Dumbass, then turn right around and open a sanding company to continue that part of his business, basically screwing Dumbass *and* Mr. Sandless in one giant swipe.

Dabb responded with; "good questions," as if patting me on the back for discovering his deception was going to help. He said he was completely aware of the non-compete and that once he made the sale, he was out of the flooring business. But to add yet another monkey wrench into this scenario, he said that he sold all his sanding equipment to his sanding crews, and now he pays them to sand by the square foot and then his Sandless guys go in to coat, creating as he put it a "win-win" for all involved.

Then best of all, he told me he was consulting with a company to help get them launched, and that he was opening an e-commerce import and distribution company and secured his first twenty-five-thousand-unit order that "left Ningbo Port", with a "little over a $4M order". Now this clown started to make sense to me after all! He looked down on me because I created this system coming out of the music world and a janitorial company and that drove him crazy. Just like Maypan, he thought that I was beneath his level and he despised me because he was so much smarter than me. Now he believed he was going to get that chance to show me!

You know, it was as I said in the last chapter. Where I was humble about what I achieved, Dabb was arrogant and believed he was at my level. I will admit I made it look easy on the surface, because I never paraded all the madness I endured to the system to keep appearances high. But make no mistake. Having the kind of success I had was rare and I knew that Dabb did not have the disposition to be able to duplicate it.

I responded to Dabb to inquire where this left Dumbass! I mean, while Dabb had a deal with these guys to sand for him whenever he needed them, that didn't mean that they would honor the same deal with Dumbass. They could have raised their rates significantly to make it so that Dumbass couldn't afford to sand any longer. Not only that, I inquired if his sanding guys wouldn't mind signing a non-compete as well to keep them from working with Dabb in the future.

Dabb responded by saying that Dumbass had no deal in place with the Sandless guys either, and that they could up as well leaving him stranded. I responded that his thinking was totally incorrect in this area. Dumbass would own the vehicles and equipment for Sandless refinishing, so that if those guys left, he could just replace them and not lose business. However, if the sanding guys left, Dumbass would have no equipment or vans at all and would instantly lose this part of the business! I also asked him if the vans he sold to the sanding guys had our decal package on them, because these sanders could easily be palming off customers thinking they were getting Mr. Sandless. Then I reminded him that if he showed Dumbass how to use regular urethane instead of our products, he would be setting himself up for a massive lawsuit from Dumbass when we terminated his franchise.

Not only that, I let him know he had another serious issue with all of this. The IRS had been cracking down on "sub-contractors" like Dabb had been using his sanding guys. Let me put it this way. He told them where to go, what time to get there, what to do, what color to stain the floor and every other detail about the customer and the job. That is not a sub-contractor by law but an employee! So now if he passed this along to the new buyer, then what? He would be selling a massive liability.

Despite me telling all of this to Dabb, I told very little to Dumbass. All I told him was that he needed to get out to see both services, to meet his crews and to do better due diligence to make sure he knew what he was buying. I never mentioned the sale of equipment and vans by Dabb, or his arrangement with his sanders, or the potential of breaking the employment laws. That was up to him to find out for himself.

All of this had Dabb on full alert, and so he told me he would pass all off my concerns to his attorney, and I sent this to Mason as well. There were a lot of legal ramifications in all this madness that had to be addressed before I allowed Dabb to sell. Again, I just wanted him out of my company. But his own game-playing and miss-management was making that difficult to say the least.

When Dabb replied, he said that his attorney wanted to speak to me about this personally. I told him that I was represented by counsel and would not speak directly to his attorney, but that Mason would take his call. Prior to that, Dumbass wrote a very short email to me saying he was not going to get financing to be able to purchase Dabb's business and I let Dabb know that as well. While I knew that Dabb had some issues that had to be addressed, he unfortunately would not be selling and so it wasn't that pressing at that minute.

Meanwhile, it was back to the other competitor issues and lawsuits. Through discovery, we learned that they obtained Mr. Sandless sealer and finish from a Mr. Sandless owner. After reading the details they provided, I realized this was not as it seemed. The owner didn't freely "give" them anything.

One of the competitor's franchisees got a job with a friend where they would stage a job for our guy to do. They were able to watch the system first hand through hidden cameras I suppose. While they claimed the technician "gave" them the sealer and finish, it was much more likely that they stole it from the technician's van when he was at lunch.

This competitor was known for doing this type of thing, called "mystery shopping" where they set up fake jobs so that they could test their compliance of their system with their owners. The person doing the fake job would identify themselves as a mystery shopper and then collect samples of what would be used so that they could send it back to corporate labs for testing to be sure that the franchise was compliant and used their product line—you know, the same product line they significantly marked up! This is the same crap they pulled on my guy, only they had no authority to obtain the products. That meant to me that they simply stole them.

It also showed the desperation of this company as their corporate entity knew what they were going to do and accepted our products for testing! They were sick and tired of getting their asses kicked when they went head to head with us. These franchise owners were being hurt by our owner where they operated and wanted some type of ammunition to use against us.

I had to fly to this company's home state with Mason for depositions. The first day they were to depose me, and the next day, we got to depose them. For their deposition of me, they videotaped me, as if that was going to intimated me or something. Their lawyer, who did all their legal work; I found to be a real prick, who decided I was the bad actor in all of this. Please! I had already been deposed by Maypan and so everything after that was going to be a cake walk. Other than that, there was nothing they found out in the deposition that they could really use in this case.

When we deposed them, it was with their top guys—the president of the company, the head manager and the lab tech who did the supposed tests. I helped Mason out by sending him a long list of questions to use, and during the testimony, I would write out additional questions on a pad for him to see so he could ask these things.

There were only a couple of good parts. The manager spoke of a franchise that failed in their hometown. When Mason inquired as to why they failed, the manager replied, "A bad business plan I guess". The franchise system *was* the business plan! I guess that answer didn't sit well with upper management. Then the lab guy told us that he tested the finish on glass, not wood. Our product only adheres to wood. So, any tests results would be false to say the least. They, as so many others did in the past, assumed that the products were the key to Sandless refinishing. They were wrong. The system is the key to the refinishing. Without knowledge of the system, they would not be able to reproduce our results, and so the medium they used made no difference. That was why their test results were so bad compared to our own third-party tests.

Just as with Maypan, the judge who would hear the case set us up for a settlement hearing to see if we could resolve our issues. The judge they put us with was a woman; a real pistol. Just like the other judge in the Maypan case, she did the usual blah, blah, blah about how settling was best for everyone. She made fun of the competitor's slogan, saying that she didn't see how in the world they could retain such a generic term. She also acted as if what they did was no big deal—easy for her to say. We had no idea at that point how many customers and franchisees received this false ad, and how much money that cost us. We were prepared to show that the massive decline we experienced in franchise sales correlated to the release of their advertisement!

After her initial announcement, the judge met with us separately. For their side, she told them that they would have to do something to get out of this. For me, she told me that she thought a slap on the wrist was more than enough for what they did. My issue was, I was confident that they were sharing this negative false ad with people looking to take a franchise and was why I sold no franchises that year. I wasn't even getting any leads like I used to. Who knows how far the damage went!

After going back and forth multiple times and making no progress, this judge was really on me to let them walk. To this point, with all the legal maneuvers, and the flights and hotels and depositions and Mason's fees, I was out sixty thousand dollars! There was *no way* I was letting them walk. When she told me that, I went off on her.

"I had two guys break into my home and they stole some music equipment I had in the living room," I said sternly to her. "Thanks to a very sharp detective, he tracked these two guys down and they were arrested. He asked me to come to the trial, but not attend—just to be around in case he needed me. He walked out of the trial to ask me my opinion on what to do next. It seemed the two thieves had brought with them to trial the equipment they stole from me. Their thought was that they would return what they stole, so there would be no harm and no foul, and those charges could be dropped. In other words, nothing more than a wrist slap.

I told the detective that this was not acceptable. I already had spent money to replace the equipment, I didn't know if there was any damage to what they were giving back to me, and they are thieves and should be punished. The detective then asked me what else could happen to make this work. I said that they should pay me for what I spent on the new equipment and at least this was a fair punishment. He agreed and that is what happened. I am not letting these guys off with a wrist slap."

I thought Mason would have a heart attack the way I went after this judge and the judge looked like she literally was going to explode!

I was however, totally willing to settle and move on from this as I had way more pressing issues. We were able to come up with a deal to settle all matters and signed an agreement that is confidential.

After this failed with this company, they then thought they would "one up me" with adding a new element to their floor service. I was already well-versed in this particular type of finish. The company that invented it went bankrupt!

To try and stay ahead of us, all they did was shoot themselves in the foot. They didn't care about their owners. If they did, they would have done the research and never forced their owners to add this expensive finish. Not only that, the service itself was two and a half times our standard service price! Who was going to pay for that?

That's the funny thing about franchising. You can try and force your owners to do things. You can't force them to do something that is good for them. You can't force them to do something that is bad for them—try as you may. This competitor's owners basically revolted without telling the corporate office. They resorted to concentrating solely on cabinet refinishing and skipping the floors altogether!

I have one owner who gets floor work from that competitor owner in his city. The guy refuses to do floors and turns them over to Mr. Sandless. I have another owner who has one in his market. He is often out doing floors and sees the guy doing cabinets. While we can and will do kitchen cabinets, it is only a very small part of what we do. They can have the cabinets which takes them a week to refinish, while we do five customer's wood floors in that same time. That works for us!

One of my new owners looked deeply into their system before he came on board with us. He spoke to all their owners in the region before making his decision. Not even one of them were doing wood floors and told him that they were "afraid" to. I no longer even consider this company competition.

As all of this was unfolding through the first two thirds of 2013, my friend Dabb started to lose his mind. Just as we settled the advertising matter in August of that year, Dabb's earnings dropped by fifty percent. The next month, another fifty percent, and the next, and the next. Then in November, Dabb reported no earnings. We sent him an enforcement notice to see what was going on. Just as I thought, he blamed me for losing his sale of his franchise—you know, the sale where he was going to sell Dumbass a shell of a business and then continue to sand thinking I wouldn't notice. Now he was "done" and said it was time for "dick measuring".

What he was hanging his hat on was a certain part of the language of our franchise agreement. While we immediately added "dustless refinishing" to our list of services in the agreement when I added the sanding element to the system, we didn't add the word "sanding" to the wording in the contract. So what Dabb hoped for was to be able to sand and we couldn't stop him. This was a wicked stretch to be honest. We listed sanding as competition and the agreement clearly stated that you can't compete with us. On top of that, this was no reason to bail on his agreement. In other words, he was never going to win this. Still, he had the balls to say, "try and stop me". I instructed Mason to file in high court an injunction against Dabb. This kind of crap never seems to end!

Once again, it was discovery and deposition times. Dabb hired a local franchise firm that the competitor company had hired to represent them here locally. These two jerkoffs already hated me with their loss in that case, and their defense of the injunction was the "kitchen sink" method. That is; the system stunk, he didn't make any money, we lied to Dabb, he never got any support, he never made any money, and oh yeah did we mention that the system sucked, and Dan was a prick defense. To counter all of this was too easy. This SOB earned sixty thousand a month for five years in this "sucky" system, including prior to us adding the sanding element. That's $3.6 million dollars for an investment of fifteen thousand dollars. *Please!*

Once again, I had to be deposed as was Dabb. This must have cost Dabb some serious bucks. The deposition was taken in Mason's conference room and Dabb had both lead attorneys from this firm there to grill me. Good luck with that. There wasn't a damn thing that they asked that showed a single thing. They tried to twist my words, twist Dabb's words, twist the wording of the agreement but at the end of the day, all they were doing was blowing smoke and they knew it. They knew that there was no way the court was going to allow Dabb to simply walk away and sand.

Then Mason questioned Dabb from a spreadsheet of questions I sent him. It turns out I was correct. Dabb had a personal thing with me and Mason explained it best.

"This guy looks down at you," he said. "He can't believe that someone like you created this floor system and the franchise system.

He threw out that you were nothing more than a janitor, who he believes is beneath him and he is incredulous that someone as "great" as him has to be subjected to you".

That was exactly how I read it as well. I love this from people who never did a damn thing on their own. That was why Dabb threw his "ten-mile run" in my face—because he was trying to say he was superior to me. That was why he threw out that he landed a "4 million-dollar deal" with his stupid new company.

As was the norm and had been done many times now, we were to meet with a judge for yet another settlement hearing. Dabb and his two lawyers were on the left and Mason and I on the right. When the judge entered the courtroom and we rose, he held our franchise agreement over his head.

"This will hold up in my courtroom!" he announced.

Well, that was about that; the fastest win I ever had. This judge met with both parties separately. I told him that I just wanted this guy out of my company, but that if Dabb wanted to continue to sand, I would let him, but he would have to pay me full term royalty. That was more than fair.

While the judge brought back both attorneys to review some materials, I ripped into Dabb. Prior to this, I went into his company database and added up how many Sandless refinishing jobs he had done in his tenure and how many dustless refinishing jobs. Sixty six percent of his work over the five years was…drum roll please…Sandless refinishing! So much for his claim that "Sandless sucked". This total POS even went so far as to purchase the URL "sandlesssucks.com" in case he wanted to launch against us. Very reminiscent of my wife's antics.

The judge in this case really took a liking to me. He asked me to explain our floor service to him and then inquired as to how he could get his floors done. I offered to do his service for free and I thought Mason was going to fall off his chair and pass out when I did this! I didn't know that the judge could not accept an offer like that and it could get him in trouble for potential "conflict of interest" or some such madness. I apologized to the judge, saying I didn't know and that I didn't want to get him in trouble. But I honestly think he appreciated the offer nonetheless.

Dabb insisted that he was "out" and wanted no part of floor refinishing any more, after all, he had his new venture that was going to be so very successful that he no longer needed to be in the flooring business. We agree to take twenty-five thousand dollars as a penalty for the royalty he cost us, and he agreed to the injunction to be out. Or did he?

After five years of this prick in my company, I *knew* 100% that he was not ever going to be out. I fully expected him to simply pick up where he left off and not skip a beat, thinking there was no way we could catch him. Mason said he would have to be a total fool, because this was a high court injunction that he was out. If he broke the agreement, he could actually have landed in jail! But I knew better, so I bet Mason a "nice lunch" if my claim came to pass.

I figured Dabb would work through his wife's family construction business to do his floors and that was how he hoped to fly under the radar. I hired a private investigator who lived right in his area to see what he could find out. This guy turned out to be great. He used his local church as the setup, as they had a wood floor in their hall that needed to be done. He called the construction business and had an estimate set up for someone to look at the floor. Low and behold, not two months after the injunction, Dabb showed up to do the estimate, even suggesting that he could do the floor "without sanding".

Mason couldn't believe how quickly we caught him, and it was exactly as I said—he went right back to it without missing a beat. Why? Pretty simple. What freaking idiot walks away for a business earning sixty thousand dollars a month? Now while he was not going to be making that kind of money without the Mr. Sandless name and website, he could easily still do in the thirty-thousand-dollar range. This guy was yet another greedy bastard.

Back to high court we went. Nothing pleased me more than to beat these two jackass lawyers who represented Dabb, who tried to twist this to put the blame on me—that *I* was the unscrupulous business owner. No, it was their precious Dabb who was unscrupulous. They both had the look on their faces of defeat; that they knew their client was a total jerk.

Dabb bounded into court like a kid at recess. "Here we are again!" he said jovially. My face scrunched up as if I was listening to a lunatic and I even said to myself, "this guy is bonker-beans". The judge took me back to his chambers along with Mason for some idle banter and asked what would make me happy. I told him my number and then he met with the dejected Dabb lawyers and the bouncing Dabb. What a loon.

Then the judge called Mason and me back to his chambers again.

"This guy is really a bit squirrelly, isn't he?" the judge asked.

"I think he is off his rocker, your honor!" I exclaimed. With that we had another agreement and Dabb had to pay a whooping one hundred fifty thousand dollar fine. This money came in at the last minute of 2013. On the books, I was negative one hundred and fifty thousand dollars. I was worried that if I did not have earnings to show, that I would not pass my audit and not be allowed to franchise. The auditor from 2012 was already indicating that if things didn't pick up, we may not be allowed to franchise. No state is going to allow a business to franchise when it seems they are failing.

But the influx of this timely fine saved the day. I paid up all the over-due bills and ended the year with just a bit of profit, enough to squeak by the audit and live to see another day of franchising. We refinished the floor for the church that we used to set up Dabb for free and they came out perfect with Mr. Sandless. So much for Dabb's bullcrap. And on top of this, Dabb's "huge deal" failed. It was some wickedly expensive tire inflator for changing a flat. Who was going to pay two hundred bucks when you can get triple A coverage for fifty?

Did I make it off the bottom yet? Was this the turn of the tide for me? Not yet, I'm afraid. Unknown to me at that time, I had not hit the bottom yet. That was coming, and I didn't even see it.

CHAPTER **15**

Take it to the Limit

WHEN YOU FIND yourself going through something like this maddening nonsense I was forced to endure, for such a very long time, and with so many people who I trusted, it is very hard to see light at the end of the tunnel. You just become numb to it all and expect the worst. There was no "hope" in my heart that things would turn around because every time it seemed it may, that went away like a puff of smoke in the wind. It was all nothing more than a mirage.

It is also impossible to see that these events were all somehow connected in a long spiritual journey, instead of just being a long series of never-ending "bad luck". I already had been forced to learn one seriously valuable lesson. Standing on principle was worthless. The first time I did this, where I totally believed I did no wrong, and would not cave to an extortionist, destroyed my savings and ultimately in the end, when I won out over Maypan, it was a hollow victory at best. Yes, he was out of my company. But I had to pay him back, this cost me an enormous amount of money for the litigation as well as another lawsuit from my former attorneys. Hindsight is twenty-twenty for sure. Had I known then what I know now, I would have negotiated to give him fifty thousand in the first month and gotten rid of him quickly. This would have saved me so very much grief and money.

It seemed this is a lesson that I really had to learn. You see, I always believed that I should stand on principle to the end. That may be fine if it isn't going to cost you anything. But the only people who win when you do this in litigation are the lawyers. It is best to compromise, make a deal and move on quickly. I did this in just four months with Corentine. Yes, that cost me thirty thousand as well. But this jerk did not get my company or system, and I got him quickly out of my company.

I proved that I learned this lesson with SxBoost when I immediately settled with them to relinquish those simple words. Yes, I probably would have won. But it would have cost me over a hundred thousand dollars just to do that. No handful of words are worth that!

I also learned that being an optimist was a losing proposition. I am sorry to say this but being a realist will keep you way more out of trouble than being an optimist. I always saw the best in people and look where that got me with my family, friends, my workers, my owners and my wife. It would be far better to not be so trusting and giving, as hard as that was for me.

But despite learning all these things, I knew I wasn't past "the test" of my life yet. I totally believed that I would know for certain when I did reach the end—it would be that easy to see. I knew I wasn't there yet, despite all I had been through. I wondered how many more body blows it would take, how much more it would cost me, how many more people must I lose in my life and how long before it all ended. Even with me feeling like I was the rock, I was still just a man, and one man can only take so much.

I never, not once lost my faith in God during the entire time. My faith was unwavering, and I knew at some point I would be delivered. Okay, possibly I would lose everything and have to start over. As long as I had my kids and God, nothing else really mattered. I was going to go where the journey took me—right to the bitter end.

Moving into 2014, I was still in a very precarious position. During the three years prior, I can't tell you how many things I tried to get the franchise side to pick up. We offered the franchise for just $10K including the equipment package. That didn't work. We offered the franchise for $15K with us self-financing $10K of that. That didn't work. Both times the owners we brought in with these things were the worst yet! When they have no skin in the game, they just simply don't care! They didn't care that they walked away from the business when they had no real investment to lose.

I tried raising the royalty and that didn't work. I tried advertising on a dozen different sites and that didn't work. Most of these sites got one lead for franchising and send it out to many clients who are advertising with them. They were nothing more than a total rip-off. I was beating my head against a wall. *Nothing* I tried worked!

In the first quarter of 2014, my ex-wife abandoned my house, leaving it to foreclosure. I petitioned the divorce court to give me the house back and they agreed. But I would have to first fight the foreclosure. I signed up through the mortgage company to claim a hardship and see if they could waive the massive fees, penalties and interest so that I could take the house back and start to make payments. I did in fact have good cause. My wife had control of the house and was awarded it prior to the divorce. I was paying her plenty of money to be able to pay the mortgage. She just decided not to, and there was nothing I could do about it.

This mortgage company was the absolute worst and what else is new. The lawyers who represented them would not accept my calls. The mortgage company itself wouldn't accept my calls—even if I could pay off everything I owed! Everyone I spoke to spoke broken English! They assigned me a debt counselor to help me claim the hardship. She was absolutely worthless. I had to submit fifty different documents via an online portal just so they could consider allowing me to make the payments to catch the house up. Honestly, it seemed to me the bank was damn determined to foreclose, after all, they would end up with a property worth a lot more than they got it for. It was so damn unfair.

After a month, they made me submit all the fifty forms again, and then after another month, to submit the fifty forms yet again, all the while not being able to speak with anyone. As this continued, the lawyer fees, the interest and the penalties kept rising. In the end, they rejected my claim completely and the only thing they would offer me is to pay the mortgage to date, as well as to pay the penalty, interest, fees and lawyer fees in full. Not a single penny did they give me to help me do this and I had three months to pay or it would fall to the bank.

I went "home" that night to my make-shift apartment and made a list of the pros and cons of trying to get the house back. I typed every single consideration on the list and when I ended up, there were two things on the positive side of the sheet, and eleven things on the negative. My credit was already ruined thanks to the business and divorce. I read them to my kids and asked what they thought. It seemed clear to all of us that trying to get the house back at that point was not worth it. It was simply going to be too much to make work, and so I made the decision to let it fall to foreclosure.

When I woke up the next morning, I felt terrible about my decision! I knew right then and there that I was supposed to fight to get the house back, and that letting it go was not the right thing to do. Somehow, through selling a few franchises and fighting and clawing, over the next three months I was able to pay off the roughly forty thousand dollars due to get the home out of foreclosure. While this was about a year and a half worth of mortgage payments, more than half of the amount due was from lawyer fees, interest, penalties and fines. It wasn't like this amount came off the mortgage total. It was a total rip off, really sticking it to me.

After being out of the home for three years, returning was way more than a nightmare. My daughter and I stopped by after the home was removed from foreclosure to assess the condition of the place. Words can't describe the horror of what this woman had done to the place. To start with, I had hedges in the front of the house that I personally planted when my daughter was just a baby. They were a single stick and I planted one hundred and fifty feet of them along the front and side of the home. These hedges were trimmed and well-maintained when I was there. They were now fifteen feet tall!

The flower beds in the front of the home now housed nothing but massive weeds. Some weeds were five to six feet high and had thorns on them. The lawn was two feet high and to be honest, I don't think there was a blade of grass. It was nothing but weeds. The backyard was even worse. I had a line of trees that I planted that ran another one hundred fifty feet along the back of the property. These were supposed to be maintained like hedges, but just a bit taller; around the seven-foot mark. They were thirty feet tall and totally out of control.

There was a large swamp maple tree which apparently died during my departure and it split in half, tearing down a side of the backyard fence, collapsing onto the deck that was ripped up and unstained, and strewn about the back yard with limb debris. The pool that I had installed was filled with this green-black swamp water, as that wasn't maintained either. It was a massive breeding ground for mosquitoes and smelled of high heaven.

Going inside the house was like visiting the scene of a crime. The odor was unbearable! It was a miracle the pipes didn't break from having no heat or electric in the home for a year. There were bags upon bags of trash piled everywhere. My wife never even bothered to take the trash out for heaven sakes! There were holes punched in many doors from my wife's lovers who were apparently violent. Part of one room was burned where it looked like she allowed a large candle to go unattended. If it burnt down, I would have done better with it than this. Of course, no such luck for me.

I had been in bad places during my janitorial days when we used to clean out abandoned apartments and homes. But this was the worst I had ever seen. After just forty-five minutes, I had to exit the home, so I could catch my breath. I was a second or two away from throwing up—it was that bad.

The next day I went to the house on my own for sanity sake. I figured I would do something to make some headway on getting things under control. There was no way in the world my kids and I could move back into that house the way it was, and it was going to take a hell of a lot of work to get it back to being live-able.

I brought with me a pump, so that I could empty out the cesspool water from the pool and while I did that, I figured I would clean out all the flower beds in the front. The pump worked well, and soon the water was flowing from my back yard to a city street drain across the street from my home. Within thirty minutes, I was visited by the town's fire marshal who ordered me to stop pumping the water. He was immediately followed by the board of health inspector.

It seems that the town idiot who I dubbed "Doofy" because he looked like that character from Scary Movie, happened to be walking by that day. I had never seen him on my street before and what else is new, there he was. He smelled how bad the water from the pool was and believe me—it *did* smell like raw sewage. So, he called the township to report me. Now I had to deal with the fire marshal and health inspector.

This health inspector kept yelling at me, saying "didn't you get my notices?" I had to repeat three times that I hadn't been there in three years and that this was not only the very first day for me, but that I had only been at it for thirty freaking minutes!

"You think you could give me a couple of days to get a handle on all of this?" I asked. "I mean my God, I have been here for only thirty minutes. You are going to have to give me more time than that!"

Apparently, this health inspector had been sending my wife multiple notices that the pool had to be emptied and the yard cleaned up, and of course, my wife ignored them. Now *I'm* the bad guy in all of this even though I hadn't been there in three years.

The fire marshal proceeded to tell me that I couldn't empty the pool into the city system.

"Then what am I supposed to do to get the water out of the pool?" I asked.

"You have to dump it little by little into the grass and let it dissipate through the ground!" he told me. That was going to take like forever! I told them to give me a few days and I would get a handle on the property and that I would comply with the pool water disposal. With that, they left me. I then moved the pump to the other side of the pool to the lawn and ran it long enough to fill up that area, then I shut it down to let it sink into the ground. I figured it would take me about two months at that rate to get it to be empty. Great.

Over the next four hours, I cleaned out the flower beds in the front of the house. I filled ten large outdoor trash bags with debris. As I stood up when I was finally done, I threw my back out. My back was literally twisted into an "S" and this being the first day of the cleanout! I ran the pump one more time for thirty minutes and as the water filled that weedy area again, I dubbed the water "Lake Doofy" in honor of the man who forced me to do this.

The following day I returned to the home with a weight belt holding my back straight. The goal this day was simple: Continue to empty Lake Doofy and install a surround area in front of the trees in the back yard. The following day, Tony and my entire team at Mr. Sandless would be coming by to cut down the backyard trees to just seven feet. The plan was to shred them with a huge machine, and then use the chippings as mulch. That's why I really needed to have an enclosure around the tree line.

Before I began, I turned on the pump again to fill Lake Doofy, then I started to install the partition along the tree line. I was on my knees for hours, banging these pieces in with a rubber mallet to build this barrier. As I hit the very last piece, which happened to be right in front of Lake Doofy, I stood to stretch my already damaged back out and my knee blew out! Since I was on it so long, my knee cap separated from and fell to the right of my leg. Since I couldn't support my weight, I fell backwards…right into Lake Doofy. I was now drenched with the sewage water of Lake Doofy.

I smashed my kneecap back into place and pulled myself up. I hobbled my way down the street to the liquor store and went in for a bottle of Jack Daniels. The clerk began to speak to me.

"You know you are covered in…" she started. I raised my hand to silence her.

"I know," I replied. "Just ring me out please."

The next day, Tony and my entire team worked to chain saw the enormous trees in the backyard down to their normal size. I asked

Tony if he met his match on this job, but he was confident that he could get the forty-five trees cut. It was a nightmare of a job. Meanwhile, I took my trimmer and attempted to cut the hedges in the front yard. This tool I had was no match for fifteen-foot hedges. I pulled myself into my SUV and headed to the store to buy some type of super-powered hedge cutter thing.

As I drove down the road with my blown-out knee wrapped tight and my blown-out back belted, and in pain, I prayed to God.

"What do You want from me?" I asked. "What do You want me to do?" I was finally there. I was at the end. I was at the bottom; the lowest depths. I couldn't take any more. After Henry, Matt, Silas, Maypan, Corentine, SXBoost, StratumAble, the Orb, Sadie, Caden, Dominic, that other competitor, Dabb and finally my wife; I had reached my limit.

Just as I prayed this, I already had the radio on, but wasn't paying attention to it. Now at that very moment, either I started to notice it was on, or it turned up louder so that I would notice. There is a blind spot in that section of highway where the radio signal can't reach and it normally either cuts out there or gets significantly lower. So perhaps that is why when the signal came back in that I noticed it was on.

In any event, I listen to the song that was being played. It was "Take it to the Limit" performed by the Eagles and written by Glenn Frey, Don Henley, Randy Meisner. This song had been out since 1975, almost forty years to the day, and though I heard it so many times before, this particular time, the words played right to my heart; right to my very soul! The words to this song never meant anything to me before that moment.

"All alone at the end of the evening," it said, and yes, I felt with losing so many people in my life that I was alone, and it was in fact "the evening".

"And the bright lights have faded to blue," meant that my dream of this company had drifted so far from where it should have been. What started with such great promise, was turned to nothing but blue.

"You know I've always been a dreamer." I always dreamed big—imagined that anything and everything was possible.

"But the dreams I've seen lately, keep on turning out, and burning out, and turning out the same." That was exactly how I was feeling; that no matter how hard I tried, no matter what I did, the results kept turning out, and burning out, and turning out, the same. The repeat of those words "turning out" was so true to me.

"So, put me on a highway," which was exactly where I was listening to that song.

"And show me a sign." I knew this was a message for me personally. This song would be my sign! And what was that message?

"And take it to the limit one more time." God wanted one more thing of me in this long, torturous journey. He wanted me to take it to the limit, one more time. Did I have it in me to try one more time?

"You can spend all your time making money. You can spend all your love making time. If it all fell to pieces tomorrow, would you still be mine?" I took this as God asking me that through all this shit, was I still His? As far as I was concerned, it all had already fallen to pieces.

"And when you're looking for your freedom, nobody seems to care," about summed up exactly how I was feeling at that lowest point of my life. If I could have gotten out, I would have. I *wanted* out and no one seemed to care what I had gone through. Who wouldn't want off this screwed up ride I had been on?

"And you can't find the door, can't find it anywhere." Again, these words were exactly how I was feeling. I wanted to find the door out, but it was impossible. I couldn't leave the company that I created as my entire life was tied to it by that point. I was also stuck with the monumental task of reclaiming my home. There *was* no doorway out.

"When there's nothing to believe in." There wasn't, other than my faith in God which remained rock solid. After ten years, all life did was show me that I couldn't believe in anyone but God. He was all I had to believe in. I didn't believe I was going to be able to turn the company around. I didn't have any idea how I was going to fix all that was so broken in my life. I didn't know how I was going to recover from such an awful ordeal.

"Still you're coming back, you're running back, you're coming back for more." Now wasn't that the truth! Through all the nightmare, I kept fighting and trying, and coming back, and coming back for more. And now there I am on that highway, with God showing me a sign, and asking me to take it to the limit, one more time.

I am going to be completely honest with all of you reading this. I did not put this together until I wrote this part of the story, and when I did, it really hit me hard. I literally sobbed. You probably missed this as well. I mean, I couldn't see it until it was right in front of my face. Before I even had the name of my company and brand, I was compelled by God to work with a singer with the goal of getting a song out to someone who desperately needed to hear that song to pull them out of whatever they were in. That was my conclusion of why I was so compelled to do the Silas Jones venture. Now here I was with God doing the very same thing to me! This had come full circle.

I wondered if God influenced those writers of that song forty years earlier on my behalf? If you look at the lyrics on their own, they don't seem to make any sense at all. But they certainly made sense to me at that moment I heard them. Why did the words mean so very much to me? It was like it was written just for me! Now while that song may have influenced many other people the same way (or maybe not), I don't put this out of the realm of my God. You see, my God says to the lame man to walk and he walks, He says to the blind man to see and he sees, He says to the deaf man to hear and he hears, He rebukes the storm and it stops, He tells the man to come forth and he awakens from death. This is the God that knows the count of the hair on my head and the God who knows the count of the stars in the sky and calls them by name. This is not that far of a reach for my God, but what an epic display when I was compelled to do the very same for someone else.

I wondered if Silas Jones was influenced to write the words to that song I promoted, because just like this song, they certainly didn't seem to have any real meaning on their own. But I knew they would to that person the song was meant for—that they would get the meaning.

God also fulfilled the "deal" we had. When I set out to work with Silas, I didn't at all know why I was being compelled to do it. I made the deal that God would show me why. Now having this very same thing happen to me, that was my answer. Someone out there was at the end of their rope, cried out to God for help, and He delivered them through that Silas song. Deal fulfilled.

This one event changed everything for me. From that moment on, every time I faced adversity, I said my new slogan out loud. "Take it to the limit!" This became my battle cry. I just knew that God's promise would deliver me if I could just push this out one more time and endure. While nothing whatsoever immediately changed, at least I had something I could focus on to get through it—to get me off that bottom rung.

I eventually got the house back under control. I ordered a huge trash container that was parked in my driveway and as I threw into it bag after bag of debris from the house, I filled the container, so much so that I had to have the trash company come out and remove that one and leave another! By the time everything was cleaned up, I was billed for *six tons* of debris! Six tons! Take it to the limit.

I went to an orthopedic specialist about my knee, but not before blowing it out yet again! I was upstairs in the home installing a new curtain rod when my drill gun slipped out of my hand. My reaction was to catch it between my legs before it smashed to the ground, and I caught it right between my knees, blowing the knee out again. Take it to the limit. This time I crashed to the floor which believe it or not was better than falling into Lake Doofy!

One night during the cleanout, it poured rain. I ran over to the house and turned the pump to face the street and emptied the entire pool out without anyone noticing. That's the way to get things done! It cost me ten thousand dollars more to get the home live-able again! It needed a new furnace, all new paint which my daughter and I did, floor refinishing, which at least I had that covered, a new bath, new air conditioning unit and new hot water heater. There was nothing that wasn't broken by my wife.

On that front, I was finally granted a divorce. I had the businesses valued, which after three years of incredible decline were not worth very much anymore. The valuation cost me yet another ten thousand dollars; take it to the limit. The judge made us meet to see if we could reach a settlement and as the norm, took to coming at me as if I was the bad guy; what else was new. Because my wife and her attorney, who it seemed to me may be sleeping with her, did not have a business evaluation, the judge was not going to accept mine; take it to the limit. He also said that I was hiding the value with things like the website and trademarks not mentioned in the report I paid for.

Listen, the guy who did my report was not at all kind to me in it, pretty much blaming me for the failure of the business. I don't know where this divorce judge was thinking I was getting a good deal there. Since by that time I was like a court veteran, I was calm and rational, explained to the judge that I was more than willing to settle, and told him that I was not the problem; that my wife and her greedy lawyer were.

You would not believe what "they" asked for. Okay let me explain. This lawyer said, "What are you prepared to give us?" as if he was married to me as well. I literally had to remind them that I wasn't divorcing him! They tried to present a case where they would get fifty present of Mr. Sandless and run it with me. My lawyer said that would be impossible and I replied, "That really would take the fun out of being divorced!" Then they asked for ten franchises, as if these things ran on their own. Remember, this woman never did anything in my company, so she didn't even understand what a franchise was.

I made what I thought was a generous offer to get her out of my life, and the judge said he would speak to "them" privately to see if he could get the job done. After an hour and a half, he called me back into the meeting room. His head was in his hands and his face was beat red, exactly as the judge was when he tried to work with Maypan. When I asked him how it went, he screamed at me.

"Well you know what I am dealing with here!" he yelled. Take it to the limit your honor. Even though it took the judge, my lawyer and I to force my wife to take a deal, she finally did, although she kicked and screamed the whole time how unfair it was to her. Let me see this unfairness. She wouldn't have to work, but I would. I would have the kids and she wouldn't have to pay a dime to their care. I would have to pay the house mortgage off or get her name off it, and I had to pay her alimony for eight freaking years. The only thing that was unfair in this is that after breaking the vows of our marriage, I had to pay her. *Take it to the limit*!

The best part of this story was after that, I had to go back to court to get credit for things I paid prior to being ordered to pay support. I was entitled to around eleven thousand dollars' credit and I had every single receipt to prove this. But my now ex-wife refused to give me credit, and so back to court we went in front of another judge. In the hallway before going in, my divorce attorney asked my ex-wife's attorney why she would not give me the credit. The guy didn't have an answer. My attorney reminded him that we had receipts and that the judge was most likely going to rule in our favor. My attorney inquired what his line of defense was going to be.

"I guess I will just have to make something up," he responded. My lawyer turned to me and asked if they were having an affair. I said it was very possible because this attorney sure seemed whipped to me. Of course, the judge not only chastised his nonsense, but I was awarded the credit as well.

Now that the divorce was over with, I started to focus on turning around the company. After listening to many owner's calls through our toll-free number system, I isolated what they were all doing wrong, and concentrated on correcting these simple things. Along with that, I contracted for a company to recreate our database system with a much easier to use format that could even be paperless if the owner wanted. Low and behold, after pushing these things for nearly a year and a half, the owners started to make more money! It is amazing what can happen when they answer the stinking phone!

My kids and I moved back into the home and had a great summer there. At first, they were very apprehensive, again, like returning to the scene of a crime. But since I changed absolutely everything in the house, it was hardly recognizable. They both said they were very happy that I was able to get it back.

That was when I knew I was off the bottom, but for a little bit of reinforcement, I was sent a message to be sure I knew this. There is a bush at the front corner of my house in the flower bed that I planted. It was given to me by my sister-in law years earlier and somehow it survived the "Purge" as we now call my divorce. We also call what we lost in the divorce "The Downturn" when we are in front of other people. Anyway, this bush by that time was rather large. It bloomed once every year with these beautiful red flowers. Then after about a week, the flowers would dry up and blow away. This ornamental was outstanding for a very limited time during the year, which was always around May each Spring.

As we were entering October that year, a single red flower bloomed on the tree. I noticed it immediately because basically, this was impossible. The tree for years always bloomed all at once. Not only was that strange, but the one red flower was right in the middle of the bush—like dead middle—and right where I couldn't miss seeing it. At first, I attributed this to being just a fluke. I supposed that one of the flowers was delayed in blooming and that there was nothing more to it than that. I figured it would be gone in a week anyway.

Two weeks later, it was still there. Okay this was getting much stranger, so much so that I now was looking at it every time I came and went from the house. It was right in the middle of the tree where we entered the house, so it couldn't be missed. I told the kids I wanted to take them on a special trip that Fall, so I pulled them out of school a couple of days and we spent a long weekend at Cape Hatteras right on the beach. It was beautiful to watch the sun rise over the ocean every morning and wake up to the sound of the surf. The hotel was right on the sand!

When we returned, my flower, that I deemed "the lonely flower," was still there, now three weeks since blooming. My daughter noticed it as well. After we unpacked, I went up to it and touched the red pedals. I expected to find them drying and for the flower to be ready to fall off. But they were soft and supple, like it was brand new. Another week went by and the lonely flower was still there, still soft, still like new. By the fifth week, I had a premonition that someone was going to take the flower. For whatever reason, that would have been heartbreaking to me. I went out and snipped the bud off the tree and put it into a book to press it. The pedals were as soft as ever. This was a miracle! It was not physically possible for that flower to last in cold weather like that for so long.

That was my sign that I was passed the limit I was supposed to take this to—that I had done it—that I had endured, and that change was coming to me in a miraculous way. The beginning of the next year, I decided that I had enough of poor owners. I raised the franchise fee to twenty-five thousand dollars and lowered the royalty to just 3% so that I could attract better owners.

That first quarter was astounding! We ended up having our best year in the franchise since 2010! Yes, we continued to lose owners who were not very good, but we brought in new ones at a record pace. With the new price, I was able to not only pay all our bills but to pay off all the business debt. My entire business is debt free to this point and we even have a savings account! It was an epic turnaround in such a short period of time and to be quite honest, I don't feel like I really had anything to do with it! This was a promise from God that if I pushed on one more time, that things would change, and they sure did.

Two years later, I sold the flagship franchise that I originally started. I paid off my home mortgage and had plenty left over to get a house on an island, nine hundred feet from the water. Many, many years ago, before I married, I told my now ex-wife that someday I would own a house on the beach on an island and that dream came true!

Will it keep up? I certainly hope so. I know one thing for sure. It is *impossible* that I will ever go through something like this again. This is more than enough for one lifetime. I believe that from here, I am to move on to the next stage of my spiritual growth, and that is to share what I have learned on this journey with others. That is why I wrote this book. If there is one thing for you to learn from this, it is to not ignore the spiritual element of your life, as *that* is the real reason for living!

I am not at all finished yet with "the rest of the story." I still have to tell you about individual stories during these years involving employees, vehicles, customers and even more owner stories. Hang on, there is much more to come as this saga continues!

CHAPTER **16**

You're Hired, You're Fired!

ALONG WITH ALL the other madness I had to endure in this long period of building Mr. Sandless, there were also workers, clients and owners I had to deal with. This section is just a sampling of all the additional madness that surrounded me during this epic run.

For whatever reason, my own Mr. Sandless business seemed to attract the same types of individuals when it came to employees. They were somewhat skilled, slightly driven, and mostly medicated. Now the medication was different than I had ever witnessed being used during my music days. The choice of drug apparently these days was "Percocet" a pain reliever, but these guys didn't ingest them. They would crush them up and "snort" them, and not just one, but five, ten or even twenty of these things!

This is sometimes the cause of the extraordinary madness that my employees seemed to get into. There are so many memorable ones over the year, I will have to stick to just the most precious memories of these past employees.

The Senseless J.R.

Heaven knows where I found J.R. which everyone called him, even though it really didn't stand for anything. His name was like "Robert" somebody, so the initials did not have anything to do with his real name. I never inquired what they stood for or how he came about having them. He came to work for me as a referral from a friend who thought he would be good at what we do. This was after he was the keyboard player in the band I put together for Silas. Little did I know that not only would J.R. change my mind about something very important, but that despite his ineptitude, I would use him to develop the script that is still in use in the company today.

Prior to his hiring, I used to say that the Mr. Sandless system was so easy, that "I could teach a monkey how to do it!" I was proud of the fact that the system I created was like "paint by numbers", making it so that anyone could paint a picture. You follow the steps; the floor comes out great. It was a logical step by step process.

Along came J.R. who was not an unintelligent fellow. He worked on cars and motorcycles and played keyboards in a band. So, he had aptitude. What I was soon to discover was, he didn't have a drop of common sense. There is a big difference between intelligence and common sense. Someone with intelligence could read a book to find out how to do something, while someone with great common sense can just do it without reading about it. Most people have at least a smidgeon of common sense, but J.R. had none.

The problem this presented was that the Mr. Sandless system was one hundred percent common sense based. The way it was laid out should have made sense to J.R. But it made no sense to him at all.

For example, there are three buckets used in the system, color coded so that you *know* which comes first, second and third. They were red, white and blue so following that, red is first, white is second, blue is always last. A person with no common sense can't grasp that! For example, there was a guy I hired who stopped by the office looking for work who had twenty years of experience sanding. We were desperately busy, so I hired him immediately and took him with me that very day to service two apartments in the city.

I explained the system to him step by step including the "red, white and blue" buckets, and since we had two units to service he got to see the system twice that day. Surely the next day he would be able to grasp the basics of what he did two times the day before. But the very next day, servicing another two apartment units, he didn't retain a single thing he had done *twice* the day before! He kept getting the buckets mixed up, which you can't do in this system or you could ruin the floor job!

Once again, I explained that the buckets were in the order of the flag; red, white and blue. He nodded and said "Oh" as if he hadn't heard this several times the day before. Where we were in the system was the first bucket or red. What did he do? He grabbed the *blue* bucket of course! I stopped him again, explain again the order of the buckets, and once again he seemed to get it. Did he grab the red bucket? No, he grabbed the blue again! After ten times of this madness, I told him to stop.

I walked to the balcony of the fourth floor of the building I was in and called Caden who was on another job in the city with another new hire.

"Caden if you do not get this guy off the job with me, I am going to throw him off this balcony!" I told him. With that he sent his guy down to me, and I instructed my sander guy to go to Caden who maybe could handle him better than I could.

When we returned to the office, Caden and I sat out back and talked. He told me that the sander guy I had hired was no good, and that he was never going to grasp the system. Now this isn't because he didn't have common sense. It was because he had no sense at all! Whether he was brain dead from twenty years of breathing in toxic urethane or was brain dead from years of pill popping, it was no matter—he wasn't going to work out. Just as we finished talking, the sander guy came back to see us sitting there.

"I'm sorry, this isn't going to work out," I told him.

"So what time do you want me tomorrow?" he replied.

"You don't understand. I don't want you in tomorrow. You are fired. I am letting you go!" I told him.

"So, what does that mean?" he replied. To this day this remains the single longest firing in my entire life! I could not get this guy to understand that he was fired! It took nearly an hour to get him to pack up and leave. Normally I would have been livid. But it was lucky for him I was too tired to get aggravated after doing the two apartments nearly by myself.

Now this story takes me back to J.R. who was not totally "senseless" like this sander guy. Before I explain J.R. to you, I wanted to show you just how bad an employee could be! J.R.'s problem as I explained was *common* sense. He had the reaction time of a snail and none of the other guys wanted him on their jobs. So, it came down to me to work with J.R. as my helper. It's no wonder. At one job, there was low ceilings, and there was a ceiling fan that was running as J.R. was mopping. The mops were long, and you had to be careful because they could easily hit into something low hanging.

J.R. raised the mop and it hit the blades of the moving ceiling fan. What does a normal human being do when something like that happens? Normally the reaction would be swift, where you would duck to avoid the fan. But not J.R. He stood there holding the mop as the fan hit against it, breaking every single blade off it. The guys on the crew with him had to chip in to buy a new fan for the customer. So of course, with these kinds of things, they didn't want J.R. working with them.

There was a time I was with him where we were servicing a decent size hall for a church. The hall was down a long, cramped corridor from a kitchen. I laid a tarp on the kitchen floor and decided to use the kitchen as the staging area for the job instead of blocking up the corridor or the hall itself. We could just bring things as we needed down the corridor instead of trying to navigate everything through that tunnel. This is using "common sense" in preparing for the job.

It came time for the rinse of the floor and I instructed J.R. specifically.

"Go to the kitchen and bring back both rinse mops," I told him. That would be the mop from the white bucket and the mop from the blue bucket. J.R. nodded and I didn't think much of it because he had been working with us for six months by then. He should already know how the system goes. But when I turned to look, J.R.

was wheeling the one white bucket, wringer and mop down the corridor.

"No J.R., *no*!" I called out to him. "Just wring out the mop in the white bucket and the mop in the blue bucket and bring just the *mops*! We don't need to have the buckets blocking up things moving up and down the corridor!"

J.R. nodded and said "Oh" as if he got it. But let me explain. This is like he flipped the light-switch, and the light was indeed on. It's just that it wasn't on in the room J.R. was in so to speak! Leaving the white bucket at the edge of the corridor of the room we were servicing, next thing I knew J.R. was now coming down the corridor with the blue bucket, wringer and mop! It was like my words meant nothing to him. No common sense!

There was another time we were working on a third-floor apartment that had very old pine floors. The boards on this floor had massive gaps between them from the aging of the wood. J.R. being J.R. pulled the red bucket in an awkward manner and toppled it over, sending four gallons of solution onto the floor. What would a normal human being do? Perhaps quickly pick up as much liquid as possible with the mop? Not J.R. who stood there watching the solution run through the boards and into the ceiling of the apartment below us!

One of my favorite J.R. stories is the time we were refinishing three rooms in a restaurant in the city. The place wanted to open for lunch at noon, so we had to hustle to get the job done. In one of the rooms, there was a board with a large gap. I had a water-based product that could be used to quickly fill the gap and since the color matched the floor exactly, it wouldn't even be noticed. Since I was already busy, I explained to J.R. how to do this.

"J.R. I need you to fill that gap for me," I said as I pointed to it. "This stuff is water based and it has been in the truck, so it is cold. So, take the tube, shake it up, kneed it, shake it up again, kneed it again *before* you open it, because due to the cold, the water has separated from the hard material and you have to mix it back together again to use it". J.R. shook his head as if he understood. But given his track record, I assumed he did *not* understand, and I repeated the instructions again to be sure he had them.

"Shake up the tube, kneed it, shake it up and kneed it again *before* you open it, okay?" J.R. nodded several times as if he got it as I reached my hand out to pass him the tube. Now picture the scene as if it is a movie. J.R. is to the left, I am to the right. I reached my right hand out to hand him the tube, and at the same time, I started to turn my body to walk away from him. Picture this in slow motion. Cue the music and it is the theme song "Chariots of Fire". J.R. took the tube as I continued to turn. The music was playing. J.R. started to turn away from me, as my right foot was about to take the first step away from him...

"Oh shit!" I heard him exclaim, before my foot even hit the ground. He had opened the stinking tube and the water spilled out of it and onto the floor! At that moment, the obscenities that flew from my mouth were an epic rant. The people in the restaurant all heard both what I said as instructions to J.R. and then my reaction to what he had done, so they were all laughing. The other worker I had with me, who is going to get his own story unfortunately, said he could hear me screaming over the vacuuming he was doing.

After so many screw ups, I decided to try and transition J.R. to the office where he could answer incoming phone calls. I figured this could really work out because at least he could explain our service to someone. The day before I had him try this, we were out servicing a customer's floor who had maple floors in the kitchen, dining room and hallway. The area under the table in the dining room was all gray and I wasn't sure it would all come out. The customer told me that this spot was why he called us and that if I couldn't get it out, he didn't want to do the job. I asked him to give me five minutes and I would let him know. I poured our solution on a small area of the gray spot and after five minutes, just kind of rubbed it with my sneaker. I could see the color come right back, so I told him we were good to go. The floor came out like brand new.

The next day, J.R. took his first call and this is what I heard.

YOU'RE HIRED, YOU'RE FIRED!

"Mr. Sandless this is J.R., can I help you?" There is a pause as he listened to the caller then he responded to them. "Gray areas? No, we can't do anything with them. Thanks for calling!" With that he hung up without getting their name, their phone number, anything! I was livid! I took an empty water bottle that was on the desk and threw it out him. It bounced off his thick head.

"What the hell is the matter with you?" I screamed at him. "We just did that f***ing job yesterday with the gray area! What do you mean that we can't do anything with gray areas?" It was at that moment that two things dawned on me. First, was that I was completely wrong. I could not teach this system to everyone. Second, what I deemed so very easy to sell was anything but. I would have to develop a way to teach someone how to sell the service, for surely we would have owners with no common sense just like J.R.

For the next three months I sat in the office with J.R. and wrote up every insane, nonsensical thing he would say on the phone to a potential customer. Then I would tell him, "Don't say that, say *this*!" until I had the entire sales script written up. I had been selling all my life and the sale of this service was so very easy to me because no one wanted to sand, and they were calling me for the sale. It was too easy! But I never thought about a novice coming into this with no sales experience. So, in such a roundabout way, having J.R. as an employee turned into a blessing.

When things got slow, I laid him off. He told me he wanted to go back to school for computers and that he appreciated being laid off. But that isn't free to me. I kept him out on unemployment for as long as I could and finally recalled him after four months. He fought and screamed and cried and said I was a bully, so I didn't do anything and let him ride out the full six months of unemployment while he continued school.

Years later I was out with my now ex-wife and some friends at a local bar and J.R.'s band was playing there. This band had no sound tech, so the "common sense" thing to do was to have the sound board on the stage in case there was an issue that needed to be addressed.

But instead, I noticed J.R. had the sound board *off* stage. The very first song, there was wickedly painful feedback and two band members had to jump off stage to try and fix the issue.

When I went up to say hello to J.R., I asked him why he had the sound board off the stage and pointed to the space right next to him and suggested that would be a better place to have it.

"That's where we put it," he explained. That was his "reasoning" for the off-stage placement.

"But wouldn't it make more sense to have it where you can quickly make changes instead of having band members leave the stage to fix something like feedback?" I asked.

"No because that is where we like to have it," J.R. replied. I could see that wisdom was still out of his grasp.

A year later, after discovering my ex was having a mid-life multi-boy adventure, J.R. posted on her social media page that he was happy I would be getting a divorce, wrote that I was an "asshole" and tagged my daughter in the post! This wouldn't be the first employee that I heard back from after getting rid of them, that's for sure. Other than the empty water bottle to the head, I did no wrong by this man! I was kind to him that I even kept him on, and even more kind to allow him to remain collecting unemployment. I wrote him a private note and ripped him, but he then tried to rub my marital issues in my face saying how proud he was of his long-standing marriage. Get over yourself pal! I would rather have a brain than your wife!

Fireman Dylan

Up next was a large overbearing type ginger of a kid by the name of Dylan. I believe he was in his twenties, so more "man" than "kid" but he seemed immature for his age. Dylan wanted to become a full-time firefighter. For the time being, he was on the volunteer force. He was the kind of kid who because he was large, bullied his way through life.

Anyway, we had in the system this non-Mr. Sandless product for the removal of mastic. It was all natural and did a great job to get glue off the floor when a glued-down carpet was removed, so that we could refinish the floor. There was a job we were doing that had mastic on the stairs, and Dylan was assigned to do the removal.

It is a fairly easy process. You apply the solution to one step at a time. You kneel on the step below it, use a scraper to get the mastic off, then do the same moving down one step at a time. I suppose because the lead tech who was on the job didn't explain this or it could have been that Dylan didn't want to be told how to properly do the job, he took it upon himself to cover three steps with the solution. That meant he could barely reach the first step without getting the solution all over himself.

From what I gather, because of his size, Dylan got tired and couldn't keep leaning to reach to the step that was three away from him. So, he decided to sit on the lower step, essentially sitting in the solution he laid on that step. What an idiot!

As it turns out, ginger skin is not particularly the best thing to have when sitting in mastic remover! Before very long, especially with his weight pressing down on his ass and him squirming around on the step to reach the area he was working on, Dylan's ass skin started to burn off! Who would have known?

I was not too happy about this I can tell you! I mean what an idiot! He had to be rushed to the hospital and of course, OSHA was called, and I had to produce a material safety data sheet on the solution. Luckily it was natural and non-toxic. It even had no hazardous effects for burning skin. It was just his ginger ignited it or something.

If that was all for this goofball, then he wouldn't have made this book. But alas there is more! Being a firefighter, you would think this dumb ass knew better than to play with fire. A few days after his butt healed and he was back on a job, Dylan was sitting next to co-worker William, called "Willy" who will also have his own stories in this section. They were driving at sixty-five miles an hour down the highway after completing their job for the day. The brilliant Dylan, whether bored or just plain stupid, decided to take a chisel, place a lit lighter under the tip until it was glowing red. Then Dylan looked over at his co-worker and branded him with the glowing chisel, right on Willy's leg, while driving down the highway at sixty-five miles an hour. I kid you not. Needless to say, I "fired" him immediately upon hearing of this event!

On Again, Off Again Willy

Speaking of Willy, he has one of the most interesting careers here at Mr. Sandless, having been fired and re-hired the most of any other employee. I hired a drugged-out kid as a carpenter before I found Willy. He had worked with Willy before and said that he thought he would be a good hire. Willy had been sanding for ten years and the company he was working for was having trouble. I gave him a chance to try this. Most sanders do *not* make good Sandless refinishing technicians as they always want to revert to sanding.

Back in those days, we serviced a huge area since we were the only Mr. Sandless as we had not begun to franchise yet. That meant there were some jobs well over two hours away, as we serviced the entire region. After working a handful of months, Willy and a helper had to drive to another state to service a job. I didn't know if he was seasoned enough to be able to do the job himself, especially given that it took him nearly three hours to get there.

As I suspected, the customer called me and said they were not happy. I made a deal to accept less than what we charged so that I could get Willy out of the job and back on the road to get home—given the long distance. As he normally did, Caden got involved, called Willy as he was driving back and bitched at him about the job. Willy took offense and let Caden have it that he thought the system sucked, the company sucked, that everything sucked.

Caden then made it much worse when he told me the conversation and said that clearly Willy would never make lead tech given the way he felt. I waited for Willy to come back and at 9 P.M. that night, I unceremoniously fired him. At that stage of my life, after all I did to bring the company to fruition, I didn't want to hear it from anyone that the system didn't work. By that time, I personally had serviced more than a thousand floors with no issues. So, to me, if there is an issue, it is on the technician not the system and so I tended to agree with Caden.

A little while later, that drugged-out carpenter quit, and I had a need for someone to fill the spot and hired another guy from that sanding team by the name of Miles, who yes will have his own stories as well. You have no idea yet!

Miles seemed decent when he came on board and saw how crazy busy we were. He talked me into giving his good friend Willy another chance. I figured it would easier to fix what was wrong with Willy than to train another new employee, so I got him back and explained to him what Sandless refinishing actually was.

Everything seemed to be doing fine for a couple of months until one Monday morning I received a call from a "client". It seems she loved the job we did for her over the weekend, except that we had left behind some items that she wanted to make us aware of. Only I didn't know this client. She wasn't in our system and we had nothing scheduled for that weekend. After asking for more details, I quickly determined that Miles and Willy took it upon themselves to service a client "on the side". If that isn't bad enough, they used my company van to do the work.

As it happens this customer didn't have their cell phone numbers, but she did remember the van and that is why instead of them, I got the call. I am not big at all on theft and both Miles and Willy were fired, Willy now for the second time.

Now you can't fault me because it was during this time the company was exploding at the seams! During that year, we had forty-five new owners come on board, training nearly every single week. On top of that, my Mr. Sandless was exploding, and I was working on launching my next franchise system, Dr. DecknFence®. It was lucky my head didn't come off!

When things were crazy, and I needed help, I brought back both Miles and Willy after a terse dress down. They both came back and seemed more enthusiastic than before and a few more months went by. Then I received a call from a customer who said that the four crew members who were in the van were smoking pot in her driveway! I was too busy that day to handle it, so I told Caden to find out who was on the job and to take care of it.

Caden was very anti-drug and told me that we needed to get rid of anyone who was doing drugs at Mr. Sandless. I had a policy of basically don't ask, don't tell, but don't dare do it while at work. I really didn't care what they did in their off hours. Not only that, one of the guys in the van smoking weed that day was Caden's brother Dominic, who is going to have his own stories as well. This is twisted, isn't it?

Anyway, Caden didn't like Willy very much and took it upon himself to fire him making this the *third* time Willy was fired from Mr. Sandless! This was right around the time I was having issues with Silas. It popped into my head that Willy could come in as an assistant for Silas, learn what he does, so that if Silas departed, I could have someone to do what he does. I contacted Willy and asked him to join me in the franchise department, now making it that he was hired and fired <u>three times each</u>!

Willy vs. Haley

Unfortunately for Willy, the yo-yoing of his life was to continue. After Silas left the company, everything fell on Willy to handle—all the franchise administration work that Silas did. While he was somewhat capable of doing this, Willy had no real educational background for the work. I brought in a woman by the name of Haley to replace Willy, who I was then planning on sending back into the field doing floors.

Haley had all the degrees and she was certified in all the software that we use in the company. Her resume was perfect for the job. I had Willy work with her to try and explain what to do and how to do it, but that didn't work, as Haley believed she was smarter than Willy and didn't need his help. So, after trying for a couple of days, Willy departed for the field, and Haley took over his job at corporate.

As is the course of things at this madhouse, things did not go well for either. Haley believed that she needed to clear out the way Willy did things and create her own systems to use from the ground up. Not a very good idea at all. In a maddening effort, she deleted absolutely everything we used and created that both Silas and Willy used to administer to the system. She deleted all the email from owners and staff, which is never a good idea. Then she double deleted them by emptying the recycle bin on her computer so that nothing could ever be retrieved.

Meanwhile Willy was on a job and had a little accident. Instead of using the cloth tarps we have on all the trucks, Willy and his team used black plastic garbage bags to protect the area of carpet at the top of a set of stairs they were doing. Not a very good idea as plastic on carpet is very slippery.

When Willy was going up the steps with an open can of stain, and stepped on the plastic bag, suddenly he became a surfer, slip sliding down the stairs, spilling the stain everywhere! These stairs were the kind with no riser, so the stain could flow freely onto the stairs, the walls and on the carpet below. It was lucky he didn't break his neck!

Meanwhile I needed things from Haley and she couldn't produce them. It seemed her master plan to rebuild all the systems from scratch had failed miserably because she deleted anything she needed to look at in the first place! On top of that, to attempt to cover for her miss-deeds, she bought the rest of the staff lunch from the Turkish Pizza shop of poison across the street and promptly gave most of the staff a case of food poisoning!

I am a big believer in local small businesses. So, when a new pizza shop opened across the street from our offices, I was thrilled. Now when we had visitors to the office, I could take them just right across the street for a bite to eat—how convenient would that be? So, on their grand opening, I took the entire staff over for lunch. The food was unfortunately horrible! I introduced myself to the owner, who said he was Turkish. The guy cooking looked to be the same. But in no way should anyone open a food establishment when they can't even cook!

I didn't hold back and told the owner that it wasn't any good, and that is when he told me that the "chef" had no experience at all. He was just "winging" it. About a month later, he called over to me and said that he had hired a new cook—who could actually cook! So once again, I did the "nice" thing and brought the staff over for lunch. Thankfully it was real food this time!

The very next day I had visitors and took them over for lunch. I told them how good the food was just the day before. But when I entered, I noticed the old guy back their cooking again. I went up to the owner and asked what happened to the real cook? He quit after just one day! But it was too late for me to just leave, so four of us had lunch there. What we ate, I can't say. While we were trying to get the food down a woman called in to complain. Apparently, she ordered "chicken wings". I could clearly hear her on the phone as she told the owner angrily that what he gave her was not "chicken". God only knows what it really was!

By the end of that day, all four of us who ate there were throwing up! That would be the very last time I would ever eat food from the Turkish Pizza Shop. When Haley brought food from there for everyone, I was the only one not to partake and was thankful I didn't!

Now back to Willy's job. I had to hire a painter to repaint this guy's walls. I didn't charge him for the job we did, an $1,100 gift and $600 for the painter. The only thing left was the rug under the stairs that was in the hallway. That little section had to be replaced. I figured the $1,700 was more than enough to cover for this. But the owner was looking for blood.

He came up to see me and handed me a bill in the amount of $4,500! When I asked what it was for, he said it was to replace the carpet. I told him that this wasn't going to happen and that I was going to turn it over to my insurance company. What a total prick. We are talking about a three by ten-foot piece of carpet. His "estimate" was to replace the entire carpet in the home!

After just ten days, I fired Haley. Her clean sweep of all the data and systems turned into a nightmare and we had to rebuild the systems on our own from scratch because we were the only ones who knew what should be in it. She had no knowledge at all. I brought Willy back in the office once again (how many times now?) and he has been at the administrator position ever since. Willy found email on her computer that Haley had sent to her friends, saying that she thought she was perfect for this job and that she believed she had a career here at Mr. Sandless. Unfortunately, education and being "book smart" is not enough when it comes to the real world.

Back to the idiot with the $4,500 carpet. After twenty-five years in business, this was the first insurance claim I had ever filed. The insurance company sent an adjuster to look at the "damage". He noted the hallway carpet had stain on it and that it couldn't be cleaned off. We already knew that. But he also noted that the carpets in the other rooms were not affected and on top of that, were totally different colors than the carpet in the hallway! This guy was just trying to scam money off me. The adjuster also noted that the hallway carpet was more than twenty years old and depreciated to nil. The insurance company sent the guy a check; for one dollar.

Infuriated and thinking he still had a claim, this knucklehead filed a complaint with the Insurance Bureau of my state, claiming that my insurance company was jerking him around. The case was examined and in a rare case of bureaucrats making the right decision, they upheld the one-dollar payment. Geez!

The Stoners

There were some employees who for the life of me I just can't remember their names, but certainly do remember their antics. There was the kid who I hired and told to be at the office first thing Monday morning. He was a no-show, so I had to go out and do the scheduled job myself. About noon he called me with some wild story about why he couldn't make it in on time. I fired him immediately, and to this day he remains the quickest firing of my life. He hadn't even worked a single hour!

There was a kid we hired as a helper who was a pill snorter. Of course, when potential workers come to interview, they are not all highed-up. But subsequently they show their true colors. This rocket scientist on his first day of work was so screwed up, that he collapsed on the job. He passed out and slammed face first into the floor. He was so stoned that he didn't even put his hands out to stop himself from falling and broke his nose on impact. On top of blood on the freshly finished floor, the boards had an imprint of his freaking nose. I had to pay for a board replacement for the customer to get his stinking nose plant out of the floor!

Yet another stoner was hired for our outdoor work. My manager at the time, Tony, who as it seems will continue the pattern with his own story as well, stopped by to check on the kid who was supposed to be staining a fence that day. When Tony pulled up, he couldn't believe what he was seeing. This knucklehead kid passed out on the lawn. What made this one interesting is that the stain sprayer was in his hand, and the stain was shooting all over the lawn, kind of a like a colored sprinkler system!

Now I couldn't fire this kid just yet because he said he had passed out from "heat exhaustion" even though it was sixty-nine degrees that day! If I had fired him, he would have been able to come back at me. As luck would have it or drugs, our boy on his next job decided he was a carpenter, pulled out a huge table saw from our installation van so that he could cut a tiny piece of trim. Let's just say the trim wasn't cut, but the tip of his finger sure was! He sliced part of his finger right off!

This had to be reported to my insurance even though this kid had no authority or training to even use a giant table saw. Fortunately, this kid went away on his own…literally! He was arrested, probably for drugs and kind of disappeared on his own. I heard through the grapevine of my other employees that he was threatening to sue me. For what, I have no idea. I think he believed that once he was cleared to return after the injury by worker's compensation, that I didn't give him time to come back. But I couldn't because we couldn't reach the kid because he was in jail!

As for Tony, his infamous story involved stain as well. We had a ton of opened and used stain we needed to get rid of to clear room in our storage for new supplies. I instructed Tony to load it up and take it to the place where the township accepts hazardous products. But Tony said he was just going to toss it into our trash dumpster for regular pickup. I told him that was not a good idea, but then I got distracted and Tony went ahead with his plan, not mine.

His plan would have worked if the trash truck driver who emptied our dumpster just picked up the trash and left. Instead, after he dumped the contents of the dumpster into his truck, he ran the trash compactor to make room, crushing all the stain cans that were in our dumpster like a giant pile of oranges. The stain poured from the trash truck, covering our parking lot. Nothing we tried would remove it.

Tony felt terrible, so he contacted the fire department and had them bring a truck, so they could use their powerful hoses to wash away the stain. I still have the video I took that day of the fire crew trying to power wash the driveway—not making a dent in the stain. We finally had to reseal the driveway to get rid of it!

Back to other employees, the drug culture seemed to take hold almost as soon as I started to hire at Mr. Sandless. The very first carpenter I hired was a hell of a nice guy by the name of Benny. He was very good at replacing floor boards and doing trim work and was a very hard worker. The only problem was he was a major pill-popping stoner!

Benny would tell me stories of his days with a sanding company, like the time the house almost caught fire.

"I just got done slapping a coat of finish on this floor, when I smelled something burning," he once told me. "I looked over and saw some smoke coming out of the sanding bag." For those who don't know, this is the bag that holds the saw dust that came off the floor during the sanding. Benny continued:

"I opened the bag to see what was going on and saw that the damn bag was on fire! If I waited a few seconds longer, the room would burst in flames as the finish was still wet. I opened the window and threw the bag out as it burst in flames and I almost hit a woman walking her dog!"

Despite his good work when he came in, Benny was always late because he couldn't get up after popping so many perks. After about a month, I had a good long talk with him. I told him that he wasn't getting any younger and that he needed to worry about his future. He wasn't a kid but in his late 20's. I told him that I really liked him and that he could have a long career with Mr. Sandless and even elevate as the company grew. Then I told him he had to clean up his act.

His response was that he wasn't interested in stopping popping the pills and so I fired him. That kind of thinking I could never understand.

Miles was another one who was a pill popper. I call them that, but again, this "modern" drug user crushed the pills up and snorted them. I didn't think Miles was that into drugs when he first came to work for me. He seemed more like the "pot" kind of guy. But he must have been influenced by others here and he too started with the pills.

I had him working as a manager for a short while but it all got out of hand. I mean he was falling asleep right in the middle of work! I couldn't even have a conversation with him because he was so out of it. I eventually fired him as well. But Miles is also featured in an unbelievable story about a visitor I had for a franchise presentation in another section of this book.

As I think back, there were so many druggies, I can't possibly list them all here. There was Blake who came from a well-to-do family and had all the appearances of a clean-cut kid. But I should have known he was a drug user since it was my drugged-out family friend Henry who brought him into the company! Still he was a good worker and always showed up on time. It was with Blake that I finally figured it all out.

You see when all these guys are hired, they had no job and so they had no money and so they had no drugs! These prescription drugs cost about a dollar per pill. But when you realize they did eight to ten pills per day, it got to be expensive. When they had no job, they had no money for drugs and is why when they came to me, they didn't have the appearance of being a drug user.

However, once they were working and making money, they *did* have the money to buy drugs! Therefore, the longer they worked, the worse they got. The more they did, the more they need to do to keep that level of "high" and so the worse they got.

Anyway, Blake lasted only a year. I got rid of him when he started to get bad with the pill popping about six months after my loving family friend departed. From what I heard, his family found out about his drug use and tried to get him to stop, but that he wouldn't. Then a few years later, he turned his car head first into a trash truck and was instantly killed. What a total waste of a life.

Two other guys I hired for our outside work have similar stories. Bob and Max were good at the outset with my Dr. DecknFence. When they came to me, they both seemed clean and once again after getting money from their work, the drug use started. I believe Bob got into perks when he hurt his back and they were prescribed to him. From there it just escalated. Then I think Bob got Max into them as well.

After a few years I had enough of looking at them. The deterioration from the drug use was unmistakable. I laid Bob off and never recalled him. Sometime later he got into a fight at a local bar. The guy he fought returned with a knife and cut him up badly. He was very lucky to have survived.

I fired Max after another worker reported to me that he drove far away during a break from doing a job, to a known drug area, and in open view and broad daylight, and bought drugs from his Mr. Sandless vehicle. I liked Max and sat him down in my office to try and get him to get into some kind of program to get clean. He totally denied everything of course, but I said that just looking at him I could tell he was popping pills. I fired him but with the promise that I would take him back immediately if he went through a program and got clean.

He was on my Facebook friend list, so I could check in on him.

He continued for some time being an absolute mess. If anything, it seemed to get worse once he wasn't working and he was lashing out online.

About two years later, he stopped by my office. He said he had been clean for nine months, had a job and regained his life! He thanked me for trying to set him straight and thanked me for giving him the opportunity to work. I shook his hand and said I was proud of him. That is the first and only ex-employee to return better than when they left. In the back of my mind, I had fired so many people during this company that I thought there would be a decent chance that one of them would return to me and *shoot* me. I am thankful that didn't happen as well!

CHAPTER **17**

The Power-trippers

BEING A LEADER to me is a very natural thing. The "boss" leads by strength of character. My work ethic, my communication skills, my empathy for understanding the work all equates to people wanting to naturally follow me. I don't call at all upon my power or authority. Great leaders do not need to do that, and I can only recall doing that one time with Silas.

I've learned what being a leader is by watching those that allow power to go to their heads. When I was very young, I was driving out of a development with my girlfriend, heading to a party she wanted me to take her to. As I pulled out onto the exit road, she was confused about the directions and this is *way* before cell phones and GPS. I stopped there in the road because no one was coming in either direction while she figured out which way to take.

Just as she said to go north, and I started to turn that way, a car came up on the south side, more than one hundred yards down the road. In other words, nowhere near us yet. He could clearly see that I was in the middle of the road, but I quickly straightened out and started to drive north. Suddenly, this total jerk moved from the south lane to my north lane, basically coming at me head-on. He accelerated as I began to break, wondering what in the world he was doing. I had no choice but to get off the road. The SOB ran me off the road!

When he passed by, he forcefully pointed at me, and indication that he wanted me to stay on my side of the road. His insignia clearly indicated that he was a fireman. This is what I mean by power going to someone's head. His "power" was that he was a fireman, and don't get me wrong here, a very noble and dangerous profession. But in no way does that give him the right to become the law and the judge by forcing me of the road to "teach me a lesson" or whatever power trip he was on. He was a fireman not a policeman. Besides, he was nowhere even close to me. So, he became judge and jury of me as well. Power trip. This is like several workers I had in Mr. Sandless.

Behemoth Ken

The first was Ken, a behemoth man who came on as a technician. At first, he was a very skilled worker. He worked his way up from helper, to lead tech, and then to trainer in the system. He was so good, I sent Ken to New Guinea to launch our new owner there.

About the only trouble I had with Ken was with this one contract I had. The head maintenance man was the one we worked through to fulfill the refinishing of the units they wanted done. He was a nice enough man and didn't bother me one bit. But for whatever reason, he was rather effeminate where he could have appeared to be gay. That didn't matter to me one single bit as I always treated everyone with equal respect and his private life was none of my business. On top of that, he could have been straight for all I knew! He never said anything to me and it didn't matter to me at all.

But with some workers; they made folly of this guy behind his back. Believe me, if I caught them doing it, there would have been a reckoning, but they never did it around me. I just heard it through the grapevine.

Anyway, this contractor told me and said he had words with Ken. He told me that my guys all know they must use the service elevators and that he caught Ken riding the resident elevators instead. After he told Ken that he needed to use the service elevators, Ken called him a "faggot". Great. I apologized for Ken's terrible remark, told the guy that I would dress him down, and said that he would no longer be sent to do work there.

When Ken got back I approached him to inquire what had happened. Of course, and as expected, he pretty much blamed the other guy. By that time, I had employees for over twenty-five years, and knew exactly the best way to handle the situation. I let Ken hang himself, and once he did, I told him that I knew what he called the guy. With that the curtain was pulled back and Ken knew he was toast. All I did was write him up, but I told him that what he did would not be tolerated again.

Other than this, Ken seemed on the surface to be a model employee. But then that power thing happened. At around his sixth year with me and toward summer, Ken felt he no longer needed to work. He would come in the office in the morning, leave to go to a job with two workers, open the job, have the client sign the paperwork, set the workers up to do the job, and then he left. Normally around 3 P.M. he would return to the job site, collect payment and bring the workers back to the shop. Due to his size, these helpers didn't dare say a word.

After a month or so of this abuse, one finally had some gumption to speak up. Ken told him he would basically kick his butt if he said anything. Now that the cat was out of the bag, Ken amped it up even more. He felt he was "owed" the privilege of just opening the job and not doing any work because he was "the boss" or as I like to call it, the "fireman" of the job! From then on out, after Ken opened the job, he instructed his guys to do all the work, then to call him when they were close to finishing, so he could return! Ken became his own boss!

After another month of this, the workers finally had enough. Did they tell me? Of course not! They told another worker, who told another worker, who told another worker until through the grapevine, I heard about it! I used to tell the guys in the field all the time to not mess up out there because I always heard about it. Always all things would eventually find their way to me!

Once I heard about it, I set the plan in motion to catch Ken in the act. I had Willy take a day and a camera to go and hang out at Ken's house to see if he showed up there. Now due to the smallness of the street he lived on, there was no way Willy could get a picture of Ken being there without being seen. While a photo was out, at least Willy could be a witness.

Sure enough, Ken showed up back home at 9 A.M. when he should have been on a job. Willy witnessed Ken mowing his lawn and sipping iced tea on his porch. What a lovely thing for me to be paying someone for! Once Willy made his report to me, I fired Ken. I had a bunch of workers and my manager at the time who asked me if I wanted them there given the size of Ken. I told them not to worry about it, because I could take care of myself. After I got Ken to admit he was home that very afternoon, I fired him.

Now if that was the end of the story, that would be one thing. But it doesn't end there. Ken filed for unemployment compensation. Can you imagine ripping me off for two straight months, being caught doing it, and now expecting to be paid for being fired? I contested the application and due to the lovely way business owners are treated by the government, I would have to go to a hearing to prove my case.

Now let me say right now that this was never worth me paying a lawyer to represent me. If it was any other court related issue, I would take my business lawyer with me. But these things were not worth the costs. I mean, how could I possibly lose when the guy was robbing me? Of course, I have said that before, only to lose the ruling in the end, even when all the evidence was on my side. Those judges at that department simply hated me! I was always made to feel like I was the bad guy, because I gave someone a stinking job!

When I got the notice for the hearing, I was told who the judge would be. It was this woman who really, *really* hated me! Oh great! I had never won a case with this woman! I knew I had an uphill battle. But again, Ken admitted to me that he was home that day while on my pay. That is theft by the law and I had every right to fire him. What kills me about this judge is she is smoking hot! Believe me, somehow that makes this that much worse.

The case goes on. We are sworn in. We are recorded, then evidence is taken and testimony and cross examination, the whole kit and caboodle. He gives his side. I cross examine him and get Ken to admit he was home where he should have been working. Ken pulled out this guide where years earlier I said that I would pay them a full forty hours if the job was done each day. I object to the guide because I couldn't check to see if it was altered. She overruled me and admonished me that I must accept what was in it. I explained that the guide meant he had to do the work, not that the job got done by his co-workers and that I proved beyond any doubt that he stole from me that day. This judge would not allow me to bring in what the other workers told me, that this had been going on for two months. But all I needed was to prove one act.

After we were done, she said she would mail the results. When I got them and saw I lost, I couldn't believe it. Her ruling was that since I only proved one case of theft and not a pattern, that he was entitled to unemployment. I looked up the law myself and it said clearly that to fire for theft only had to be *one* case proven, not multiple. She was going against the law and probably only to spite me. I'm the business owner so I am the oppressor.

I turned it over to my attorney who filed a motion at the state capital to overturn the judge's ruling and of course this cost me some six thousand dollars! He used the very law I found to state that only one case needed to be proven and I had every right to fire Ken. The state had a hearing over this, and there was no way in the world they were going to rule against me because I would have taken this to the state supreme court! They ruled in my favor and against the judge and Ken.

That was the last time I could show my face in that building. From then on out I sent someone else to represent us. And we haven't lost yet, so it *was* me! I freaking hate injustice!

Hands-On Hunter

The next power tripper was another ginger by the name of Hunter. I had hired a handy man to come to my home to install a ceramic tile floor in my bathroom. This guy did such a nice job with the installation, I asked him to come and work for me as a lead technician and he agreed. Hunter was a very skilled guy; a very detailed worker and he learned the system well and became a trainer for me just like Ken. In fact, both were in the company at the same time and rotated back and forth doing the trainings.

For the most part, the other employees couldn't stand Hunter. He was one of those kinds of people who could never shut up! He could talk on and on about worthless things and he would always voice his opinion strongly about these worthless things, as well as to kind of get in your face and ask, "You know what I mean?" repeatedly. So, his demeanor was less than appealing for the other workers. I wound up pairing him with a helper who didn't seem to mind.

It also didn't bother me that much because I am a talker myself. But what I would do when I was with Hunter that others didn't do, was to guide the conversation by asking him a question about a more interesting topic. Then at least it was conversation about something I was interested in and it seemed to work the handful of times I worked with him. For example, there was one time I had to go to a job about two hours away to help our owner there do a large bar job. Hunter was set to go, but no one else wanted to be in the car with him for that long of a period! So, I got stuck going. To be very honest, it was a great trip! I would rather talk and be engaged for the two hours of driving than to be bored to death or just be listening to music.

As it normally happens and just like the case with Ken, Hunter too started to let the power trip get to his head. He became very "bossy" to the other workers and because I got along with him, he had an attitude as if he was "un-fireable" and untouchable. His trainings were not going well because instead of teaching and letting the new owner do the work, he did it himself because he wanted it done correctly. I had to explain to him several times that the point of "training" was to let the owner do the work. But really his biggest issue was bossing around the other workers.

The longer it went on, the more brazen Hunter grew. He developed a chip on his shoulder the size of a railroad tie! This reached a peak during a training with a female owner. Now this owner was already a whack job. She was fifty years old, not particularly attractive, and one of those artsy kind of people, stuck up, superior to everyone, and from a small area in a southern state where all the people from that area are like her. So, she was already super-sensitive to start with. I mean for heaven sakes; she came to me crying after the first day of training because she didn't think it would be "that hard" of work! When I say "crying" I literally mean with tears!

Once again, I was so busy I could barely think straight during that time. Once we had Hunter and Ken doing the training, Caden stopped going out altogether, even though I asked him to oversee all the trainings. Caden is partly to blame for me having to have to assign Hunter to train this uppity woman. It should have been him to do it.

Once again through the grapevine, I heard something that I just couldn't believe. One worker who was on the job with Hunter during the training of this woman, told another worker and so forth until it reached my ears. Hunter, with huge chip on his shoulder, with power of being un-fireable coursing through his veins smacked the ass of the woman he was training! Apparently from what I heard, it was meant as a sexual, playful smack.

I didn't think it could be true. First, this woman did not ooze any kind of sexy vibe that a man would want to put his hands on her. Second, Hunter was happily married to a very sweet woman. None of it made sense to me.

I went into Caden's office and told him what I heard. He couldn't believe it either. So, on speaker we called Hunter's cell phone and I asked him if he smacked the ass of the woman he was training. He said he did, and I was dumbfounded. I asked him why and he really didn't have an answer. Unfortunately, I knew that this power trip was getting too much for him to handle.

I thought for certain I would be getting sued by this woman for sexual harassment. She was the kind of bleeding-heart type who would sue for something like this. But I sucked it up and went to talk to her about it. Right away she went there with the threat of lawsuit. Believe me I had to fight the urge to just say straight out to her to suck it up, because it was nothing permanent. The thing that saved the day was I had Hunter profusely apologize to her. I told him if he did not put on a great show and get her to back down from suing me, he would be fired, because she was at that time demanding that I do. His apology saved both his ass and mine!

And just like Ken, if the story ended there, that would be one thing, but of course it didn't. I had a worker who was female by the name of Emma who was a very attractive blonde. She had both a pretty face and a great body. I may have been hesitant to hire her with all the rest of the "dog pack" that worked for me, except that she was lesbian, and she openly told everyone that she was. I figured that would pretty much have all the guys keep their hands off her.

I liked Emma and worked with her a few times. She had a great work ethic, was meticulous at her job and I was glad to have her. She was the kind of worker that I really wanted to have in the company.

But once again through the grapevine, I heard something that not only upset me to no end, was as incredulous as Hunter's previous episode. You would think this chucklehead would have learned his lesson where he almost lost his job putting his hands on someone. I heard that Hunter was sexually harassing Emma!

I couldn't rationalize this in my head! Okay, Emma was attractive. But she was lesbian for heaven sakes! Not only that, Hunter was married! Thankfully I had a sexual harassment policy in the company so that I had guidelines to follow. I was mortified to call Emma up to my office to discuss this issue, because she did not report it to anyone or follow our guide on how to report the issues. This came to me from outside the company.

I made her feel as comfortable as possible and told her that I had zero tolerance for anything like this. Emma told me that she didn't bring it to my attention because Hunter had convinced her, and she believed, that I would never fire him no matter what. So here we have it, the power trip thing again.

Hunter was so stoked on his own bullcrap, that it made him "manlier" than he otherwise was. He believed that a romp with him would "un-gay" Emma. For weeks, he would tell Emma about his prowess in bed. Now if you saw this scruffy guy, there would be no way he would come off with this type of confidence on his own.

When Emma rebuked his advances, he started to ridicule her. For example, when she was bending over, he would get behind her and pretend he was humping her. It reached a head when during one job, he actually grabbed her by the hips, and dry humped her right on the stinking job! Emma was crying when she told me this. I wanted to execute Hunter.

I did my best "boss" thing and comforted Emma. I told her how absolutely horrible this was, and that Hunter was as fired as any human being could be fired. I told her that she could come to me at any time if any of our guys even looked at her sexually and that I would take immediate action. I told her that I would always have her back and thanked her for her great work. She was feeling better when she left my office, but within a month or two, she quit. That really pissed me off to no end that I lost a great worker because some freaking idiot on a power trip couldn't keep his hands to himself.

I really let Hunter have it when I fired him. I believe he *did* think that it would never happen, no matter what he did. Wrong! Shortly afterwards, I received an email from Hunter's wife. She said that she heard things and asked me why I fired him. I responded that Hunter should be the one to tell her and that for the years he worked with me for me to fire him that she should know it was serious. She replied that she heard he had put his hands on a female employee. I just said for her to ask him.

Well-Hung Italian Stud Chase

The third power tripper employee was a guy by the name of Chase. Once again like the other two, he was talented and could do everything in the system. He was friends with Hunter and that is how I came to hire him. I had such faith in both as far as the service was concerned that I let Hunter and Chase each do a floor for an HGTV show Mr. Sandless was featured in.

Chase's biggest problem was his blatant inability to handle any kind of authority. Any kind of power would immediately go to his head. If for example he was heading up two or three teams on a large job, he made it perfectly clear to the other workers that he was "the boss" and that the job would be done his way. Of course, as I said at the start of this section, that is no way to be a leader. If you must tell someone you are the leader, you already don't have any power!

I discussed this several times with Chase and explained that this was not going to work. The other workers would instantly withdraw with heavy-handed tactics like this. They couldn't stand it when Chase was in charge. For the most part, I assigned him a helper and for several years, I had him just working with the helper, so I could avoid any power trip issues. But over those years, I wrote Chase up at least three times for exerting too much power on the staff when in fact he had none.

As the madness and growth was happening and in between managers for my Mr. Sandless, it came that I had to put Chase as an interim manager until I could find someone else. For six months he managed the business and to be honest, he did a decent job with it. To my amazement, the position didn't go to his head. But I believe that was because I was always around.

At the end of that year, I was headed out to our yearly convention in Las Vegas with all the senior members of the company. We would be departing on Friday and would return to work Tuesday the next week. Chase was left behind to oversee things. There were three jobs scheduled for that Friday, one for Saturday and four on that Monday. Everything was set up and scheduled including who would be doing each job, the times they were to be there, the paperwork, all down to the last details. There basically was nothing for Chase to do but oversee things.

While I was in Vegas, I received a call from just about every worker I had in the field. The best I could tell is Chase went on a maddening power trip. He totally disrupted every job that Friday by rearranging the schedules, changed out the teams to do the jobs, even going so far as to switch team members to other teams where they didn't know what they were doing. The results for Friday was that not a single job was completed. The same thing happened on Saturday. Every job that was scheduled for that Monday had to be rescheduled because he so screwed things up.

But this time, Chase crossed the line. He told the staff that I gave him permission to do these changes, that he spoke to me and I gave him the "power and authority" to act on my behalf. What in the hell is the matter with people like this when power goes to their head? I suppose it is just a lack of self-worth that when they get any power, it "bolsters" their self-esteem and that makes them feel better than they normally do, so they act out.

As soon as I got back to the office that Tuesday I confronted Chase. As I usually did, I let him hang himself by trying to explain to me what happened. There really wasn't any excuse as the schedule should have never been changed. Once I got him to confirm what the others told me, that he claimed I had given him permission, I fired him for gross insubordination.

And as usual is this the end of the story? Of course not, but I did in fact save the best for last! As we started to prepare for a new manager to take over, a staff member was assigned to clear off the office computer Chase used. She brought to my attention that Chase had used our Mr. Sandless email account to set up an account on "Craig's List" where he advertised for people to fulfill his sexual needs. It would be bad enough if these "needs" were normal and sound, but they were absolutely bizarre.

"Well-hung Italian stud seeks black tranny for sexual encounter" read one of the ads. This is basically what the hundred or so ads were like. Before I knew it, the entire list was being passed around the office. If that wasn't bad enough, this "well-hung Italian stud" made a porn video that he was passing out to friends, the video made it to Mr. Sandless. I am not sure why he was so impressed with his manhood because let me tell you, this was the shortest porn probably ever made. The "stud" lasted about thirty seconds!

But wait there is more. Five months after his dismissal, I got a notice that I was being sued for a worker's compensation claim by Chase. His claim via an ambulance-chasing attorney was that I fired him because he was injured on the job. He was claiming that he blew out his knee, shoulder and arm lifting a heavy piece of equipment into a home on that weekend that I was away and that when I found out, I fired him. His attorney had him see a "doctor" who claimed that an injury to his knee and shoulder had occurred at that time and that he needed surgery and that was why he was suing.

As soon as I saw this, I asked a bunch of my workers if any of them were Facebook friends with Chase. Several were, so it was very easy to access his account. I took screen shots of all that I found there.

"Back from the gym. Great shoulder and cardio work out" was posted on March 24.

"Off to the gym" on March 27.

"Going to the gym is starting to get expensive. $218.00 for membership for the year and now I have to go out and buy all new clothes because my body is growing. Don't fit in my jean's" April 2

"Went to the batting cages yesterday. Hit so many balls I have 4 blisters on my hand. My hands are killing me" April 5

So much for his injury to his shoulder and knee after I fired him! The final one, which I did not make a copy of, was a post of him at the beginning of May saying he was drunk and fell down a flight of stairs at his house. I didn't copy this one because at that time, I didn't know what he was claiming in the lawsuit. By the time I found out about the so-called injury to his knee and shoulder, he had blocked everyone from his Facebook page and I couldn't get it. But that is how he got the injury, not on the job!

I passed all this information along to the lawyer who was assigned to take the case by our insurance company. They would have liked to settle and been done with this, but Chase refused any offer they made. He was hell-bent on a trial.

I was disposed by his attorney as well as a worker who Chase said was on the job with him when he got injured. Of course, the worker said it never happened and that Chase never said he was injured. Chase's lawyer tried to insinuate that I forced my employee to say these things. On the way out of my office after the deposition, I yelled down to the lawyer that his client fell down a flight of stairs when he was drunk and that he was going to lose, bad.

Fortunately, the way this worked is you submit all the evidence to the judge, then he has the trial just between the lawyers and Chase. My worker and I did not have to attend as the judge had our sworn depositions.

During the trial, the Facebook posts were presented to the judge. Chase lied his ass off under sworn testimony that the posts were not actually about him, but about his son. The judge didn't buy it, accepted our version and based on the Facebook posts, and found in our favor. The lawyer for the insurance company was elated and very thankful that we were active participants in the suit. I wasn't about to let this jerk win a lawsuit that was bogus. And so ends the saga of the well-hung Italian stud!

CHAPTER **18**

Cars and Gals

HAVING A FLEET of vehicles and a lot of different workers, it was only a matter of time before accidents would happen. It seemed right out of the gate to occur as soon as I had to hire so many new workers.

Right off, one of our crews leaving drove their Scion out the front of the parking lot, which goes right onto the main street in front of our building. Just looking at the smallness of that exit area you immediately know that is not a good idea. There isn't enough room to pull out and not protrude into the second lane.

But that is what they did. The car in the first lane stopped to let them come out. They couldn't make the turn and the edge of the vehicle stuck out into the second lane, where an oncoming car clipped the bumper, ripping it off the vehicle. I could hear the collision right outside my office window and I went down to see what happened. Both vehicles and occupants were parked on the side street next to our building.

My Scion had the bumper ripped off. It caught on the front passenger side tire of the vehicle that hit them, just barely scraping the wheel well. About the only thing banged up was the person's tire.

This car was driven by a woman, with what I presumed was her husband in the passenger seat. Immediately this woman started to complain that her neck hurt! Now there was no way the impact caused any damage to her neck! Okay, the bumper on the Scion is a total piece of plastic and is why it tore off, not from the force. I was standing right there as her and the husband were immediately talking about suing me! They see a company truck, the owner is right there, and they were going for the cash. Simply unreal. Needless to say, I banned all vehicles from exiting the park lot by that exit.

This was early in the company history and believe me, certainly not the last vehicle event. On her way to a job one morning, Emma smashed our truck into a parked car! There was no explanation. She just wasn't paying attention.

Max, probably in a drugged-out stupor, smashed the truck into a bus! One of the best accidents we had was with two new hires who didn't know the Sandless service. My manager at the time was going to take them to a job, get them started and then return. He drove his brand-new Dodge Durango and the two workers followed behind them in one of our Scions. Supposedly the brakes went out on the Scion and they smashed that into the back of the manager's new vehicle! Right after that, another one of my long-time guys wasn't looking when he was exiting a driveway and backed right into another car that was on the street.

Another time I had four guys on a job at a very high-end country club. They were moving our 350-pound machine out of the building to get it ready to load into our truck. But somehow all four of them didn't notice that the machine, which has wheels, rolled down the parking lot and smashed into the side of a BMW. Believe me, this could have been worse! The manager said that we were lucky it smashed such an inexpensive car, as that parking lot normally had Lamborghinis and Bentleys!

I can't tell you how many windshields I had to replace! It was almost non-stop where I would find one of my trucks with a crack windshield. Typically, a rock would kick up from the highway and do the damage, but there were many that were self-inflicted. These knuckleheads would load the vehicles up with trim and then when they hit the brakes, the trim would smash through the front windshield. Another time, somebody hit the gas while backing up and throw an air blower through the backdoor glass! And if that isn't bad enough, one knucklehead I had through a fit one day and punched what he thought was a metal panel in the back of one of my large vans. It wasn't metal, but coated glass. Not only did he break the glass, but because he was shocked it was glass, he pulled his arm out very quickly, nearly slicing off his arm—I kid you not!

There was a time when Hunter hit a dog on the highway and it destroyed the steering system of the van. On top of that he was all shook up and couldn't do the job that was scheduled that day. And there were countless parking tickets that over the years added up to thousands of dollars. These people I hired would also regularly run the toll booth with no EZ Pass and instead of being charged $5, I would be charged $30!

As I was writing this, another good one popped into my head. The Italian stud Chase was on a job just fifteen minutes from the office when he realized he had locked the keys to the Scion in it. He could have called the office and had someone bring him the spare set of keys to get in, but that would be too intelligent to do. No, instead Chase took a large screwdriver and attempted to "can opener" the car door. Now after he made the first dent in the car frame and door, you would think he would stop. But he didn't. He kept going all down the side of the door, putting in more than forty dents in both the frame and the door. It cost me more than a thousand dollars to get it fixed!

Despite the madness of all of these, there are worse events. Two workers with the name "Bill" totaled two company vehicles. The first Bill, we called "Bill Two" so as no one would confuse him with Willy. The second Bill we called "Bill Three" so that no one would confuse him with Will or Bill Two.

Bill Two worked for me for three years. While he wasn't as skilled as some of the other guys, he always showed up on time, didn't seem to do drugs, and always did a good job. I never really had a problem with him. That was, until one Friday night when he returned to the office after hours. His job ran late, and no one was there. So, he helped himself to my brand new, freshly decaled silver PT Cruiser.

For whatever reason, he was on a tear and did some massive pill popping along with drinking. Around 10 P.M. that night, he was flying down the road in my vehicle, nearly clipped a police car, then erratically turned into a stretch of wooded area, where he literally ripped the bottom of the car out. My best guess was that he was trying to get away from the cop he almost hit. The vehicle was totaled and Bill Two was promptly fired.

Returning from a job, Bill Three was alone driving the best Scion I had in the fleet. It was nearly brand new. I receive a call from a Police sergeant who informed me that Bill Three took out a telephone pole in the city and that he was driving with a suspended license!

Now when you exit the highway to get to our offices, there is a short half mile trek through a small street in the city. The speed limit on that street is only twenty-five miles an hour. I have no idea in the world how he got up enough speed to jump the curb and hit the telephone pole! He literally jumped the curb and hit the pole dead in the middle of the vehicle, causing it to snap in two and land directly across the Scion, crushing it. But he walked away without a scratch.

Of course, Bill Three was promptly fired. I had come to learn that he too was a pill popping machine! What I figure is he passed out at the wheel, his foot press hard down on the gas, and he leaned to the right, aiming the car right to the pole. There were zero signs that he tried to avoid it and there were no skid marks, so he didn't even hit the brakes! I ran into him a few years later where he told me he was clean and sober. It looked like he put on a lot a weigh as I barely recognized him.

The thing I want to point out here is that employees always think the owner rakes in the dough hand over fist, not ever considering that the cost of all this damage was huge! That telephone event cost over fourteen thousand dollars and that doesn't include the total loss of the vehicle!

Paisley

In case you were wondering if it was just the guys who did boneheaded things, think again. The first female I hired for Mr. Sandless was a receptionist for the corporate office. Once we launched the franchise division, the phones were ringing off the wall and driving me crazy. Hiring someone for this role was a top priority.

Now back then, the economy was still very hot. Just like finding an office was such a difficult thing to do, so was finding workers. I hired Paisley the moment she came in, no credentials at all, because I couldn't take another day of that phone ringing! She was just a dumb-assed kid, nineteen years old with no real work experience that I can recall. I wrote up a script for her to follow when answering the phones, and she seemed to settle into the job just fine.

Right away I could tell that "work" really wasn't her "thing". She approached work like someone who had to go to the dentist for root canal—you know, you "have to" go but don't really want to. Because of this attitude, she was constantly late getting to work. That ticked me off because when she wasn't at her desk, the phone would just ring and ring and it was such a distraction to my own work.

Paisley certainly didn't last very long, less than a year. Apparently, she had a new boyfriend who was more important than work. She began to miss several days in a row. When I finally caught up to her, I had a sit down where I explained that I couldn't allow her to work anymore if she continued to not show up. Of course, she said she would and then didn't show up for the next three days. I terminated her the next time she came in.

As is so normal Paisley immediately applied for unemployment insurance. I contested it because I had grounds to fire her and as usual I was dragged into a hearing because they never took the employer's word for anything! But the best part of this story is Paisley was accompanied to the meeting by her boyfriend. She gave her testimony and of course lied, saying I never said anything to her. I gave my testimony and said that I couldn't even count the amount of times I warned her and recounted the last time I made it perfectly clear that not showing up with end her job.

Of course, these judges never say who won, so you must wait for a "ruling" to be mailed to find out. As we were exiting, I went down the stairs first, with Paisley and her boyfriend following behind me. As I was only to the halfway point of the stairs, the boyfriend threatened that he was going to kick my ass. I stopped on the landing and waited for them to get right in front of me.

"I'm right here, tough guy!" I said to him. Paisley pulled at him to leave and he was sticking his chest out like he was trying to scare me. The funny thing is, I was more than twice his size. He would have to be out of his mind to try and fight me! As they walked off, that was the last I saw of Paisley and I later found out I won the case, one of the very few I ever won.

Crystal

For the first four years of Mr. Sandless I did the bookkeeping myself, partly because I was a control freak, and partly because I knew it would be done correctly so I could pass my yearly audits. But as the company was exploding at the seams, I decided it was time for a full- time person to be the company bookkeeper.

I take zero credit for the hiring of Crystal! At that time, I had a new receptionist and a personal assistant, both female, who were in with me for the interviews for a bookkeeper. They thought Crystal was the best fit for the company.

As is the MO of all drug users, when they come to the interview and then for work, they are clean and sober. Then a few pay checks later, once they are sound, the money started flowing to drugs. Crystal was "decent" with the books to start with. The first audit after her first year, I pretty much did on my own, so that I could show her what she needed to do for the next year without me. The idea was to not have me involved in the yearly audit because that took up three months at the busy start of each year.

The following year, as the drug consumption continued to grow, every time I would check I would find serious mistakes in the books. Crystal had a nasty habit of putting expenses as credits. I would constantly see negatives in income and positives in expenses.

Three months before the yearly audit in her second year, I reviewed all the books and had my accountant do the same, then presented to Crystal a massive list of mistakes to be corrected. Two other times after that I sent her lists of corrections to make including a guide on stating which items were priority and that she needed to start working on.

Nearly a month into the new year, our accountant called Crystal to inquire if the work was completed and if they could start the audit. Here response was "I haven't even started". The very next day Crystal called that she would not make it to work that day and told our receptionist that "there was nothing for me to do today anyway". I was furious! If the audit was delayed, I would not be allowed to open any more franchises until it was completed. By this time, it would already be April before I could start offering franchises again!

An inspection of her office revealed that even though I personally gave her a list of details that she had to attend to, it was not followed at all. Not a single item was filed and ready for review for the audit, there were stacks and stacks of notes, and papers everywhere with complete disorganization. I spent the entire day Friday, all day Saturday and Sunday to get the paperwork in order. Despite my memos stating to organize her notes and not use scratch paper, I threw out *three trash bags full* of scratch paper notes. Absolute insanity!

A review of the books showed major errors, such as expenses being listed as income, which is a major issue in an audit. I had already warned her in writing about this mistake, but it continued anyway. Given that she did not perform the minimum tasks of proper book keeping, that she failed to do anything to prepare for the audit as required, and that her office and filing was in complete disarray, and that I found hundreds of personal e-mails from her to her boyfriend which was distracting her from doing accurate work, I fired her for gross misconduct.

In fixing the issues in the books, I lost fifty thousand dollars! Crystal entered five times a five-thousand-dollar entry from an advertiser as income. So, in changing these to expenses, I lost twenty-five thousand in income, and gained twenty-five thousand dollars in expenses!

As was usual, she too filed for unemployment and down to another hearing I was forced to go. Crystal came prepared. She had an ambulance chasing lawyer with her. Despite the mountain of evidence, I had that she failed to do her job, along with the stacks of emails from her boyfriend during the day, I *lost* the case. You don't do your job at all, and I am not allowed to fire you! Isn't that simply unreal? As she walked out of the hearing, that is the last time I saw Crystal.

Charlene

Right after I straightened out the books for the audit, I hired Charlene as the new bookkeeper. Same MO again. No money, no drugs. She would get work and a job, earn money and get caught up on her bills, then the drug use started.

Charlene was about as capable as Crystal and believe it or not, made the same exact kind of mistakes. She was decent about being able to collect outstanding debts which was about the best thing going for her. During her first audit, there were massive mistakes. We unfortunately had a new auditor who was losing his mind with Charlene. He created about fifteen very complicated spreadsheets for her to fill out, basically just to bust on her so that he didn't have to route through the books to find what he needed.

That was a nightmare and we were later than ever before in getting the audit complete. I asked the auditor if it was Charlene's fault and if he created all those spreadsheets to get her to think straight and he said he did. I knew it was only a matter of time before her employment was going to end.

It seemed from what I could pick up on, both Charlene and her son were *way* into the drugs. Again, this is why it took so long to affect work. They would start out straight, pay up their outstanding bills with their pay and then once they had disposable income, that went to drugs. With opioids, the more you do the more you need to do to maintain the level of high. One pill starting out over time could wind up to ten or more pills per high. Charlene was literally falling asleep at our company business meetings or passing out would be a better description!

I finally couldn't take any more, so I pulled her in my office and told her that her drug use was obvious and that she had to clean up her act. As usual she denied it up and down. By the end of that week, we watched out the window of our offices into the parking lot where she purchased fifty pills in a bag off some woman. I fired her immediately.

Wouldn't you know it, but she applied for unemployment! That time of my life was so screwed up that I didn't even contest it. What difference would it make as I would have probably lost anyway! A few years later, Charlene began to tell people that I "embezzled" money from the company. This totally false claim gave Dominic the incentive to call me one night in a drunken stupor and threaten to "expose" my corruption. When I explained to this idiot that literally every penny in the company bank account *was* mine, and that whatever Charlene saw me take out as a draw was legal—especially because she knew about it! I can't embezzle my own money for heaven sakes! But Charlene could and from what I heard, she admitted that she did steal from me. I suppose I am a loon magnet. Can you ever imagine running a business with the host of loons that I had employed? Seems quite impossible doesn't it?

CHAPTER **19**

Crazy Clients

IT SEEMS THAT no matter what business I am in, I find myself serving absolutely bat-shit crazy clients. From my band days and working for insane club owners, agents and managers, to my janitorial days and the bizarre people I ran into there, the pattern continued with Mr. Sandless. You can read about my crazy cleaning clients in my book "True Dirt: Confessions of a Male Housecleaner (Xlibris).

Now don't get me wrong. The vast majority of clients I serviced were very appreciative and blown away by the service. I heard an awful lot of praise over the years we have been offering this service. But there are some serious hard-core loons as well whose stories just have to be told.

Mrs. Smith

For the most part, my first year was uneventful as far as clients were concerned. Every single person we served that year was very happy with the service and no issues at all. But as we continued to grow, we serviced more and more people and eventually I ran into some very interesting characters. Mrs. Smith was one of those. After her divorce became final, she was moving into a very large single home where she would house her business as well as herself. We were contracted to take up the carpets in the living room, dining room, hallway and one bedroom and refinish the floors in all those areas. Matt and Luke were with me on this job.

As soon as we got there, we all knew instantly that this was going to be a wild job. Mrs. Smith was a forty-year-old Irish woman with a slight cute accent. She was in a word; gorgeous, with a beautiful face, great hair, and an hour-glass body. She had on hip-hugger jeans and a halter top with no bra. Immediately she was all over me, so much so that as I looked back at Matt and Luke, they turned away in embarrassment. I tried to get Mrs. Smith to focus on the job I was there for.

I quickly learned that she had a large landscaping company, that she was very outspoken and gregarious, that she hated her now ex-husband, and that she found me to be "very handsome". I made the excuse that to get the work done, we would have to get right to it, and with that I was able to slip away from her.

She disappeared for some time as she was working on moving her business to this new property which was very large. While it had a home, there were large garages and storage areas and I could see she had already moved quite a bit of landscaping materials to the site. We moved along well getting the carpets out and working the floors, which were in amazing shape. As it turned out, it was going to be an easy job.

But while we were taking our lunch break, Mrs. Smith returned with several trucks and a bunch of men from her crew. We watched as she directed them where to unload the trucks.

"This one is trouble!" I told Matt and Luke.

"You want us just to leave for an hour and a half?" Matt asked me as Luke snickered.

"Don't you freaking dare leave me with this woman!" I replied. At that they both laughed.

Listen if I were single at the time, not only would I have participated in Mrs. Smith's overtones, I would have probably tried to date her. She was funny, smart, and gorgeous, a deadly combination. But I was married to the women who would eventually cheat on me, so… no I mean; I'm just not the cheating kind. To me, cheating isn't about

CRAZY CLIENTS

your partner. It is about you. What does it say about you if you are a cheater? It says you are a dishonorable piece of crap, that's what. I could never cheat because I would be cheating on my own honor. So of course, I didn't want to be alone with Mrs. Smith.

If she was divorced, why did she go by "Mrs. Smith"? Well that was the name of her business: "Mrs. Smith's Landscaping" and so that is what everyone called her.

When we entered the home to apply the next finish coat to the floors, Mrs. Smith invited me into another room to meet her "crew". There were multiple sofas in the room, and all the seats were occupied by her guys who were taking a break from the work.

As I looked around the room, I noticed that all of her "crew" were strapping young men in their twenties. But more than that, every one of them had a smile on their face as if they *all* had partaken in Mrs. Smith, and that they knew that she had her sights set on me!

After the next coat, Matt and Luke went to the truck to wait until the coat cured. As I was exiting the home from the hallway, Mrs. Smith grabbed my arm and asked for my help. She pulled out a small three step ladder and told me she needed to change the bulb in the hallway ceiling light and said she didn't want to slip. She wanted me to hold onto her, so she wouldn't fall off the ladder.

Look I know this was a total set up but what the hell was I going to do? Tell here "no thanks"? She faced away from me and got on the first step of the ladder. There were just three places for me to put my hands on her to hold her. It was either going to be by her breasts, on her bare waist, or on her hips which basically meant I would be holding her ass. I decided to go with the waist. I remember she had great skin and I couldn't believe that there I was holding this woman, so she could change a bulb. What the hell was I thinking?

She took the second step, reached and stretched her hands up to the light, then swung around as her breasts popped out of her top and right in my face. I was still holding her waist as she faced straight at me, my head between her breasts. Then she bounced around and smacked them against my face, cooing as if she was having a ball!

As I guided her off the ladder, she pulled up her top, took me by the hand and begged me to dance with her. I pulled away and she seemed so disappointed and she started gyrating for me to some really goofy music she had playing in the other room. But I slipped by her and got out of the house. I have to say that I was really flattered and really not interested. Like I said, I wasn't a cheater and so I wasn't even tempted.

I was able to finish the job for the "terribly disappointed" Mrs. Smith. Don't get me wrong, she loved her floors but was disappointed I wouldn't "play" with her. She pushed right up to me when she gave me the check for payment, kissed me on the check, then smacked my ass when I turned to the door. Of course, Matt and Luke had a field day watching me escape her all day long and they said that they didn't know how I could resist such a beautiful woman. I was more embarrassed than anything else!

Sally

Unfortunately, there were many women who hit on me while I was on the job site. There was one older woman who lived in an historic home that we were servicing. I was training that day and when I first went in, I tried to upsell her another room. She did not respond well to that, but I wanted to show my owner how to upsell, so I really didn't care. Her floors were old parquet and were going to come out great, so I wasn't worried if she was a bit bent that I tried to get more money out of her.

As the job progressed, she seemed to get more and more friendly. At lunch break, she joined me out on her patio where we sat on a table under an umbrella. There she began to tell me that her husband travels for work and she is so lonely, as she began to caress my arm. I didn't want to make a scene in front of my new owner, but as I got up to call Caden to come take my place, so I could get the heck out of there, she slipped her card into my hand with her private number and whispered "call me" into my ear. Once Caden showed up, I ran out of there!

There was another time I knocked on the door and the woman we were servicing answered in her pajamas. She had on a sheer top with only one button buttoned crossed her chest, and hip-hugger bottoms that were also sheer. I could see the works. Matt and Luke looked like "two blind mice" running into each other to try and pretend they were not looking. My heavens they were so damn immature. I introduced myself, shook her hand and walked in.

We were servicing the living room, dining room combination great room and a hallway. She had carpet on the floor and she had removed that herself to get the floor ready for our service.

"I couldn't move that hutch," she said as she walked to the kitchen to get some coffee.

"No problem, we can get that out of here for you," I replied. I motioned to Matt and Luke to take the piece out which they did.

Now when they moved it, there was a small section of carpet under it that was still attached to the floor. The client saw it and remarked that she thought she had gotten all the carpet up. I told her it was no problem at all and I would take care of it. With that, I got on my knees and started pulling the piece up and removing the staples.

"I'll get that!" she replied, grabbing her tools off the kitchen table.

"You don't have to," I said, "I got it." But before I knew it, she was right in front of me. She bent over to get the carpet out and stuck her butt right in my face. I mean it, and I am not even kidding, my nose was in the crack. What made it even worse was, she was good looking too!

As Matt and Luke turned the corner and saw what looked like the woman getting off on this, the two blind mice ran into each other again, which broke the mood for the client and she ended her fun. I think if I was alone, she would have raped me!

There was another time that we serviced three bedrooms and a hall for a woman. She was a spinster type who took care of her elderly father. The moment she saw me, she was all over me. I had to run around the table with her old man sitting there to get away from her. She had an incredible body with the full curves and hour glass look, but her head was absolutely frightening. He hair was black and in this beehive fifty's hairstyle and she had huge gray streaks in it, just like the bride of Frankenstein. And she had a black hairy mole on her face the size of a man's fist.

Now to be honest, I ran away from Mrs. Smith as well, so don't beat me up for running from this woman. It wasn't just about looks. But you have to admit, that this *does* make the situation even worse! I will never forget that day. She was all over me, rubbing my arms, and cuddling up against me. It was so bad, I couldn't stay in the house. The temperature that day was zero; the absolute dead of winter. Zero, and I spent as much time out in the truck as I could because I couldn't be in the house.

This brings me to sweet Sally, a skinny very attractive blonde who was totally my type. The first time we were at her house, we serviced her family room and kitchen. I remember that she had a bunch of dogs and there was so much hair in the family room, that no matter how much we vacuumed, we couldn't get it out of the floor. It ended up that a *lot* of hair got in the finish and there was nothing we could do about it. I thought there was no way she was going to be happy with the job we did, but Sally seemed please anyway.

For whatever reason and who knows what makes the world go around, but Sally lit up from the moment she shook my hand. She hung around and talked to me nearly the entire job. Not only was she my type, she was intelligent and funny and a pleasure talking with, so I wasn't at all upset that she hung around while I did the service. She told me that I reminded her of her father and that I thought the way he thought. I believe that a comment like that assured me that I was "safe" if she was treating me like a father figure.

Sally called me back again and booked a bedroom, which we went to service as well. I knew I was wrong and not in the safe zone the moment she lit up when she answered the door. I could smell the perfume on her as she grabbed my arm and pulled me into the house. I was fortunate enough to dodge a bullet because her friend popped by and that ended whatever thoughts Sally had in her mind for the day.

But then she called me back for yet another bedroom. Great day in the morning! If life wasn't already stressful enough, I had to figure out how to let her know this wasn't going anywhere. Once again, she opened the door with her tremendous smile and pulled me into the house. Once again, we had great conversation. Then she asked me if I could look at her computer because she thought she may have a virus. Now the computer was in a room off the family room in the back of the home. Matt and Luke would be remaining upstairs to finish the bedroom, I would be down there alone with Sally.

She took me to the room and showed me the computer as I sat in the chair and started looking through it. She placed her right hand on my left shoulder and kind of rubbed my back. I dropped my hands for a second, and I suppose she took that as a sign. With that, she sat on my lap and wiggled her rear into my crotch, as she grabbed my arms and wrapped them around her.

"I think we need to talk," I said to her, as she stopped wiggling and turned toward me, now sitting on my lap.

"You are really beautiful, really sweet, really intelligent, and in a different life, you and I could be great. But we are both married. I am going to tell you the truth. Your old man needs to start ponying up, manning up and taking care of your needs. You need to have that conversation with him because you can't be looking for this in the arms of another man." I was fortunate to have that little speech already prepared because I was expecting this kind of thing. I never really thought I would get to give it.

Honestly, she was so my type I wish I could have taken care of her in the biblical sense. On top of that, she so wanted me too and to make things even worse, this was when my own wife was separated from me in our own home. But I wasn't about to do such a dishonorable thing to both my wife and her husband no matter how great the two of us meshed. That was the last I heard from Sally.

The Aerobics Instructor

Believe me I have had battles with customers over the years. I booked one particular woman over the phone. All she had was a single living room to be done and she told me that the floors were "in good shape". When my guys got there, the floors were a nightmare. She totally lied! On top of that she became so irate when the team said she would need board replacement to get all the black stains out of her floor that she screamed at them. They called me for help and I got on the phone with her.

"Ma'am you told me your floors were in good shape," I said to her.

"I told you all about the black stains, the warped boards, the gaping holes and the paint!" she yelled back.

"No, you did not. When I asked you to tell me about your floors, you said, and I quote, "they are in good shape". You never mentioned any problems that you really do have in the floor!"

"Are you calling me a liar?" she barked.

"Yes Ma'am, I am!" I replied. I think I may be the only person in the world who can call someone a liar, or even to say I am going to kill them and still complete the job and get paid! I will tell you about the character I was going to kill coming up!

There was another female client who contracted us to remove all the carpets throughout her massive home. We sent a large team there to get the carpets out and refinish the floors for her. She called and said she stopped by that night and was not happy at all with the results or the job done for her. I drove to the home, used the passkey to get in and looked around.

I wasn't happy with the way my guys left the home either. There was a lot of dirt and debris left behind. I cleaned all that up for her, so at least there was no issues in that area. As for the floors, that was another matter. They were all mostly in bad shape. Someone had sanded all the bedrooms and didn't know what they were doing. So, there were chatter marks throughout the entire floor from the poor sanding. Only another sanding can fix that.

The area between the board and the wall was huge, so that regular trim wouldn't fill the gap. This floor obviously was never meant to be used as anything more than a sub-floor for carpet. The huge living room had the biggest pet stain I have ever seen. It was some nine hundred square feet of black! That floor had a lot of serious problems.

After she had time to review, she called me about all these problems. She claimed that Katherine, the manager at the time told her that floor board installation was free. Now no one in their right mind gives away board installation for free when first, we don't even know if she needed board installation because we couldn't see what the floors were like under the carpet and second, we charged ten dollars a linear foot for board installation, so it wasn't cheap! No one is going to offer that for free. It isn't like it cost us pennies to do!

Along with that, she of course had issues with the floors. I tried my best to explain to her that we didn't cause the pet stains, we didn't cause the sanding marks because we didn't sand her floors, and we didn't cause the gaps in the walls. But she wasn't having any of it. She demanded we install boards to replace the pet stains for free and she had not paid me a cent for the four thousand two hundred dollars she already owed me. I told her straight up that she had to make me whole before I did any more work for her.

Things got ridiculously heated. She started f bombing and so did I. She called me the D word, I called her the C word. I mean we were going at it on the phone! We finally agreed to meet at the home to discuss the issues. I told Caden and Dominic that they would be coming with me because of all that we said to each other on the phone, I needed a buffer between us. We all jumped in a company Scion and we headed to the home.

I pulled the car into the driveway, and the woman pulled next to me to my right, so I couldn't see her. Caden and Dominic got out as I hesitated to meet her and stayed in the vehicle for a second or two. Instantly I could tell something without ever looking up. She was "hot". Now how in the world could I tell this? Because of the way both Caden and Dominic greeted her. I could hear in their voices that rose up that she was something else. As I looked over, she came to the side of where I was parked to open the door to the home and all I could see was her rear end.

"*This* is what I was fighting with?" I mumbled to myself. You could set a glass on that ass.

After a lengthy explanation of what caused the problems and issues in her floors, I got down to the brass tacks with her. Caden and Dominic were like two lap dogs, each to one side of her, basically taking her side against me! "Yeah, *give* her the boards, *give* her the boards!" They would have done back flips if she asked! She apparently was an aerobics instructor and had written a couple of books about having a superior derriere, but she looked more like a model if anything. I practically had to drag them away from her when it was time to leave and I swear I saw their tongues hanging out of their mouths! She did wind up paying me in full and that was all I cared about.

Jasmine and Sam

Several years later, a friend told me that a woman she knew would like to get to know me and that she may be sending me a Facebook friend request. This was of course after my divorce, so I said it was fine, and I found out her name was Jasmine. That very night, a Jasmine sent me a friend request and I accepted.

The next morning, I received a private message from Jasmine. Apparently, this was *not* the woman I was told about, but some other Jasmine! How weird was that? This Jasmine told me she had our services and that she was not happy at all with the outcome. She said she was "crying" over the condition of her floor. I responded politely to let her know my private Facebook page was not the appropriate place for this and that our company had its own pages where this could have been sent. I also said I would investigate the job that was done.

As luck would have it, bad luck that is, her floor was serviced by Max who was on his way out the door because of his drug use. I was not too happy that he slopped up her floor, so I had my manager order him back to the house to strip off our product and start over. He did just that but slopped it up again. At least that is what Jasmine said through her husband Sam who called to tell me that she was crying over the floor yet again. I didn't see it the first time, so I was taking this woman's word for it that it was slopped up.

There was no way we could strip the floor again, so I had our dustless team go down to sand the floor, stain it and finish it and end this madness. I was bending over backwards to help this "crying" woman but to be dead honest, I shouldn't even have gone down the first time, because this woman signed off at that time that she was satisfied! I should have never gone back down, because once you sign that you are satisfied, you can't change your mind.

It was this third service where things really got heated. The floor was sanded, Jasmine and Sam picked the color stain they wanted, and the floor was then stained and ready to be sealed and finished. My guy called me and said that they changed their minds! They didn't want the color that *they* picked! I got Sam on the phone since Jasmine could no longer talk to me because of her fragile crying state! I really let the guy have it, saying that if they changed color, we would have to sand it yet again!

This idiot was adamant that it had to be changed, and so our *fourth* service to the floor started again. At this point, I was thousands in the hole for this job that was originally priced out at just $550! But this is the loony customer who I created a "stain waver" for that stated that customers pick a color and sign that this is the color they picked, and that if they changed their minds, and we had to re-sand the floor, they would have to pay us to sand again! Enough is enough!

Unfortunately, I was already stuck on this job because Jasmine was crying yet again. She was in fact out of her mind over her precious floor! It was then sanded again, stained the new color they picked, and the loon husband signed that he was satisfied. The very next day, Sam called me and said she was beside herself with grief and she hated the floor and was crying a river. Once again, the fifth time, we sanded the floor. Once again Sam signed off that he was happy with the floor. Once again, the next day he called me that Jasmine was suicidal.

"She may as well kill herself because we won't be back," I told him. "We cannot satisfy that which cannot be satisfied. I feel very sorry for you Sam."

Since somehow Jasmine "wore the pants" in the family despite her mental instability, and to maintain *his* sanity, Sam went on the attack against us. He sent me pictures of the floor and claimed that we destroyed them.

"Sam if you will sign a release that I can use the pictures you sent me, I will take out a billboard on the highway, put your pictures up on it and have the caption 'Get showroom results like this with Mr. Sandless!' Your floors are absolutely gorgeous."

Okay so here is the real deal. The first time we did the floor Jasmine asked them to go darker. The second time darker. The third and fourth times darker. This fifth time she went natural. The floors, being very light had a heavy grain which became much more apparent with the light color than the dark and that is why she hated them.

I turned it over to my insurance company and they—without my knowledge, gave them $5,000 freaking dollars to get rid of them. They still were not happy. They went on to badmouth me all over every negative online site they possibly could—me personally. People like this really take the joy out of life. I should have never done the service the second time and swore I never do this again for another customer. Once that form is signed for satisfaction, that is the end of it!

Sean

One client remains to this day the most difficult to book. She had called me twenty-six times, and I am not even kidding! She could not make up her mind if the service was right for her. Eventually, she "allowed" me to service a small hall in her enormous McMansion home that was in a posh neighborhood. Me, Matt and Luke had to drag

CRAZY CLIENTS

all the equipment up two flights of steps just to finish one hundred square feet to prove to her that Sandless refinishing was for real.

After she looked at the hall, she agreed that we could do her entire downstairs. When we returned to do that service, I met her husband who was going off to work. He was a big-wig lawyer who came across to me instantly as a "blow-hard" kind of guy. We serviced all the rooms and they came out great but ran into a very small problem. We use blowers to speed up the dry time of our products, and the air knocked a small picture frame down and the glass broke on it.

As I was closing out the job, she remarked how great the floor came out.

"We are having a party this weekend," she said. Why don't you leave some of your cards and I will hand them out to our guests for you?"

"I have to be honest and don't think you will do that," I replied.

"Why is that?" she asked in response.

"I've met your husband. He is going to tell everyone he spent ten thousand dollars to have his floors sanded. He will never want anyone to know that he only paid Mr. Sandless three thousand."

"You are probably right!" she replied. I had this guy pegged. Anyway, after she wrote the check, she seemed like there was something more.

"Okay so what are you giving me?" she asked. I pulled my hands apart to indicate I had no idea what she was talking about.

"The picture frame you broke," she responded. "Are you going to pay for that?" I reached in my wallet and pulled out a ten-dollar bill, which she accepted for the cheap, plastic picture frame. Too much!

But the second most difficult client to book has an even better story. Sean called me eighteen times before booking service. I just knew he was going to be difficult because he was so unsure of himself. He insisted on seeing a floor that we serviced, and I was fortunate to have just serviced a Reverend's parsonage down the street from Sean and the Reverend was kind enough to allow Sean and his wife in to see his floors. They both had the same kind of parquet flooring.

The Reverend called me and told me that Sean and his wife did visit, and that they got into a fight in his home because they couldn't agree if they wanted the floor as shiny as his floors were! Can you imagine being invited into someone' home, then having a fight instead of waiting until you leave? They fought right in the Reverend's home!

Anyway, Sean finally booked. We were to do his entire downstairs including moving and replacing the furniture. His floors were dark and dingy from built-up old wax, so I knew that once I got the wax off, the floors were going to look amazing. I wasn't worried that Sean wouldn't be happy—I *knew* he would be.

Matt, Luke and I got to work with those guys moving the furniture out of the house and with me starting the system. As I turned to the one part of the hallway, I ran right into Sean who excused himself to get around me. As I moved down the hall, I bumped into him again behind me. As I rounded the corner from the hall to the living room, I ran into him again. I put down my tool and told him we had to talk.

"I need you to pick one of these things," I said to him. "You can get in your car, go have a nice long lunch and when you return in four hours, I will put a smile on your face. Or I leave, or I kill you." He seemed a little taken aback, so I explained.

"You see it is either you leave, or I leave, or I kill you. Because you are driving me crazy getting in my way to try and keep an eye on what I am doing. And that isn't going to work. If you stay and I stay, I will most likely end up killing you. So, make your choice. Either you leave, or I leave. Which will it be?"

"I guess I can take a long lunch," Sean said dejectedly. He believed he was going to be on my hip the entire service.

"Good choice Sean, good choice!" I said. "When you come back, I will put a smile on your face!"

After that I could concentrate on the job and as I said, once I got the wax off, the parquet was nearly like new. The color brightened up and popped on the floor showing a spectacular look. I snapped a bunch of before and after pictures to be sure that if I had trouble with Sean I would have evidence on how great the job came out.

When he returned, Sean started to cry.

"You certainly did put a smile on my face," he said through tears running down his cheeks.

"Just a check is all I need to wrap this up," I replied, shaking my head of the insanity of this guy. Listen folks, it is a floor! You walk on the damn thing! It isn't "life or death". It's just a freaking floor! If you get this wrapped up about your floor, how in the world do you handle real adversity and trouble in your life?

Dime Spot Susan

Speaking of over the top reactions was Susan. We did a typical job for her, servicing a living room, dining room, stairs and hall. The team that was on the job called me at the office to report they were leaving, and everything was looking good.

But then I received a call from Susan who literally was sobbing on the phone. She explained to me through tear-filled bawling that there was a "spot" on her floor. I swear, and I am not even kidding, it was like someone had died. I assured her that we would come back and address the issue to her satisfaction and set up Miles to go back to her house the very next morning.

No less than a half hour after he left the office, Miles called me to say everything was fixed. I inquired what in the world could have been the issue that had Susan so upset. He told me there was a spot on the last step that was the size of a dime. He rubbed a little bit of finish on it, it disappeared, and then he asked Susan if she was happy. She acknowledged she was, and with that he left. And for a spot the size of a dime, she was crying to me on the phone? You will have to forgive me when I have come to say "No one died, it's just a damn floor" when I have endured clients like this!

Lindsay

The very first complaint in company history remains one of my biggest regrets. It was June of 2007, well into our second year of franchising and more than ten thousand customers served. One of our owners did a three room and hallway job for Cindy who booked him for the service, then had her husband there to oversee the work.

Cindy's husband told the owner that the floors came out beautifully and even gave him a tip. But when the darling Cindy returned home, she hated them and called us up to raise holy hell. Three rooms and a hallway for a lousy $900 and to be dead honest, I saw the before and after pictures and the floors were amazing. There was nothing to complain about.

But being new to this, we ordered the owner to give a refund. That bugged me since that moment we made him do that and from that time on, I said the hell with it. Once they signed off that they were satisfied, we would not be returning their money. From then on in it was up to each individual owner.

Paint Spot Loon

I quickly learned to get rid of whacky customers as swiftly as possible. In the beginning, if I had what I thought was a loon on the floor, I would pass them to the leading sander in the area. But once I had a run-in with StratumAble, I would send all loony customers to him, even going so far as to tell them to tell the owner that I was the one who told them to use his service!

Out of all the jobs I was ever on, I only walked from one. I was at the home that Matt and Luke and I were going to service. When I knocked on the door, the woman client literally jumped on all fours on the floor in the foyer at our feet. Matt and Luke started to giggle as usual. I threw them a wink and then I joined our loony client on the floor.

When I got down, I noticed she was pointing to a drip of paint on the floor that had adhered to the finish. She was pointing to the spot, which was the size of a pin-head with her index finger. I joined her and pointed to it as well.

"Do you see it?" she asked me.

"Yes", I responded. "Does that drive you crazy?" I asked.

"Yes, it does!" she replied.

With that I got up from the floor and told the woman that we were leaving.

"You are not going to do my floor?" she asked in a shocked voice.

"No, I am sorry, you are a loon. No one who ever visits you is going to get on their hands and knees to inspect your floor!"

Muffy and The Ascot

I will end this section with a favorite of mine. Prior to franchising, we received a call from a very affluent area in a town far from our serving area. Since it was a large job, I booked it.

When we went up to the house, it was another McMansion, with a sixteen-foot mahogany door that was probably more expensive than my entire garage! When I knocked on the door, a gentleman answered who was wearing an ascot around his neck. Instantly Matt and Luke began to laugh, and I had to turn and glare at them to get them to control themselves. But it was funny. I mean, who wears one of these things around the stinking house? The gentleman explained his situation of why we were there.

"Muffy and I are having a holiday affair at the residence. We will sand when we go to the Hamptons in the Spring," he explained to me, sounding very much like Thurston Howell from the old television show "Gilligan's Island" as he raised his neck and grabbed at the ascot. In other words, he wanted our inferior service to cover for the party and he would later "do it right".

I explained that would be fine and we got to work. The Ascot left for work, leaving his precious Muffy to attend to our work. Muffy was smoking hot—a cheerleader type who was very friendly and once again, once we got to talking, was way too into me. But since this was a huge job, I had plenty to do, so I ignored her prancing about the house in short shorts. She bent over so many times to get me to look at her that it became boring. How did I know for sure? I could see her looking back to see if I was looking.

When the Ascot returned from work, he adjusted his neckwear, as he preened and looked over the floors we had just completed.

"Muffy and I will no longer sand" he stated. Ah yes, another satisfied customer.

CHAPTER **20**

The Whacky World of Visitors

FOR MANY YEARS, I would have "open house" franchise presentations as well as individual meetings to bring new owners into the system. We had people visiting us for franchises before we were even ready for franchising!

Colton and Xander

One of those visitors was a mid-westerner Colton and his business partner Xander that I mentioned way earlier in this book. Somehow, they had discovered Mr. Sandless and thought the system would be great for their state. In fact, this was one of these early "big-wigs" who thought he could swoop in and grab up as much of the company as he could for "cheap", getting in on the ground floor so to speak.

Colton was the money guy and Xander, more friend than business partner would be the guy to actually run the business for Colton. They also had another guy who they would set as the overall manager of the business. Xander would concentrate solely on sales, the manager would handle the day to day operations. On the surface, they seemed to be sincere and have their act totally together.

They came to meet me at my original office in 2005, about a year before we were even able to franchise. I tried to make that shoebox of an office look like something was going on, but it was difficult to be "impressive" in six hundred square feet! Still, having five trucks and ten guys working there, it looked more like a bee-hive than an office and I believe they could see the massive potential of the business. They expressed desire to expand Mr. Sandless throughout their state. While I would basically be "giving" them the franchises at a meager five thousand for the first one and just two thousand for each option territory, I felt that having someone with the financial wherewithal of Colton would be an overall asset. Once he was established, I could bring on others like him and expand the franchise system rapidly.

Once we had our Uniform Franchise Offering Circular (UFOC), the ridiculous name the government came up with for our franchise "disclosure", Colton jumped right in and we had a deal for the expansion. He would become the first Mr. Sandless dealer in the USA, but not the first franchise owner as that now-infamous distinction goes to Dobbie of Canada. More about his story coming up!

Now if everything had gone like Colton and Xander had planned, Mr. Sandless would have been off to a terrific start. I personally trained Xander and their new manager Elliot so that they started the service at the highest level. The training went great and by the time they departed, they both were fully able to service floors.

Within a day or two of returning, Xander called to tell me that Colton released him from their agreement! Apparently, they had a contract over what would be performed and who would perform it and apparently it was a very one-sided agreement, with Colton getting the lion's share. Colton had in the agreement where at will he could buy Xander out for the whopping fee of one dollar and that is exactly what he did after they had some type of falling out. I believed at the time that Colton felt he had Elliot and wouldn't need Xander at all to run the business.

Now let me tell you, if I knew this I would have *never* given Colton as much territory as I did. I knew that Colton wasn't going to be working in the business, and I was fine with that because Xander *was* in fact "the man". He was much hungrier for success than Colton who already was successful. My belief in Xander is what led me to sign the deal, not my faith in Colton. There was no way I could do anything about this, as there was no type of clause in the Franchise Agreement to give me an out for something like this. I would just have to try and work through it.

The franchise location was launched in their state's biggest city as the first part of their company. From there they were to expand to other parts of the state. But first they had to make this city work. There were so many problems that I don't even know where to start. Elliot, who was the weakest in the system between him and Xander, would field the calls, make the bookings and would send out two new hires they had to do the service. Elliot wasn't trained on the phone at all, and the two workers were not trained at all in the system. Can you imagine a more ridiculous opening of a business?

In his first month, Elliot delivered…nothing. He had dozens of calls and booked absolutely no one! The growth of the brand was dependent upon this first USA franchise's success and I was horrified! What if our success couldn't be duplicated? While I didn't really believe that, I needed answers and I needed them quick. I flew out to their location the manager I had at the time for my location, a very capable woman by the name of Katherine, who as I said earlier, pronounced her name "Kathereen" for some strange reason. She would sit with Elliot and see what he was doing so we could figure out what in the world was wrong.

Katherine called me the next day and said it was very simple. Elliot was not following our script and he was pricing by square foot instead of our package pricing. She worked on him for another day to correct these issues and then she flew back. With these two simple changes, Elliot booked twenty thousand in work the very next month. The day was saved, or was it?

No, now came the untrained workers who messed up every single job they touched! Once again in panic mode so that other owners who may consider coming on board with us would not think our training was so poor, I flew Caden out to work with these guys. He would basically train them on the job so that we could quickly correct the issues as well as to keep the income up for this new location.

It was hard to believe how much effort and commitment I had to put into this first site to make it somewhat functional. For the years it was in existence, it was our number one complained-about location. In fact, this site was the very first to have a complaint posted about them online, starting a trend that would last to this day with online "hate" posts.

While some people make this such a big deal, to date we have something like thirty- eight online complaints. Having serviced literally tens of thousands, that is really a very tiny amount of complaints. Besides, a third of those were from sanders trying to bash us, and another third from totally irrational customers. That left less than 15 that were truly complaints. But even if I multiplied that by one hundred, that still gave us a 99.9% customer satisfaction rating.

Anyway, they serviced this woman's floor who was not too happy. It seems she had a kitchen floor with prefinished boards, that were glued down on concrete. Elliot's team ripped out some of the bad boards and attempted to glue back real wood boards instead of replacement prefinished boards. The real boards didn't match at all, not in the way they looked or even their height. They were higher than the original boards for heaven sakes.

The comedy of errors on this were so easy to see. The two guys working were not carpenters and had no business attempting this. You don't replace prefinished boards with real wood. But to start with, we would have never recommended pulling up glued-down boards. Of course, the brain-trust there never called us for tech support, so we couldn't tell them any of these things.

We were not even aware of the job or the complaint until we saw it online. This woman was a lawyer and she wasn't nearly as upset with the destruction of her kitchen floor as she was with Colton not returning her calls. Both not reporting the complaint to us and not answering the customer's calls were a breach of his agreement with Mr. Sandless.

But here is the thing that killed me most. I spoke to this woman to find out what we could do to help her. Eight hundred dollars. That's it. That is all she wanted and for that she wouldn't even have posted online against us. I forced Colton to pay her, but once a negative post is online, it *never* comes down.

For the next several years they basically dicked around with the business until Colton found himself with a girlfriend. I was introduced to Madison when Colton brought her with him to an open house sales class I was having, to increase sales from our owners. By this time, we had more than thirty, so it was worth putting on this type of "boot camp" sales lessons and service specialty training lessons.

Madison was a "trophy" kind of girl, more plastic than human. You know the blonde "Barbie" type with the voluptuous figure, who loves being the center of attention. She tried her charms on me several times that weekend, bending and posing in provocative stances for me, then glancing over to see if I was looking. But I was married and not at all interested, so she moved on to some of the other owners who were at the lessons. Believe me she had Caden and Dominic at her beckoned will! They look like her two lap dogs following her around.

One of those owners was a kid in his mid-twenties by the name of Jack. Jack and his father purchased a large area adjacent to my franchise. I will never forget as I was doing my three-hour long sales class, that Jack sat in the row behind and to the right of Madison. I don't think he heard a word I said, as his eyes were transfixed on Madison and his mouth hung wide open in amazement of what he was soaking in. Pure eye candy for sure!

Of course, this was a turn-on for Madison, who during the break stood right in front of Jack and took some sort of sexy pose that I could never contort my body into, basically projecting her enormous breasts and butt out at the same time for Jack to see. I swear the poor kid looked like he was going to faint!

Unfortunately, Madison had the mistaken belief that she was way more than eye candy and believed she could manage the franchise for Colton and turn it into a winning venture. But she was pure dumb ass! I took her and a few others to an estimate with me where I explained the use of the script, when Madison stated how she spoke to clients.

"I always tell them the truth," she told me in the car that day. "If they have rotten boards, I tell them they have rotten boards!" I had to explain to her why it was a bad idea to tell a customer they had "rotten" boards!

As it turned out, the tandem of Madison and Elliot produced no better results than what they had achieved before her. I really tried hard to support this site and gave multiple classes to both Madison and Elliot in the hopes I could turn it around, but it was hopeless. The only guy who could have made this work was the guy that was bought out by one dollar!

Eventually Colton proposed to Madison, who sported an enormous diamond on her finger at our next convention. When asked about the situation by other wives and women there, Madison boldly pronounced her love for Colton by saying she would never leave a man who could pay for a ring like that. Now isn't that gold-diggingly precious?

That was unfortunately not true, and they did in fact break up before marriage. Colton was devastated, and the franchise was a disaster, so I convince him to consolidate the territory he had and release all the rest of the state to us. After we discovered that Elliot had left the business, and one of his workers was running the franchise and hiding work from us, we basically forced Colton to cut his losses and turn the franchise territory back over to us. That ended a six-year run of the worst managed franchise ever in the system.

Dobbie

The "dubious" honor of being the first Mr. Sandless Franchise falls to Dobbie who was a Canadian "entrepreneur" if you can call him that. He had a couple of other franchise type ventures in the past that seemed a bit more miss than hit and he wanted to try his hand at Sandless Refinishing. Of course, I put all my resources into launching the franchise system in the USA, and with a Canadian now very interested, I had to retain a Canadian lawyer to convert our USA UFOC to the Canadian CDD. Got to love government acronyms!

THE WHACKY WORLD OF VISITORS

Just as Colton struggled, so did Dobbie, but in a different way. While he was certainly more hands on and did a decent service, he was more just "dicking around" with the business than being serious. He was the kind of guy with just not enough gas in the tank for the full run, if you know what I mean. After a few years, Dobbie sold his franchise to a relative, and we were thankful that we would then get an owner who wanted to make a go of it.

The funny and rather strange part of all this was after his two year non-compete elapsed, Dobbie took a franchise with my nearest competitor StratumAble! I mean why in the world would he leave the world leading refinisher at that time to join a much less effective and known system? But it gets worse. After a couple of years, he gave up on that franchise and joined my other competitor, SxBoost. They threw his name at me to try to make it look like we sucked so bad that he had to leave us and go with them.

But now for the icing on this ridiculous cake. After a couple of years of doing well, and during the time Dobbie was now doing SxBoost, the relative started to have family issues. First his wife passed away and that sent him into a bad spiral. The business almost crawled to a halt when I called him to see what was going on. This guy reported to me that he was basically depressed because of the loss of his wife, that his one kid was very sick, and that his other kid was "living an alternate lifestyle". This guy wasn't big on being gay apparently and took that personally.

He said he would try to sell the business and if he couldn't, he would sign it back over to us. I waited several months and heard nothing from him. I decided to call and see where he was at. To my blistering surprise, the call went to the voice mail of Dobbie! I left a message of who I was for Dobbie and told him I would squash him like the bug he was if he continued to palm off our customers to his SxBoost franchise. Then I called the other guy and told him I would squash him like a bug if he didn't immediately cease all advertising and shut off his phone. He did, but never signed the franchise back to us and that is the last I have heard from either of them.

Timmy

Prior to his firing and before he was deeply indulged in pills, my worker Miles told me that his family was interested in taking a franchise with us. He said that his father was in maintenance and was retiring and they thought this would be something that would be good for him to do. His family wanted to consider taking a franchise in a state right next to ours, but they couldn't come to a presentation until early evening. I set up a time for them to visit with us that seemed would work for them, a 7 P.M. meeting.

Probably a year before that meeting took place, I heard either from Miles or one of my other workers that Miles had a brother who was handicapped. I had no idea what the handicap was, just that he was.

Now back to the meeting with Miles's family. There with me that evening was Caden and Silas. All three of us were in our downstairs office where my franchise ran out of, waiting for Mile's family and from there we would take them upstairs to our corporate offices to have a franchise open house sort of meeting.

Right at 7 the front door opened, and three people walked in, one who appeared to be the father, the other the mother, and the other, Mile's brother. Unfortunately, there is a small entryway to that office and it is blocked by a privacy wall. So, all three were crammed in that small corner. With three of us trying to introduce ourselves to three of them, well it was a total mess trying to do it in that corner space. So, after trying to shake everyone's hands and introduce ourselves, I announced that we should all just move upstairs to the conference room where we would be more comfortable. I was able to shake the mother and father's hands, as well as the brother who introduced himself to me as "Timmy". Perfect!

It was obvious that Timmy was autistic or something like that, which I assumed was what I had heard about him being "handicapped" meant. Silas squeezed by everyone and led the way upstairs, with the parents and Timmy following and me and Caden right behind. Nothing so far out of the ordinary to speak of except that on the way up, we were told that Miles would be coming a bit later.

Once in the conference room, Timmy sat at the head seat of the conference room table to the left of me. There was a seat left open to his immediate left that I suspected they were saving for Miles. Then the mother was in the next seat and the father in the next. Silas sat on the right and opposite of Miles across the table, and Caden sat to his left. I stood in the middle of the room by the white board and began my presentation.

I handed everyone a short confidentiality statement and instructed them to sign the form which I then collected. Timmy's handwriting was so bad that all I could recognize was the "T" in his name. The rest was just a mess.

I had done this presentation more than one hundred times. I wrote it from scratch, and it was polished and rehearsed. As I began, Timmy seemed to be a bit agitated. Again, I am not sure what his affliction was, so I didn't know if this was normal, or if he really was agitated. Only about five minutes in, I showed a picture of a wood floor that was bad and started to talk about what we could do with it. It was at that point that Timmy yelled out to me.

"When is the abortion going to start?" Timmy spouted. He obviously wasn't just mildly autistic, but severely. Immediately I turned from the white board and looked at Timmy's parents. I mean if Timmy was going to go off, I figured they would be trying to calm him down. But they just acted like he didn't even say anything at all. I figured that they were immune to his antics and that since they ignored him, I should do the same. So, I turned back to the board and continued the presentation.

Timmy had other ideas. He started to yell bizarre things, like about abortions, and that he got his girlfriend pregnant, and that he needed some drugs. I kept glancing to the parents and they didn't say a word or bat an eyelash. I looked over at Silas and Caden. Both had their heads held low as if they were trying to retreat from the table. I obviously wasn't going to get any help from those two at all.

But I was starting to lose it! It seemed every time I started, Timmy would interrupt me. I figured the best thing to do was to try and engage him to figure out what his motives really were.

Back to another floor picture and Timmy was asking me if that was the abortion.

"Do you mean the floor is an abortion, or did we abort this project" I wheeled around and asked him.

"When is the abortion going to happen?" he replied. I tried a second time.

"Do you mean this abortion about the floor? What are we talking about here?" I asked. He didn't even look at me, and acted like I never said anything to him, exactly as the parents were doing. I glanced over again at Caden and Silas with the look of "help me you fools" on my face, but their heads were still down as they tried desperately not to react. I turned back to the white board and I swear I started to talk to myself.

"I can't keep going like this," I said quietly under my breath. "This guy is bonkers!" After determining I needed to take a break, I asked everyone if they would like a bathroom break. Of course, they all agreed—anything to get out of that awkward moment! We got some bottles of water out as everyone took turns using the facilities. It was at this time that Miles joined us and said hello to everyone. With that I invited them all back into the conference room.

Miles took his seat right next to Timmy and his mom. As soon as I started the presentation again, Timmy started to rib his brother.

"Oh, *I know what you did to your girlfriend*!" he said to Miles. I stopped and looked at Miles who seemed a bit embarrassed. I thought to myself that Timmy was about to spill the entire family secrets as he continued.

"You got your girlfriend *pregnant*!" Timmy told Miles. "When is the abortion going to happen?"

As I looked back over, Silas was nowhere to be found! He had left the meeting and locked himself in his office! What a total coward. Caden was also no help at all, burying his head down and away from everyone. This was all going to be on me it seemed.

After Timmy called out several more times about the abortion, I couldn't take any more. I announced that we should all go downstairs so I could show them a working franchise site. I had to do something to stop the madness!

As we made it downstairs, Timmy started again.

"Do you think all religions are the same?" he asked me.

"Actually, no I don't think they are the same at all," I barked back at him. "I don't think they are the same at all!"

"Then why don't they all give abortions?" Timmy responded. With that I shook my head and turned to get everyone to the back room. As I did, out of the corner of my eye, I saw Caden grab hold of Miles's arm and pull him out of the office. Timmy thankfully stayed in front of the office as the parents followed me to the back-storage area of the office.

As I was explaining the different solutions we have in the system and how we use them, Miles entered the room and whispered something into his mother's ear. I was guessing that it had to do with Timmy. But the mom exclaimed with a shocked look on her face "NO!" in a very loud voice. What the hell was going on, I thought?

Miles ran over to Caden and whispered something to him, and then Caden quickly moved to the front of the office to confront Timmy.

"*Who the hell are you?*" I heard Caden scream to Timmy. I turned to the parents.

"*Wait*, are you telling me you don't know Timmy?" I asked.

"*NO!*" they both exclaimed. "We just thought he was here to see the franchise presentation like we were!"

As it turned out, Timmy had followed the parents to our office from Delaware thinking he was going to an abortion clinic. In other words, Timmy was out of his mind. I couldn't believe that the parents thought he was legitimately there to see us, and we all thought that Timmy was their son, especially having Miles sit right next to him and engage him. This had to be the strangest meeting I have ever had!

The Providence Man

This final story shows how totally screwed up franchising can be. Never in my wildest imagination did I figure on people abandoning a business they paid for like I have seen in this company. Take the stay-at-home dad who had nine kids in a state out west. His wife, a professional photographer wanted to get him out of the house and she bought a Mr. Sandless franchise for him for a very large area.

He came out to train looking very sullen and did as little as he could while he trained. When he returned, they ordered and received their franchise equipment and supplies. Then they went silent. We tried repeatedly to reach out to him to see where he was, but the truth was, he didn't want to work, and never opened the business.

Another guy did a massive amount of due-diligence before he came on board. It took him six months to make up his mind to finally sign on, and that included visiting with one of our owners to see the service. He came up from his southern state, trained, received his franchise materials and opened for business. He struggled on the first couple of jobs and then went silent. A month later, he wrote to tell me the business was not for him. So, he returned all the equipment and supplies, and we released him from the franchise agreement. I tried to get him to give it a run by having him just run the business and I would send him someone to do the work for him to get him started. But he just wanted to find another job and leave, losing more than forty thousand dollars in the process.

But by far the worst of all of these was this guy from Providence. He had realtor experience, so he understood how we fit in the marketplace. But he was an older gentleman and I feared that he may struggle with the physicality of the service. I told this to him and pushed him to get a younger worker to come to training with, but he said he would rather learn first, then get someone later.

After the first day, he came to my office and did say it was too demanding. We agreed that he would just watch the service the rest of the training, and when he returned to Providence, he could hire someone and send them back for training.

When he was home, he contacted me about getting his franchise supplies and equipment, then like all the rest, he went silent. I will never forget this. It was on a Sunday afternoon about a month later, and I received a cryptic email from this Providence man, stating that he could no longer do the franchise. I thought about this and figure that if this was due to a negative thing, he would tell me. I figured that maybe he inherited money and no longer needed to do the franchise business, but that he feared telling me this because he was worried we would come after him for a penalty or something.

I explained in my response that if this was the case, we would not come after him and just release him. Just like the other guy, I offered to send him one of my guys to work the business for him to get it started. He literally wouldn't have to do anything, and we would run it for a month or two for him to get him on his feet. But he replied that he thought it was funny that I thought he hit the lottery or something but said that wasn't it, and that he would think about my offer. That was the last I ever heard from him. How freaking strange.

Epilogue

While there are so many more stories I could tell, I think by now you get the picture! I never would believe that starting a franchise system and brand would cause so much insane reactions. While at this moment, I still own Mr. Sandless and continue to operate as its CEO, and things in my life are way more balanced and secure, the craziness has certainly not stopped.

Just in the past year, I had a new master franchise owner for another country literally steal Mr. Sandless and give it to his father's carpet cleaning company. That cost me a hundred grand to stop. Another owner who had left the system and was promoting his own company and using products that were not ours. When we tried to stop him, he "lawyered up" immediately. Instead of a lawsuit that we would clearly win and to force him out of business, I allowed him to pay the entire royalty he would owe to term and leave Mr. Sandless. I took the money and bought myself a fantastic truck!

The craziness continues, and I assume will continue for as long as I own the company. I am being sued by a customer who claims to have had Mr. Sandless refinish her floor but has no contract and made the check for payment out to some guy. There isn't a shred of proof they have to be able to win a case against me, but I have to fly to their state and fight anyway. At the same time, I am being sued by a blind guy in another state saying he can't "see" our website—I am not even kidding.

These kinds of things will unfortunately continue and by now, I am numb to them so much so that I take them like a grain of salt. I have no plans on retiring any time soon but do plan on continuing to write books about the adventures of my life. I hope you read another that I have written soon!

www.ingramcontent.com/pod-product-compliance
Lightning Source LLC
Chambersburg PA
CBHW070718160426
43192CB00009B/1229